Contents

Introduction iv

Unit I: Getting Off on the Right Foot

1. Planning the First Day 3
2. Being Part of the School Community 11
3. Working with Parents 17
4. Planning for the Substitute 28
5. Personal Goals and Growth 40

Unit II: Getting Ready to Teach

6. Content Sources 56
7. Content Organization and Analysis 64
8. Objectives 68
9. Diagnosis 72
10. Paper Grading and Record Keeping 82

Unit III: Getting to Know Your Students

11. Interest Inventories 92
12. Anecdotal Records 98
13. Learning Styles Inventory 105
14. Time-on-Task Studies 123
15. Sociograms 128

Unit IV: Behavior Management

16. Problem-Solving Strategies 134
17. Encouraging Student Responsibility 142
18. Reinforcing Positive Behavior 146
19. Contingency Management 149
20. Student Behavior and Consequences 157
21. Using Support Staff 164
22. Weekly Progress Reports 167

Unit V: Instructional Management

23. Routine Management 174
24. Whole-Group and Small-Group
   Management 181

25. Integrated Small-Group Activities 190
26. Prescriptive Instruction 202
27. Skill Groups and Individual
   Conferences 213
28. Learning Centers 219
29. Self-Selection Activities 223
30. Work Contracts 229

Unit VI: Instructional Interaction

31. Questioning 238
32. Values Activities 249
33. Field Trips and Guest Speakers 255
34. Combined-Class Activities 266
35. Peer Helping and Tutoring 283

Unit VII: Instructional Environment and Materials

36. Classroom Environment 294
37. Interactive Displays 307
38. Homework 315
39. Developing Instructional Materials 324

Bibliography 332

Introduction

SO OFTEN the most frustrating problems associated with teaching are the basic management problems encountered every day. This book offers practical advice and management strategies for beginning and experienced teachers alike.

Being A Successful Teacher provides specific guidelines for helping students develop responsible learning behaviors, improving your organization and time management, and sharpening your goal-setting and problem-solving skills. In addition to providing strategies for successful teaching, this book was designed to help you increase not only your professionalism, but also your confidence and enjoyment of teaching.

Following the text in each chapter are a few worksheets to help you:

▶ assess your current materials, programs, and strategies.

▶ specify your goals in a particular area.

▶ plan and organize for new materials, programs, and strategies.

▶ implement new ideas and techniques.

▶ keep track of resources and references for future use.

▶ evaluate the success of the new ideas you've tried.

A number of the planning sheets are reproducible so that you may use them in future years.

Whether you're feeling frustrated by teaching, a bit overwhelmed, or just ready for a change, help is available. May this book contribute to your success and happiness in the classroom.

Being A Successful Teacher

A Practical Guide to
Instruction and Management

Jane E. Bluestein

Fearon Teacher Aids
Belmont, California

In memory of Dr. John L. Morgan

Acknowledgments

I wish to thank a number of people without whose help this book could never have come into being:

To Larry Knolle, Doris Gow, and Dave Champagne at the University of Pittsburgh, who introduced me, during my graduate training, to much of the content on which this book is based.

To Phyllis O'Brien, former colleague, with whom several of these programs and management systems were developed.

To the interns from the 1980–1981 and 1981–1982 programs and to the other talented teachers in the Albuquerque Public Schools who contributed their ideas, programs, materials, and support.

And to Marian Morris, who got me through my first year of teaching.

ISBN 0-8224-6791-7

Printed in the United States of America

1. 9 8 7 6 5 4 3 2

The first edition of the present work was published by I.S.S. Publications, 1982, and entitled *The Beginning Teacher's Resource Handbook*.

UNIT I

Getting Off
on the Right Foot

Chapter 1

Planning the First Day

ONE ASPECT of teaching that sets it apart from other jobs is the fresh start each fall. Every new year brings different faces, different problems, and different opportunities—a chance for new teachers to try out the ideas and techniques they learned as student teachers, and an opportunity for veteran teachers to work with a new group. Each new year presents another step in the learning process and offers exciting opportunities to grow—to learn new content, implement new programs, refine management techniques, collect new materials, or simply face the new challenges that each group presents. So even if you've got twenty years under your belt, every first day will be, in many ways, entirely new.

There is a flip side to these exciting new beginnings. What other profession confines you to the same group of clients, in such close contact, for such a long period of time? Although your classroom climate and your relationship with your students will change and evolve throughout the year, the first day is important because it sets the tone for the entire year. While you can emerge successfully from an awful first day, the advantages of getting off on the right foot are clear.

The following guidelines have been developed to help you get through your first day. They focus on planning, structure, and attitude, and have been designed to keep things moving and organized.

Guidelines for a Successful Beginning

Your Environment and Activities

1. Have your environment in order. Make it as comfortable and functional as possible. Organize furniture, materials, and supplies. Keep the organization *simple*. Have materials in the environment for the students to see (such as displays), to use (books, pencils, etc.), and to stimulate thinking (for example, a door sign, question of the day, or active bulletin board).

2. OVERPLAN! Arm yourself with a written list of activities and discussion topics. As well as you can, account for every minute of the school day in your plans—and then plan some more! Keep your students busy! Vary the planning in terms of types of activities, levels of participation, and types of behaviors required. Undirected free time can elicit a variety of undesirable behaviors which may otherwise be avoided.

3. You do not need to get everything going at once. Your first day may include diagnostic activities, the first activities in the books, and warm-up and review in some areas. You won't lose much ground if your reading groups don't start on day one.

4. Develop plans for getting acquainted. Also, discuss schedules, classroom maintenance, safety procedures, and supplies locations. Finally, high-success curricular activities that will "warm up" your students can help them get started. Don't forget that, for the most part, students are excited to be there and ready to start, too.

5. Plan some time for practicing routines, movements, and care of materials. Your students may need instruction and practice in using the pencil sharpener, putting the caps back on the markers, taking books from the shelves *and* putting them back properly, moving from one part of the room to the other (without losing pencils, getting lost, or hurting themselves), and so on. The fewer assumptions you make about their abilities, the fewer problems you are likely to encounter in your planning.

6. Pace yourself and your students. Plan interactive activities between pencil-and-paper work. Allow some movement after your students have been sitting for a while. Be sensitive to signals that they are confused or tired.

7. Have materials prepared and available for students. Try to anticipate where the students will be for each activity, how you will get them there, what they will need, and how long it will take. Think through your directions (including the points you are tempted to assume they know or understand), and develop some contingency plans in case something goes awry.

Your Structure and Expectations

1. Keep rules simple and to a minimum. Don't find yourself in the trap of having a lot of rules to enforce. You will probably develop some commonsense ideas about the use of the hall pass or pencil sharpener, for example, but you can cover general classroom behavior by one simple statement about courtesy and safety that stresses the importance of not interfering with anyone's learning (or your teaching). Just about everything else will fall under that one rule.

2. Minimize the need for students to make choices and decisions until they learn your routines and expectations. Assume that you may have to help them develop decision-making skills and other responsible learning behaviors during the year.

3. Depending on the students' previous classroom experience, it may be wise to begin the year by keeping things simple and highly structured. The environment, organization, and standards of the first few weeks will not necessarily reflect what will be happening in the room later in the year. Keep your long-term goals in mind. Remember that even if the students do not have many opportunities for decision-making during those first few days, they will have an easier time once they have a familiar framework in which to work.

Your Attitude and Teaching Role

1. Know your needs and limitations. Anticipate as much as possible. Be aware of what behaviors you will and will not accept in the classroom. Think through strategies and responses. Commit yourself to being consistent—following

through on what you say, modeling your behavior to reflect the way you would like your students to act, and following through on long-range goals.

2. Be an adult. The students neither expect nor want you to be their peer. Your students will look to you for leadership and direction. You have a whole year to help them develop self-management skills, but you won't be much help unless they perceive you as organized and competent.

3. Work hard to establish a positive classroom climate. You will be spending the next nine or ten months with these students. Although you are committed to being an adult, you can still be friendly and human. You will be no less a leader for laughing and enjoying your students.

4. Respond to disturbances calmly and firmly. Avoid the temptation to overreact or to "talk" an incident to death. When problems arise, you have an opportunity to model and encourage problem-solving techniques. Likewise, starting out the year with positive intervention strategies can help you set the tone for *self*-control rather than teacher-control.

5. Try to solve problems on your own, but record incidents and discuss them with the principal or parents at a later date if the problem persists. Use common sense in handling disruptions and try to perceive specific problems as *behaviors*—not as personality problems.

6. Maintain flexibility and a sense of humor. Regardless of your previous experience, each group's dynamic is different. What worked last year might not go so smoothly this year. What took twenty minutes in the past might take five with this group. Be prepared for unexpected changes and interruptions—things you *can't* control. First days can be a little crazy at times.

Add any of your own ideas here: _____

_____

_____

_____

_____

_____

Developing Your Plan

Each teacher has a mental picture of how he or she wants the year to go. Translating this picture into actual plans may not ensure a perfect first day, but it will help you determine how realistic your picture is. Planning is a way of committing to a purpose, and it will help you accomplish your goals.

The planning sheets at the end of this chapter have been supplied to help you think about where you want to be and how you plan to get there. The first planning sheet (page 7) asks you to consider your goals and expectations. You will then need to decide how you intend to reach these goals through your plans for your classroom environment, management, and activities.

Remember that you are more likely to achieve your goals if your plans focus on what you can control: your own behavior, organization, and attitude, for example. Even if you do everything "right," things may still go wrong. Expectations, no matter how well expressed, carry *your* commitment; they will not generate cooperation unless your students are also committed. (Suggestions for encouraging students' commitment to cooperative behavior are presented in Unit IV.)

Planning Activities

The first day is full of introductions. You will introduce, or reintroduce, yourself. Some students will meet one another for the first time; others will reacquaint themselves after the long break. In many instances, you will be meeting your students for the first time, even if you've seen them around (or heard about them) for the past few years. In addition, you will also be introducing room arrangements, materials, new equipment, rules, and routines. These introductions will occupy at least a part of your first day.

Personal introductions involve interaction, and any "Who am I?" type of activity will help you and your students get to know one another. A few ideas are suggested below:

1. Provide, or have students make, nametags. Wear one as well.

2. Ask each student to tell something special about themselves. For example, you can go around the room and have each person tell: what they can do well, what they're looking forward to the most this year, what the most exciting thing was that they did during the summer, what they like to do after school, and so on. Share information about yourself as well.

3. Prepare a list of "characteristics," such as:

Plays an instrument	*Likes the (local team)*
Has a cat	*Has an older sister*
Has been to the zoo	*Has been in an airplane*
Likes to play (a particular game)	*Likes spinach*
Has seen (a particular TV show/movie)	*Likes the color yellow*

   Leave a blank line after each characteristic. Have the students move around the class and ask the other students if, for example, they play an instrument or like spinach. The students should then write the names of the other students on their lists next to the characteristic that describes them. Students can put a name on their list only once. Set a specific time limit (five to ten minutes) after which you call the students together and ask them to talk about their lists. (Did anyone find someone who has been to the zoo? How many of you got ten or more names? Was there a characteristic you couldn't find a match for?) This activity works well when the teacher participates as well.

4. Have your students print their names down the left side of a piece of paper. Next to each letter, have the students write a word or phrase that begins with that letter and also tells something about them. For example:

   Jovial
   All excited about tomorrow's game
   Nice to animals and most people
   Excellent chocolate chip cookie maker

   Have students share their name lists and post them on the bulletin board. Provide an example using your own first name or your "teacher" name.

One word of caution: If you've been in a school for any amount of time, you will know that certain students carry "labels." It may be impossible to avoid hearing that Mabel is a brain, Jackie is a slob, Monique is a pest, or Robin is trouble, but you can avoid allowing past perceptions—including your own—to color your behavior and affect your students' chances for success in your room. The more you can clear your thoughts of expectations based on gossip or past performance, the more likely each student in your room will get a fair start.

Introducing rules and routines will include little student participation other than some discussion and practice. If you choose to talk about rules, try to keep things positive and simple. Some possible topics or activities might include:

- taking a "tour" of the room, although students will remember where things are much better once they have a reason to use them.

- taking a tour of the school, especially with younger students, and pointing out the office, the auditorium, the gym, the cafeteria, and so on.

- practicing fire drills or pointing out fire exits.

- assigning books, seats, cubbies, lockers, and so forth.

- taking attendance; demonstrating attendance procedures that involve the students.

- discussing the schedule for the day; discussing the weekly schedule, including physical education or library time.

- specifying materials students need to bring from home for class, such as money to buy lunch or milk, or items needed to participate in some activity.

- collecting any money, notes, or materials brought from home.

- distributing materials for class and notes to take home.

- assigning helpers.

Other ideas: _____

_____

_____

_____

Clearly, the introductions and managerial activities described above will take up only part of a day. Students may also be anxious to get into the swing of academia and do some *real* work. While you don't need to get every program going during the first week of school, use this time to establish an atmosphere that encourages students to work.

On the first day you may wish to teach the first social studies lesson, introduce the math books and conduct a pretest, or assign the first spelling lesson. You may also establish "story time," language drills, show and tell, or a few minutes for whole-group silent reading. Consider drawing attention to one of your bulletin boards or a sign in the room that students can respond to or work with during the day. Assign some high-interest, high-success activities such as an interest inventory (another "about me" activity), a coloring or drawing activity, or a word search or other puzzle. Connect some of the high-interest activities (including breaks and recess) to some of the other activities you want completed so that participation is encouraged by additional activity.

Given the above suggestions and your own ideas, plan your first day, giving consideration to your goals. Beginning with the students' entrance to your room, describe your strategies, activities, materials, and management. Anticipate how long the activities will take, and, if possible, underestimate the time involved.

For each activity, consider the learning behaviors your students will need to successfully complete the task. What will you do to ensure that the students have the prerequisite skills before attempting these activities? Do any of the activities require decision making, movement, self-control, sharing, working independently, or working cooperatively? How will your management and direction account for students' behaviors in each situation?

You may want to save your plans and, at the end of the day, note what went well and what you should reconsider before using next year. Note any ideas that will make these plans work more smoothly in the future.

You may never again plan anything in such detail. Still, your first day may not work out exactly as planned, but your plans *will* get you through the day and make you feel—and appear—confident and organized. And that's a great start.

Planning Sheet: First Day

Goals and expectations: _____

_____

_____

_____

_____

_____

_____

Environmental plans:

Furniture _____

_____

_____

Supplies/materials _____

_____

_____

Decoration _____

_____

_____

Stimulation _____

_____

How will your preparation of the environment help you reach your goals and fulfill your expectations?

_____

_____

_____

_____

_____

_____

_____

_____

Planning Sheet: First Day's Schedule

Time	Strategy: what you will do	Activity: what students will do	Materials	Management considerations
8:00				
8:15				
8:30				
8:45				
9:00				
9:15				
9:30				
9:45				
10:00				
10:15				
10:30				
10:45				
11:00				

Time	Strategy: what you will do	Activity: what students will do	Materials	Management considerations
11:15				
11:30				
11:45				
12:00				
12:15				
12:30				
12:45				
1:00				
1:15				
1:30				
1:45				
2:00				
2:15				
2:30				

Time	Strategy: what you will do	Activity: what students will do	Materials	Management considerations
2:45				
3:00				
3:15				
3:30				
3:45				
4:00				

Chapter 2

Being Part of the School Community

TEACHING IS, by nature, an interactive occupation. Yet, because you spend most of the time in your classroom interacting with students, the scope of your interaction with other staff members may seem rather limited at times. Despite this occasional sense of isolation, you are a part of a school community that is defined by history, location, traditions, interpersonal dynamics, rules, and the characteristics of the staff, students, and parents.

This chapter will examine three kinds of involvement with the school community: working in the school and the community, being a part of a professional staff, and working with the principal and administration. The chapter is intended to enhance your interpersonal relationships in school.

The School Community

Teachers who have been a part of a school community for a long time have an advantage over a newcomer because veteran teachers usually have a greater sense of the school's climate, the needs and history of the community, and the interpersonal dynamics of the school personnel. These teachers tend to know many of the families in the community, and are known themselves, either through personal contact or reputation.

At the end of this chapter is the School Community Survey. You may find some of the information you need to complete the survey in school records or by talking to administrative personnel, parents and parent organization members, or other teachers, particularly those who have been with the school for a while.

The survey will help present a picture of the sociological, cultural, and historical elements of your school community. This activity has been included especially for beginning or new teachers who have entered the school within the past few years. The survey will help teachers understand the structure of the school community, gain a sense of belonging, and acquire a context for working with students, parents, and school personnel.

The School Staff

Familiarity with the school community may improve your sense of confidence and belonging, but it is less likely to affect you on a day-to-day basis than your relationships with the other adults within your building.

If you've been a part of your school's adult population for a while, you are somewhat established within the internal community. In some schools, new teachers—whether first-year or transfers—may have some difficulty getting settled or being accepted into the existing interpersonal structure. However, even for "old-timers," this structure is dynamic and will be affected by administrative or policy changes, scheduling or assignment changes, the growth and development of individual members, and the addition of new people from one year to the next.

Certain behaviors are more likely than others to win acceptance and promote a personal sense of comfort and inclusion. The following suggestions may be most helpful to those individuals who are new, or to those who are dissatisfied with their personal relationships with their peers:

1. Be friendly and open. If you are new, initiate conversations and gradually get to know individuals one by one.

2. Attempt to "fit in." Without compromising your individuality, dress and behave within what appear to be acceptable limits for your particular school. Professional competence and credibility may be hard to establish if you maintain an outrageous appearance or have an abrasive personality.

3. Build your support system by identifying one or several members of your staff with whom you feel comfortable and capable of developing a close working relationship. Approach people with a blend of confidence and openness—even if you are new, you're willing to grow and you know what you're doing there!

4. Make sincere offers to help or share ideas and materials if the need arises. Respond to specific needs or situations. Statements such as, "I see

you are doing a unit on dinosaurs. I have a great set of stamps/coloring dittos/activity cards you are welcome to use," may be more effective than, "You can borrow my materials."

5. Participate in school activities and social activities that involve the staff.

6. Contribute to discussions that concern you.

7. Respect the relationships that exist in the school setting, and accept the differences in teaching styles and philosophies.

8. Give coworkers space. Be sensitive to their needs and interests. Many may be very willing to share or talk with you, but keep in mind that they have their own schedules, workloads, and time demands. Do not be one of them.

9. Be especially cautious about expectations or demands. If you give, do so for the sake of giving.

10. Use discretion in publicly sharing information about yourself, your students, or your teaching. Be aware of how much of your conversation contains the word "I."

11. Avoid other surefire turnoffs such as:
    ▶ using the teacher's lounge as a soapbox.
    ▶ complaining about students, school policy, other teachers, or even parents—it's unprofessional and annoying.
    ▶ whining about your problems or bragging about your latest success in the classroom, which can mar your professional image.

12. Listen carefully to people.

13. Avoid the following attitudes, which will be perceived as insecurity: "Everyone seems to know what they're doing except me" and "Nobody around here cares/works/tries as much as I do." Both attitudes wear thin quickly and neither is likely to be true.

Working with the Principal

Although you may have few encounters with your principal, your relationship with him or her can have a strong, pervasive impact—positive or negative—on your teaching experiences. Your relationship with the principal can effect everything: the ease of getting supplies or clearance for a field trip, the outcome of a parent complaint, or even your professional evaluation.

Following are some ideas to help you develop a good working relationship with your principal:

1. Principals vary in their degrees of supportiveness, authoritarianism, and interpersonal capabilities; they also differ in their priorities and values. Try to get a sense of where your principal stands. Regardless of his or her expectations or view of teachers, your job is to be a professional.

2. Above all, principals probably want to be informed about significant problems or incidents occurring in the school. Set up some system of communication for instances in which a conflict arises with students, parents, or other staff members; you implement a new program or make a major change; or you plan something that involves other staff members, students in other classrooms, parents, field trips, or guest speakers.

3. Make sure that the office gets a copy of any communications about school business that you send home or outside of the school.

4. Invite your principal to your classroom to observe your environment, materials, or teaching, particularly if you have something special to share.

5. Invite your principal to your classroom for parties, presentations, or special events involving the students. Perhaps have the students construct the invitation.

6. Avoid relying on the principal to handle your discipline problems. In addition to being a potential annoyance, you convey to your students an inability to manage your own class-room. In this regard, recruit assistance within the guidelines set by the administration.

7. Be professional! You can demonstrate a high degree of professionalism:
    ▶ in your appearance and language.
    ▶ by being on time.
    ▶ by leaving good plans for a substitute.
    ▶ by turning in well-prepared plans, reports, and materials by the deadlines requested.
    ▶ by following and supporting school rules and policies.
    ▶ by registering complaints or proposals for change with discretion and through the proper channels.

School Community Survey

School name: _____

Significance of name: _____

_____

Number of students in school: _____

Number of students at each grade level:

    Preschool _____   Special Education _____   K _____ 1 _____ 2 _____ 3 _____ 4 _____

    5 _____ 6 _____ 7 _____ 8 _____ 9 _____ 10 _____ 11 _____ 12 _____

Number and description of mixed-age or multigrade classrooms: _____

_____

What types of classes other than regular academic classes exist in your school (for example, types of Special Education, Art, Music, Physical Education, Instrumental, and so on)?

_____

_____

_____

Private schools serving the same community: _____

_____

To which school(s) will your students go when they leave the highest grade at your school?

_____

_____

_____

What other support personnel serve your school?

    Full time _____

    _____

    Part time _____

    _____

Describe the racial and/or cultural composition of the student population: _____

_____

_____

_____

_____

Describe the socioeconomic status of the student population: _____

_____

_____

_____

Describe the educational backgrounds of the parents of your students: _____

_____

_____

_____

Describe other relevant characteristics of the community in which you teach (for example, stability/transience, family patterns, parents' employment):

_____

_____

How long has the school served this community? _____

In what ways has the community changed during the last five to ten years? _____

_____

_____

_____

In what ways has the school changed during the last five to ten years? _____

_____

_____

_____

Does the school have an active parent organization? _____

    What is its membership? _____

    How frequently, and when, does it meet? _____

    _____

    Who are its officers? _____

    _____

In what ways will the information on this survey help you in your interpersonal relationships and interactions with the staff, parents, and children?

_____

_____

_____

_____

_____

Working with the Staff

Identify someone in your school community that you perceive as being "a real professional." What behaviors and attitudes has this person exhibited to give you this impression?

_____

_____

_____

_____

_____

_____

What have you done to foster positive working relationships with the other staff members in your school?

_____

_____

_____

_____

_____

_____

_____

_____

Are you satisfied with your relationships as they now stand? _____

_____

_____

If not, what do you plan to do to improve the situation? _____

_____

_____

_____

_____

_____

_____

_____

_____

Working with Your Principal

What have you done to foster a positive working relationship with your principal? _____

_____

_____

_____

_____

_____

_____

Are you satisfied with your relationship as it now stands? _____

_____

If not, what do you plan to do to improve the situation? _____

_____

_____

_____

_____

_____

_____

Reflection: In what ways have the exercises and information in this chapter been helpful to you in developing your interpersonal relationships at school?

_____

_____

_____

_____

_____

_____

_____

_____

_____

_____

Chapter 3

. . . .

Working with Parents

BECAUSE PARENTS are such a vital and dominant part of the lives of your students, they are likely to become a big part of your professional life as well. Communicating with parents is as important as setting up reading programs or taking attendance. Your behavior with parents will influence their attitudes toward and involvement with you, your class, and the school.

Too often, interactions with parents are limited to exchanging brief "hellos" on Open House night, or receiving parent signatures on report cards. Frequently parents and teachers are silent, knowing one will hear from the other as soon as something is wrong. For this reason, both groups are often unnecessarily defensive or cautious, narrowing the potential value of each as a resource to the other.

The information in this chapter reflects the assumptions that parents have a right to be informed about their children's progress, performance, achievement, and behavior in school; to inquire about your content selection and instructional strategies; and to be involved, as much as possible, in their children's education. Granted, some parents will be less involved than others, but assume that with few exceptions, parents are interested in their children's school lives and hold academically high aspirations for them. This statement holds true for parents of all social and economic levels, including parents of educationally disadvantaged children.

A successful relationship with parents is often enhanced by regular and informative contacts with them. Building a foundation of trust, openness, and communication can be especially helpful when problems arise. This chapter will present some guidelines for parent-teacher conferences, whether through home visits, phone contacts, or in-school meetings. In addition, ideas for sharing information about classroom programs and activities through class newsletters will also be discussed. Another strategy, sending brief, weekly progress reports about student behavior, will be discussed in Chapter 22.

Written communications and personal contacts are both effective in building relationships with your student's parents. The two can differ, however, in the purposes they serve, the preparation they require, and the impact they have. Conferences, whether face-to-face or on the telephone, are far more personal than notes or newsletters. In personal contacts the dynamics are more involved, more immediate, and more inclusive. Variables such as appearance, body language, tone of voice, or physical proximity and positioning, absent in written communications, can have tremendous impact—positive or negative—in a face-to-face conference.

Home visits

There are basically three types of parent-teacher conferences: a phone conference, a home visit, and an in-school conference. Home visits are sometimes required early in the school year by schools or districts to set up initial contacts and help teachers become familiar with their students' home environments. These visits can be particularly valuable to a beginning teacher or a teacher new to the community. Likewise, when a parent is unable to come to the school, a home visit might be arranged.

All home visits should be set up in advance so that the parents can be prepared for your arrival. Some special safety considerations regarding home visits might include planning the visits to occur during school or daylight hours; planning to go with another person, such as a team teacher, the counselor, or an aide; and letting the school know where you are going and when you will return.

Phone Conferences

Phone conferences may be most useful as brief contacts regarding some specific content, such as a reminder about a field trip or a discussion of a particular incident. Phone conferences can help avert later conflicts if some incident occurs between you and a student, or between a student and a classmate. Getting your version to the parent before the child does can often prevent serious miscommunications or the anxiety of a parent wondering why "the teacher never called me about that." Likewise, a positive phone call can be a powerful reinforcement when a student has a particularly good day or week, or when significant improvement occurs.

If your students have telephones in their homes, you have a handy vehicle for supplementing newsletters and progress reports, for checking in with parents you haven't seen or heard from lately, or for reversing a trend of negative reports. Whenever possible, avoid calling parents at work, during dinner hours, or after nine o'clock unless you've been advised beforehand that doing so will not be disruptive. Keep phone calls short, professional, and to the point. Focus the discussion on that parent's child, and avoid discussing other children, other teachers, unrelated incidents, or your personal life. Unless the calls are consistently negative or annoyingly frequent, these contacts usually convey a sincere sense of interest and involvement, and will be appreciated.

In-School Conferences

When a pattern of problems emerges or when you have a great deal of general information to share, the in-school conference is probably the best choice. Meeting parents in school is a bit more formal than telephoning, and it requires a number of additional considerations.

Before the conference:

1. Notify the parent of the purpose, the place, the time, and the length of time allotted for the conference. Consider the parent's schedule and offer choices whenever possible.

2. Prepare the materials you will need. Review the child's records and gather work samples. Have everything you will need on hand and be very familiar with the student's performance and progress before the parent arrives.

3. Plan an agenda, listing items you wish to present or discuss.

4. Arrange your meeting environment to provide comfortable seating and eliminate distractions. The parent is at an immediate disadvantage by being on your turf. To help avoid power implications, arrange the environment so that you and the parent are in the same-sized chairs and sitting side by side, rather than face-to-face across your desk.

During the actual conference:

1. Welcome the parent and establish a positive atmosphere for the conference.

2. State the purpose of the meeting and whatever time constraints exist. Following your agenda, share the information as planned. Take notes if possible and encourage the parent to do so as well. Provide pencil and paper if necessary.

3. Encourage information sharing, comments, and questions. Listen and be sensitive to verbal and nonverbal cues. Validate and address the parent's concerns and note the parent's responses.

4. Discuss and note various actions you and both parents may take in future dealings with the student. Plan a time and a way, if possible, to follow up on these intentions.

5. Summarize what you've discussed and end on a positive note.

After the conference:

1. Review the conference with the child and share relevant information with other school personnel, if appropriate.

2. Mark your calendar for a planned follow-up.[1]

General Guidelines

In any personal contact with parents, certain behaviors will facilitate a positive outcome. Consider the following suggestions:

1. Maintain your professionalism at all times. Your professional image will be reflected by your appearance, language, attitude, and the subjects you discuss.

[1] Suggestions provided by the University of New Mexico Institute for Parent Involvement, 1979.

2. If you have planned the meeting beforehand, be on time. End on time as well, particularly if you have other appointments or classroom duties to resume at a specified time.

3. Work toward a mutual goal: the child's success in school. Do not presume to care more about the student than the parent does.

4. Respect the parent-child relationship. Your shared time with a student gives you a limited knowledge and familiarity compared to that of the parent. Your relationship with the student can contribute to the parent's understanding, but the parent's relationship to the child can enrich your understanding even more.

5. You have specialized knowledge that makes you qualified for your line of work. Do not use that knowledge against the parent by using jargon or by talking down to him or her.

6. Your professional opinion counts. Be prepared to back your observations, explanations, and decisions with documentation.

Dealing with an Aggressive Parent

You will seldom have problems with parents who share your perception that their child is doing fine. It is when discrepancies arise in the parents' and the teacher's perceptions, or even when both agree that the child is having problems, that difficulties may arise. Should you encounter angry, hostile, or verbally aggressive parents, your behavior can help reduce the stress and negative feelings.

Do:

  ▶ listen.

  ▶ write down what the parents say.

  ▶ when the parents slow down, ask what else is bothering them.

  ▶ make certain you address all their concerns.

  ▶ ask them to clarify any complaints that are too general.

  ▶ show them the list and ask if it is complete.

  ▶ ask them for suggestions for solving any of the problems they have listed.

  ▶ write down the suggestions.

  ▶ speak softly if they speak loudly.

Don't:

  ▶ argue.

  ▶ promise things you can't produce.

  ▶ take on problems that aren't yours.

  ▶ raise your voice.

  ▶ belittle the parents' concerns.[2]

Documenting Parent Contacts

Consider developing a system for keeping track of your contacts or attempted contacts. Documenting contacts can provide another dimension for the student's records and data file as well as protect you in the event of later questions or conflicts.

Probably the simplest record-keeping form is a blank 3″ × 5″ (or larger) index card. You will need one for each student. Keep the cards in a separate file or envelope, or clip the card to the student's record file. On the card, write the student's name as well as the home phone and the parent's work number, if applicable. Use the card to record the dates of home visits, phone contacts, and in-school conferences, as well as notes or unscheduled parent visits. A sample card might look like this:

```
Rodney Stevenson              234-5555(h)
    Mother (3:00-11:00p.m.)888-4000(w)

9-16 Mother sent note about medication.
9-23 Called about playground incident.
9-25 Mother called to check on behavior.
10-30 Father came to ask about handwriting
       problems. (unscheduled)
11-4 Both parents in-school conference.
11-20 Note from mother requesting
       psychological testing.
```

After noting information on the card, you might:

  ▶ file the mother's notes of 9/16 and 11/20 in the student's folder.

[2] Guidelines provided by the University of New Mexico Institute for Parent Involvement, 1979.

- describe the incident of 9/23 in the anecdotal record file, or on a slip of paper to be filed in the student's folder.
- file notes in the student's folder about telephone or in-person contacts.

Regardless of the form you use or the filing and storage methods you select, documentation of parent-teacher interactions and attempted contacts should be easily accessible and clearly written. The parent contact record should indicate the date of the contact, the form of the contact (for example, phone call, home visit, note, scheduled conference, or drop-in), who initiated the contact, and the purpose of the contact. Also include dates and times you were unable to reach the parent by phone, whether you received no answer or a busy signal, or left a message (and with whom). Indicate no-shows and any follow-up you may have attempted.

All other information, including detailed notes of meetings, descriptions of incidents, plans for follow-up, or outcomes of contacts, should be noted and filed separately. Keep all related papers handy in the student's folder, noting the date and event to which the materials refer.

Class Newsletters

Another way to keep parents involved in classroom activity is to use a newsletter. While conferences, progress reports, and report cards tend to focus on the progress and performance of a specific child, the newsletter dispenses more general information and can be used to clarify curricular goals and describe new skills, strategies, and concepts introduced in class.

Newsletters can announce special programs and events (field trips, holiday parties, or guest speakers) and encourage parents to participate in these and other classroom activities. In addition, a newsletter can give a context for progress reports and report cards.

Guidelines for Class Newsletters

Newsletters can be formal or informal. They can be handwritten on a ditto as a letter or typed with headings in newspaper format. Send them home consistently at least once every four to six weeks. Consider the following guidelines:

1. Newsletters can give the parents information such as:
   - what the class is studying this week/month in various subject areas.
   - changes in format, grouping, and environment.
   - new goals and directions.
   - special events or projects; special contributions of students.
   - upcoming programs, projects, or events.

2. The content and language of the newsletters should fit the community and be written with the parents' interests in mind. Newsletters should contain information that the parents would like to hear and should avoid technical language and jargon.

3. Newsletters can directly involve parents by inviting them to participate in activities, attend programs or presentations, contribute materials from home for school activities, or remind students to do certain things or bring in certain items.

4. Newsletters are usually written by the teacher but may also contain student-written articles about class projects, field trips, or new programs. Newsletters may also contain samples of students' work, such as poems or writing that illustrates current topics. If student work is included, be sure that each child will be featured eventually.

5. Newsletters should be shared with your students and with the principal.

You may want to use the following sheets to reflect on and evaluate the methods you use in communicating with parents.

Reflection and Evaluation: Home Visits

Have you made any home visits this year? If yes, for what purpose(s)? _____

_____

_____

_____

What safety precautions did you take? _____

_____

_____

Were all the students' homes visited? _____

_____

What were the parents' responses to your visits? _____

_____

_____

_____

What did you gain from the experience? Were you satisfied with the outcomes of your visits? Is there anything you might do differently in the future?

_____

_____

_____

_____

Have you recorded your home visits? If so, how? _____

_____

If you have not made any home visits, why not? Do you plan to make a home visit for one or more of your students?

_____

_____

_____

Will making home visits become a regular part of your teaching duties? If so, how? _____

_____

_____

_____

_____

_____

Reflection and Evaluation: Phone Conferences

Do all of the students in your class have a phone in their homes? Do you have their phone numbers and their parents' work numbers on hand?

_____

Do you use the telephone to contact parents? If yes, how often and for what purpose(s)? _____

_____

Do you call from school or from your home? _____

_____

Have you spoken with the parents of each student through phone contacts? _____

_____

Have your calls been mostly positive (about student progress, achievement, or improvement), negative (about problems or misbehaviors), or neutral (reminders or general questions about the student)?

_____

How have the parents responded to your calls? _____

_____

_____

How have the phone calls been helpful to you? Were you satisfied with the outcomes of your contacts? Is there anything you might do differently in the future?

_____

_____

_____

_____

Have you recorded your phone contacts? If so, how? _____

_____

_____

If you have not used the telephone to make contact with parents, why not? Under what circumstances, if any, do you plan to do so?

_____

_____

_____

_____

_____

_____

Reflection and Evaluation: Parent Conferences

Describe the conference phases you have experienced. Which steps have you followed, omitted, or added?

Preconference _____

_____

_____

Conference _____

_____

_____

Postconference _____

_____

_____

Did you record the conferences? If so, how? _____

_____

_____

In what ways were your conferences successful? _____

_____

_____

_____

_____

How might they have been better? _____

_____

_____

_____

_____

Is there anything you might do differently in the future? _____

_____

_____

_____

_____

_____

Reflection and Evaluation: Dealing with the Aggressive Parent

Have you ever had an encounter with an angry or aggressive parent? If yes, briefly describe the circumstances:

_____

_____

_____

_____

_____

_____

_____

How did you handle the parent's anger and aggression? Which of the guidelines did you follow?

_____

_____

_____

_____

_____

_____

Do you have a tendency to do any of the "don'ts" described on page 19? If yes, describe. What might you do differently in the future?

_____

_____

_____

_____

_____

_____

_____

_____

_____

Reflection and Evaluation: Documenting Parent Contacts

How do you keep track of each of the contact methods listed below? Where are these records located?

Home visits _____

_____

Phone conferences _____

_____

In-school conferences _____

_____

Notes sent by parents _____

_____

Notes sent to parents _____

_____

How have these records been helpful in noting student progress? As support data in placement meetings or conferences?

_____

_____

_____

_____

_____

_____

_____

_____

Are you satisfied with your record-keeping system? What changes have you made? What might you do differently in the future?

_____

_____

_____

_____

_____

_____

_____

_____

_____

_____

_____

Planning Sheet: Class Newsletters

Duplicate this sheet for each newsletter you plan.

Purpose: _____

_____

_____

Date to be sent: _____

Format:

    ☐ letter   ☐ newspaper   ☐ other: _____

    ☐ handwritten   ☐ typewritten   ☐ computer written

Topics: _____   Written by: _____

_____   _____

_____   _____

_____   _____

_____   _____

For articles written by students:

    First drafts due by _____

    Correct drafts due by _____

Production: Person   Date

    Typing/writing will be done by _____ _____

    Layout/pasteup will be done by _____ _____

    Reproduction will be done by _____ _____

Notes for next time:

_____

_____

_____

_____

_____

_____

_____

_____

_____

_____

Reflection and Evaluation: Class Newsletters

How frequently have you been sending home newsletters? Have you been sending them on a regular basis?

_____

_____

How have the newsletters served the purpose(s) for which they were intended? How have they changed in:

purpose? _____

_____

format/style? _____

_____

content? _____

_____

production? _____

_____

What types of information do your newsletters contain? _____

_____

Have you received any feedback from the parents regarding the newsletters? _____

_____

What are your feelings about using newsletters as a means of fostering good home-school relations?

_____

_____

_____

Have you received any feedback from the students regarding the newsletters? _____

_____

How do you feel the newsletters have helped the students in your class? _____

_____

_____

What are your plans for using the newsletters in the future? _____

_____

_____

_____

_____

Chapter 4

Planning for the Substitute

YOU WILL PROBABLY have to miss a day or two each year because of illness or emergency. The school system is prepared for these absences with substitute teachers who are assigned to continue the instructional process, or at least maintain order, until you return.

A note about substitute teaching: there is probably no job more difficult in the entire educational system. Substitutes are vulnerable to continual unfamiliarity and confusion. They are rarely in one place long enough to establish their commitment and consistency. Students, aware of the substitute teacher's temporary status, are frequently unwilling to make a particularly good impression. You, therefore, have a responsibility to the substitute, to your students, and to the school, to help the sub survive his or her experience in your classroom.

While you may not be held accountable for the behavior of your students in your absence, your efforts to make a continued routine by leaving plans and information for the substitute can make the difference between success and disaster. The sub's convenience is only one purpose of this activity, however. The other is for your own peace of mind.

When You Have to Be Out: The Substitute Folder

Some teachers come to school when they are very ill because they consider it too much trouble to plan for a sub, or because they don't recognize they are ill until the last minute. Being at school and being too ill to work is not fair to the students. In addition to functioning at less-than-optimum efficiency and competence, the teacher may expose the students to the illness.

One option is to rise at 4:30 A.M., prepare plans for class, and drop them off at school before the sub

gets there. While this option would seem to hold even less appeal than the first, many teachers do manage to come in early enough to leave plans for the day. Another option would be to not bother leaving plans for the substitute teacher. This choice, however, is unprofessional and downright cruel.

Guidelines for Preparing Materials for a Substitute

1. Prepare a "Substitute Folder" containing survival information such as:
   - where to find the students in the morning if they do not come directly to the class on their own.
   - a copy of the schedule including the times for recess, lunch, and dismissal. For library time and physical education, indicate whether it is necessary to accompany students, and if necessary, tell the sub where to take students and where and when to pick them up.
   - a schedule of important times that notes "pull-outs" (students who go to other classes or resource people out of the room). For pull-outs, indicate the names of the students, where they go, and at what times.
   - a list of subjects and activities. Indicate times, procedures, and where to find materials (including teachers' guides).
   - emergency lesson plans.
   - ideas for extra time, including perhaps games and familiar time-fillers. Indicate the names and locations of any resource books and materials if available.
   - an explanation of the environment including location of work centers and seating charts.
   - a fire drill map with instructions.
   - class rules and procedures.

- dependable helpers, including students and teachers; names and locations of the principal, counselor, translator, and other resource people.
- special needs of particular students (for example, non-English speakers or hearing-impaired students).

2. Have available an extra set of dittos (already run off), story starters, task cards, puzzles, and so on. Set these materials aside specifically for the substitute's use. Plans should include activities that students will enjoy doing independently (and quietly), activities that will take up some time.

3. Try to keep things as simple as possible for the sub. Make sure plans are clear and manageable, and that all materials are accessible.

4. Minimize changes in routines and activities, but use caution in requesting that a sub conduct special programs or routines such as committees, reading groups, or individualized conferences.

5. Talk with your students beforehand about the possibility of an occasional need for a sub. Discuss your expectations, and identify specific ways they can help the substitute.

6. Do not request or expect the sub to run off dittos or grade papers.

The substitute folder materials on pages 30–39 are reproducible so that you may use them more than once.

Planning Sheet: The Substitute Folder

Before gathering the materials for your substitute folder, consider the following questions:

What plans and materials will you need for a substitute? Are your "substitute plans" different and separate from your regular plans?

_____

_____

_____

_____

_____

_____

_____

Which parts of your regular routine would you like the sub to carry out? What provisions do you need to make to ensure that these routines continue smoothly in your absence?

_____

_____

_____

_____

_____

_____

_____

_____

Which parts of your instructional program do you not intend to assign to a sub? What materials, routines, and plans do you need to provide in place of them?

_____

_____

_____

_____

_____

_____

_____

Which items in the guidelines of this chapter do you need to prepare for a substitute? Is there any other information you need to provide in addition to those items suggested in the guidelines?

_____

_____

_____

_____

_____

_____

_____

Where do you plan to store the substitute folder and related materials? Who will know where these materials will be kept?

_____

_____

_____

_____

_____

_____

_____

How will you prepare your students for a substitute? _____

_____

_____

_____

_____

_____

_____

_____

_____

_____

Information for the Substitute

To the Substitute Teacher:

I have prepared this folder to help you in your work with this class. I hope the enclosed information, plans, and materials will contribute toward a successful and enjoyable experience.

The day starts at _____ A.M.

Where to find the students in the morning:

☐ The students come directly into the classroom.

☐ The students line up outside the classroom door.

☐ You must meet the students at _____.

GENERAL SCHEDULE

	Monday	Tuesday	Wednesday	Thursday	Friday
8:00					
8:30					
9:00					
9:30					
10:00					
10:30					
11:00					
11:30					
12:00					
12:30					
1:00					
1:30					
2:00					
2:30					
3:00					
3:30					
4:00					

You will need to accompany students to _____ on _____

    at (time)_____(location)_____ and pick them up

    at (time)_____(location)_____.

You will need to accompany students to _____ on _____

    at (time)_____(location)_____ and pick them up

    at (time)_____(location)_____.

You will need to accompany students to _____ on _____

    at (time)_____(location)_____ and pick them up

    at (time)_____(location)_____.

You will need to accompany students to _____ on _____

    at (time)_____(location)_____ and pick them up

    at (time)_____(location)_____.

STUDENTS WHO LEAVE CLASS FOR SPECIAL PROGRAMS

Student	Activity	Leaves for: Person	Location	From/until

SPECIAL DAILY/WEEKLY ROUTINES

Routine	Day(s)	Time (from/to)	Procedure	Materials needed	Location of materials

SUBJECTS AND ACTIVITIES

Subject	Procedures/emergency plans	Location of materials

CLASSROOM LAYOUT

(Work centers, seating chart, locations of materials shown.)

FIRE DRILL MAP AND INSTRUCTIONS

VALUABLE RESOURCE PEOPLE

Name	Title	Where to find	Can help with

ACTIVITIES FOR EXTRA TIME

Activity	Procedure	Materials needed	Location of materials

Special class rules, procedures, contingencies, and consequences: _____

_____

_____

_____

_____

_____

_____

DEPENDABLE CLASSROOM HELPERS

_____ will help with _____

_____ will help with _____

_____ will help with _____

_____ will help with _____

_____ will help with _____

_____ will help with _____

_____ will help with _____

_____ will help with _____

SPECIAL NEEDS OF PARTICULAR STUDENTS

Student	Special needs	Special procedures/resources

I hope that this information has been helpful. Please let me know how the day went and if there is anything else I need to add to these plans. I hope you enjoyed your stay in our classroom. Thank you again for being here.

Sincerely,

Chapter 5

Personal Goals and Growth

THIS CHAPTER contains a series of exercises for you to complete at different times during the school year. All of the exercises are intended to help build confidence and direction, and to provide a context for the thousands of decisions and plans you will make throughout the year. In a profession that offers little positive feedback, a teacher needs to recognize his or her own successes. The emphasis in this chapter is on the positive—what you *can* do and what you *have* done.

Your Teaching Philosophy

The first exercise (page 41) has been designed to help you consider your ideas about teaching and about your role in the classroom. By committing to paper a broad philosophy of education, you may be able to clarify the ideas that shape your interactions, environment, and activities.

Remember that personal philosophies are dynamic and subject to the impact of experience and reflection. You will probably find that your teaching philosophy will evolve and change during the year. Plan to compare the statement you made at the beginning of the year with your teaching philosophy at the end of the year.

Competency Record

The next set of exercises (pages 44–47) helps you to identify what you believe are the characteristics of a good teacher. You will be using this list throughout the year to recognize your competent performance in the classroom.

Long-Range Goal Planning

The exercises on goal planning (pages 48–52) help you to identify goals in three broad areas: student behavior; materials and environment; and grouping and teaching strategies. Consider your goals for the first two to three weeks of school, and then decide what it is you want to accomplish by November, by February, and by the end of the year.

You will have the opportunity to develop your ability to set goals by periodically evaluating and updating them as you fill out the "Reflection and Evaluation" sheets (pages 49–52).

Weekly Reflection

The "Weekly Reflection Form" (page 53) is designed to be duplicated and completed on a weekly basis. Use this form to describe your growth and improvement. Note any new strategies, ideas, or materials you have used during the week and evaluate them. Record your classroom achievements for that week.

Baseline Survey: Your Teaching Philosophy

Complete this survey during the first week of school.

Describe your philosophy of education/teaching, including your role as a teacher. When you finish, fold the page over and staple it shut. You will review this statement at the end of the year, when you complete the reflection activity.

_____

_____

_____

_____

_____

_____

_____

_____

_____

_____

_____

_____

_____

_____

_____

_____

_____

_____

_____

_____

_____

_____

_____

_____

_____

Follow-Up Survey: Your Teaching Philosophy

Complete this survey during the last month of school.

Describe your philosophy of education/teaching, including your role as a teacher. Use this statement for the activity on the next page.

_____

_____

_____

_____

_____

_____

_____

_____

_____

_____

_____

_____

_____

_____

_____

_____

_____

_____

_____

_____

_____

_____

_____

Reflection: Your Teaching Philosophy

Complete this survey after the previous follow-up survey (page 42).

1. Open and reread the baseline survey (page 41) you completed at the beginning of the year.

2. Reread the follow-up survey (page 42) you recently completed.

3. Answer the following questions:

How are your current feelings similar to the ideas you expressed earlier? _____

_____

_____

_____

_____

_____

_____

_____

How are your current feelings different from the ones you expressed earlier? _____

_____

_____

_____

_____

_____

_____

_____

How does the more recent statement of philosophy indicate personal and professional growth?

_____

_____

_____

_____

_____

_____

_____

Baseline Survey: Competency Record

Complete this survey before or during the first month of school.

In the space below, list the characteristics you feel describe a good teacher by completing the following sentence:

A good teacher _____ .

List as many ideas as you can think of; make at least ten statements. Feel free to add to the list during the year, but do not make any changes in the comments you've already made.

_____

_____

_____

_____

_____

_____

_____

_____

_____

_____

_____

_____

_____

_____

_____

_____

_____

_____

_____

_____

_____

_____

_____

Reflection and Evaluation: Competency Record

Complete this exercise at regular intervals throughout the year, at least at the end of each month.

Using the list of statements that you generated in the previous baseline survey (page 44), select any characteristics that applied to you *at any time* during the month. Use the exact language you used to complete the statements in the survey. Do not qualify or negate the statements in any way, but *do give examples of when you exhibited that behavior.* Remember to add any new characteristics to the original list as they occur to you.

September _____

_____

_____

_____

_____

_____

October _____

_____

_____

_____

_____

_____

November _____

_____

_____

_____

_____

_____

December _____

_____

_____

_____

_____

_____

January _____

_____

_____

_____

_____

_____

February _____

_____

_____

_____

_____

_____

_____

March _____

_____

_____

_____

_____

_____

April _____

_____

_____

_____

_____

_____

May _____

_____

_____

_____

_____

June _____

_____

_____

_____

_____

_____

In what ways did this activity provide evidence of personal and professional growth during the past year?

_____

_____

_____

_____

_____

_____

_____

_____

_____

_____

_____

_____

_____

_____

_____

_____

_____

_____

_____

_____

_____

_____

_____

_____

_____

_____

_____

_____

_____

_____

Baseline Survey: Long-Range Goal Planning

Complete this exercise before or during the first week of school.

In the chart below, fill in the boxes to indicate *specific* goals you would like to achieve in each of the categories listed.

	Materials and environment	Grouping and teaching strategies	Student behavior
Within the next two to four weeks			
By November			
By February			
By the end of the year			

Reflection and Evaluation #1: Long-Range Goal Planning

Complete this evaluation at the end of the fourth week of school.

Examine the goals you set in the previous baseline survey (page 48) for the first two to four weeks in school. In what areas have you achieved your goals?

_____

_____

_____

_____

_____

_____

_____

_____

In what areas were your expectations unrealistic? _____

_____

_____

_____

_____

_____

_____

_____

How do you feel about the goals you have set for the rest of the year? What changes or additions do you propose?

_____

_____

_____

_____

_____

_____

_____

Make the necessary changes in the baseline survey.

Reflection and Evaluation #2: Long-Range Goal Planning

Complete this evaluation in November.

Examine the goals you set in previous baseline survey (page 48) for this time of year. In what areas have you achieved your goals?

_____

_____

_____

_____

_____

_____

_____

In what areas were your expectations unrealistic?

_____

_____

_____

_____

_____

_____

_____

_____

How do you feel about the goals you have set for the rest of the year? What changes or additions do you propose?

_____

_____

_____

_____

_____

_____

_____

_____

Make the necessary changes in the baseline survey.

Reflection and Evaluation #3: Long-Range Goal Planning

Complete this evaluation in February.

Examine the goals you set in the previous baseline survey (page 48) for this time of year. In what areas have you achieved your goals?

_____

_____

_____

_____

_____

_____

_____

_____

In what areas were your expectations unrealistic? _____

_____

_____

_____

_____

_____

_____

_____

_____

How do you feel about the goals you have set for the rest of the year? What changes or additions do you propose?

_____

_____

_____

_____

_____

_____

_____

_____

Make the necessary changes in the baseline survey.

Reflection and Evaluation #4: Long-Range Goal Planning

Complete this evaluation at the end of the year.

Examine the goals you set in the previous baseline survey (page 48) for the end of the year. In what areas have you achieved your goals?

_____

_____

_____

_____

In what areas were your expectations unrealistic? _____

_____

_____

_____

Comment on the goals you have set, your implementation, and the changes you have made:

_____

_____

_____

How do you feel about your ability to set goals as a teacher? _____

_____

_____

_____

Given the benefit of your experience and skills, how will your goals for the first month of school be different next year?

_____

_____

_____

_____

_____

_____

_____

_____

_____

Weekly Reflection Form

Week ending Friday, _____

New ideas, materials, strategies implemented: _____

_____

_____

_____

What went well or improved in your classroom? _____

_____

_____

_____

What was a problem, or did not go well? _____

_____

_____

_____

How can you remedy what you've described above? _____

_____

_____

_____

Other goals for next week: _____

_____

_____

_____

Evidence of growth: _____

_____

_____

_____

Comments: _____

_____

_____

_____

UNIT II

Getting Ready
to Teach

Chapter 6

Content Sources

BEFORE YOU DRAFT your first lesson plans and prepare your first assignments, you will face a number of broad questions about the direction of your teaching. If you are new to teaching or to a particular subject or grade level, you may be wondering, "What do I teach?" or "What are the kids supposed to learn in this class?" If you're already familiar with the content, you may be considering past experiences, or new ideas and materials, that will inspire you to make certain changes in this year's program.

Walk into any classroom and ask the teacher, "Why are you teaching this?" and you are likely to receive a variety of answers. Many factors determine what is taught in the classroom: the availability of materials, mandates from the school administration, and so on. This chapter examines sources of teaching materials and evaluates their usefulness. What you teach in your class will be drawn from many, if not all, of the sources described below.

Curriculum Guides

The teacher who states, "I'm teaching this topic because it's required," is, at least in part, using the curriculum guides provided by the district or by the school. School districts determine, in varying degrees, the content to be taught at specific grade levels. Curriculum guides may include general goals and specific learning objectives; suggest materials and lesson plans; and indicate specific texts to be used by the teacher at specific grade levels. These mandates are generally broad-based and often do not address individual student needs. In some instances, however, suggestions for remedial or enrichment activities may be offered.

Curriculum guides can provide some consistency within a district and also provide a broad context for the parts of the curriculum teachers address at particular grade levels. If you visit any two fifth-grade classes in a given district, however, even in the same building, you are likely to see some differences in what is being taught, because teachers use a variety of content sources.

Adopted Texts and Teacher's Guides

Teachers often adopt the content of the textbooks assigned to them and teach that content in the same sequence and format presented in the book. Teachers' guides generally offer information, objectives, materials, and activities for the teacher.

These materials are often designed to minimize the need for teachers to do extensive research, organize curriculum, design activities, and prepare additional instructional materials. As with curriculum guides, these materials usually focus on general content, although remedial and enrichment activities may be suggested.

While adopted texts and teacher guides may provide a solid foundation for teaching, they are written for a very broad audience and may present materials that are unsuited to the academic needs or to the cultural or ethnic backgrounds of the students. Many teachers, therefore, adapt or supplement the textbook curriculum to meet the needs of their students.

Students' Interests

Some teachers identify student interests and experiences in order to select appropriate topics, books, and materials for the class. Surveys, interviews, and inventories are especially useful for providing student-selected alternatives, planning grouping arrangements, and motivating students by tailoring content to their preferences and experiences.

Students' Academic Needs

Talking and listening to students, observing them working in the class, and examining their work can reveal special needs or gaps in their prior preparation. Diagnostic exercises can confirm strengths and weaknesses in particular skill areas. Observing and diagnosing individual student needs allows you to provide instruction for students at levels appropriate to their experiences and acquired skills, levels at which they can experience success and growth.

Responding to students' academic needs may mean special attention for an individual or a small group. You may need to reinforce and strengthen the entire group through review before introducing new content.

Students' Social and Psychological Needs

Problems that seem to result from poor self-concept or lack of social skills may prompt you to plan activities, design grouping arrangements, and select materials that will enhance students' growth in those areas.

The Community

In many areas, the interests of and feedback from the parents and the community may shape what is taught. A community might adopt consumer skills courses that the business community perceives as necessary. Safety programs might be instituted as a result of an incident in the community, or an antilitter campaign generated by civic interest. Other community-related classes might deal with a county or state fair, a rodeo, a festival, or any event that draws large community participation.

Teacher Interest

At times, a teacher's special interest, ability, or experience will inspire activities that will enhance the curriculum. Students may learn a song in French; learn how to weave, make tortillas, take pictures, care for pets; or learn to play a new game due to a teacher's special skills, knowledge, or experience in those areas. Students may also see slides of another country or view a special collection as the teacher finds a way to relate these things to educational content and student interest.

Making the best use of these different sources requires you to be sensitive to a wide range of needs—not only those of the students, but also those of the district, the administration, the parents, the community, and yourself. At times, these needs may seem to be at odds with one another. For example, you may be assigned a math book that starts with fractions and then find that some students can't add whole numbers.

Observation and diagnosis of student behavior and academic capabilities can help you justify selection of content outside the scope and sequence suggested by a textbook or curriculum guide. Defending your decisions will be easier if you know the objectives, sequence, and structure of the curriculum; have evidence of the skills and knowledge your students possess; and can relate student needs to the long-range goals of the district.

Reflection and Evaluation Chart

In the following chart (pages 58–61), indicate what you are teaching in each subject area. For example:

MATHEMATICS
Place value to millions
Division by two-digit numbers
Measuring the area of a rectangle

SCIENCE
Weather conditions and instruments
Predicting seasons and changes

Below each content description, identify the source(s) that led you to select that content.

Reflection and Evaluation: Content Sources

	Language Arts	Mathematics
Units, topics, concepts, and skills I teach or plan to teach		
Curriculum guides		
Textbooks		
Student interests		
Psychological/ social needs of students		
Academic needs of students		
Parent and community interests/ special events		
My interests, abilities, experiences		

	Reading	Spelling
Units, topics, concepts, and skills I teach or plan to teach		
Curriculum guides		
Textbooks		
Student interests		
Psychological/ social needs of students		
Academic needs of students		
Parent and community interests/ special events		
My interests, abilities, experiences		

	Science	Social Studies
Units, topics, concepts, and skills I teach or plan to teach		
Curriculum guides		
Textbooks		
Student interests		
Psychological/ social needs of students		
Academic needs of students		
Parent and community interests/ special events		
My interests, abilities, experiences		

	Other:	**Other:**
Units, topics, concepts, and skills I teach or plan to teach		
Curriculum guides		
Textbooks		
Student interests		
Psychological/ social needs of students		
Academic needs of students		
Parent and community interests/ special events		
My interests, abilities, experiences		

Reflection and Evaluation: Materials Resources

Use the following key to indicate which materials you are using in each subject area:

* Main resource(s) used

x Supplemental resource(s)

o Not used or not available

Resource	Language Arts	Math	Reading	Science	Social Studies	Spelling	Other:
Adopted text							
Adopted workbook							
Supplemental texts/ workbooks							
Commercial kits/games/ materials							
Teacher-made handouts							
Teacher-made games							
Comments: (strengths/ weaknesses of the materials)							

Reflection and Evaluation: Content Sources

In completing the two previous activities, what patterns emerged? _____
_____
_____
_____

To what degree do you feel the sources of your teaching are consistent with:

the mandates of the district? _____
_____
_____
_____

the input from the community? _____
_____
_____
_____

the needs and abilities of your students? _____
_____
_____
_____

To what degree have you included your own interests and experiences in the curriculum you are teaching?
_____
_____
_____

How does your record-keeping/data-collection program support your choices? _____
_____
_____
_____

Are there content sources available that you are not using to full advantage? If so, what plans do you have to include alternate sources?
_____
_____
_____

Chapter 7
·······································
Content Organization and Analysis

MAGINE THIS SCENE: You are a middle school math teacher. The textbook you use starts out with a chapter on factors and multiples. On the first day of class, your students come in, and you start to teach. In a short time, you know you have a problem. Although a few kids are busy taking notes and working out problems, most of them face you with blank stares and bored looks. You quickly assign some "review" work, only to discover that many students are not able to work these problems either. Then you assign something even easier; still, many students are lost. Now what?

Unfortunately, this situation occurs with surprising frequency, particularly when a teacher presents the same content to everyone in class, regardless of the students' prior experience or knowledge. A problem arises when a teacher's decision to teach certain content is based solely on "what's in the book," without consideration for student needs.

Despite the pressure to get through the curriculum and keep up with the other classes at your grade level, teaching students without diagnosing their educational needs can create problems. You may be working with any or all of the following:

1. A group of students who already know what you are teaching.

2. A group of students who are intellectually prepared to learn the material.

3. A group of students who have no idea what you are talking about and are not yet intellectually prepared to acquire the concept or skill you are teaching.

Your tendency may be to direct your teaching to the middle group (number two). In doing so, however, you may doom at least one group to failure and thereby leave yourself open to a number of behavior problems that are apt to arise when students perceive themselves as incapable of success.

Clearly, the solution to this problem is to match your instruction to student needs, allowing all the students to experience success, regardless of their academic backgrounds. Assessing their backgrounds before you start teaching will help you determine what you need to teach, and to whom. However, before you can design and administer a pretest, you will need to identify the scope of the content and the sequence of skills your students will need.

This chapter presents the processes involved in developing a group or sequence of skills—a preliminary step in diagnosis. The content organization that evolves from this diagnosis will help you provide a foundation for individual prescriptions and skill group placement. The list of skills will also help you in choosing materials, planning, and pacing.

Please note that this process will not necessarily be useful in all parts of the curriculum. Skill sequences and analyses are often available in curriculum guides and teachers' editions of texts. The activities in this chapter will help you create your own organization of skills to supplement the others.

To organize skills, begin with a broad concept and then break it down into parts or components. This process is called *task analysis*. Content may first be organized into categories or groups of skills. In some instances, certain skills within a given category may need to be learned before a student can acquire other skills.

For example, imagine that you will be teaching a class in photography. To begin, you might break the subject of photography down into the following categories:

Operating the camera   *Using light*
Processing film   *Creating special effects*
Composing photos

You may have noticed that each of these categories can be broken down further into a number of component skills. For example, operating the camera involves a number of skills, including loading film into the camera, adjusting the meter to the proper film speed, and focusing. In addition, there is a logical sequence to learning some of the skills. Learning to develop film is not a prerequisite to taking a good picture, but in most instances, being able to focus a camera is.

The middle school math teacher whose students are having trouble with factors and multiples, may wish to consider the various skills the students were supposed to have learned in elementary school, at least the skills they need to understand factors and multiples.

In completing a task analysis, you may find that you can teach a group of skills in any sequence you desire. When you teach science, a unit on plants does not depend on your students' understanding of a unit on simple machines; either unit may be taught first. Each unit will then consist of a sequence of skills.

Sequential organization suggests that certain tasks need to be performed before other tasks can be successfully attempted. As you organize tasks, arrange them in the order in which you feel they should be taught. Consider that the simpler, more concrete tasks should precede the more complex tasks.

The ability to analyze and organize the component parts of broad concepts that you plan to teach is essential to effective teaching. Task analysis will help you connect various parts of the curriculum, prepare assessment materials, identify gaps in student knowledge, and plan instruction and remediation accordingly.

Planning Sheet: Task Analysis

Identify a skill area you would like to develop. Keep in mind that the area you select will be broken down into a sequence of component skills and will be used for actual diagnosis, placement, and instruction of your students.

For the skill area you select, list all the skills involved. State each skill as specifically as possible.

Skill area/concept: _____

Component skills: _____

_____

_____

_____

_____

_____

_____

_____

_____

_____

_____

Prerequisite skills: _____

_____

_____

_____

_____

_____

_____

_____

_____

_____

_____

Planning Sheet: Content Organization

STEP 1:

Look at the list you generated in the previous activity. Organize the specific skills in the way you think would be most logical for instruction. Consider the degree of concreteness, the interrelations, and so on. Add any skills you may have omitted and check to see that each is stated as specifically as possible. You may also wish to check your sequence against those suggested in textbooks and curriculum guides.

STEP 2:

Code the component skills in each skill area. Coding makes future reference for diagnosis and record keeping much easier. You may wish to use a capital letter for the broad concept and numbers for the component skills. Your coding system should cover all the skills involved in that part of the curriculum (for example, all the mathematical operations skills you want to teach, including prerequisite skills).

_____

_____

_____

_____

_____

_____

_____

_____

_____

_____

_____

_____

_____

_____

_____

_____

_____

_____

_____

Chapter 8

Objectives

REGARDLESS OF the content sources you consult and select, your instruction will be aimed at helping students achieve specific goals. Once you have determined the students' needs and set curricular goals, the next step is to develop activities and materials that will help the students reach those goals. The foundations for your planning are clearly stated objectives that describe the behavior your teaching is designed to bring out.

Stating objectives not only helps you design materials and select teaching strategies, but also helps you determine how successful your instruction has been.

Many teachers resist identifying objectives, complaining that they teach intangible content that cannot be concretely defined or evaluated. Challenging this view, Robert Mager points out that "if you are teaching things that cannot be evaluated, you are in the awkward position of being unable to demonstrate that you are teaching anything at all. . . . Intangibles are often intangible only because we have been too lazy to think about what it is we want students to be able to do." [1]

For the purposes of this chapter, an objective is defined as "a description of a performance you want learners to be able to exhibit before you consider them competent. An objective describes an intended *result* or instruction, rather than the *process* of instruction itself" (Mager, p. 5).

In order for an objective to communicate your instructional intent, it must contain the following components:

▶ Performance—a description of what the learner will be able to do.

▶ Conditions—a description of any important circumstances under which the performance will occur.

▶ Criterion—a description of how well the task must be done by the students.

[1] R. F. Mager, *Preparing Instructional Objectives,* p. 73.

The Performance Component

The performance must be stated as an observable student behavior. "Understanding" or "appreciating," for example, are terms which are too broad to be observable. On the other hand, "Demonstrating an understanding (or appreciation) of . . . by (performing an observable task)" is specific enough to be assessed.

Clearly stated performance components also simplify evaluation. By identifying expected behaviors, you will see the success of your instruction when those behaviors are performed by your students. In addition, when you identify this component clearly, you are more likely to evaluate it honestly. For example, how can you determine whether your students know the numbers from one to ten? Having the students count the numbers aloud, write the numbers, or fill in an incomplete sequence may appear to be legitimate ways of assessing that knowledge in the absence of a specific objective, despite the difference in the actual skills involved. Specifying any one of those tasks as the performance component of the objective will make it more likely that you will evaluate *only* that behavior.

Below are four pairs of objectives. In the first example, the tasks described are not observable. The second objective in each pair *is* stated as a directly observable behavior.

The students will know the three primary colors.
The students can name (or list) the three primary colors.

The students will remember the fire-drill rules.
The students will walk single file, silently, to the correct exit and and wait in line by the school fence.

The students will understand how to change a tire.

The students will follow the procedure for replacing a flat tire with an inflated tire.

The students will identify compound words. *The students will circle the compound words.*

Notice that, in the second example in each pair, you can *observe* the students performing the tasks as you have described them.

The Conditions Component

Conditions added to the performance component help clarify the objective further. Conditions establish the limits of the performance situation by specifying, for instance, the types of tools, materials, or behaviors allowed or disallowed. The examples in the previous section only present the performance. They have been rewritten below with conditions under which the task will be performed.

Given a box of eight crayons, the students will select the three primary colors.

Without referring to the emergency map and directions, the students will walk in a single file, silently, to the correct exit and wait in line by the school fence.

Using the tools in the trunk, the students will follow the procedure for replacing a flat tire with an inflated tire *on the Driver Education car.*

The students will circle the compound words *on the sports page of the morning newspaper.*

The Criterion Component

The third component of the instructional objective is the criterion component, which describes *how well* you want the student to perform a particular behavior. In setting criteria for performance, remember that you will have to provide instruction to help students fulfill the objective. The performance criteria also communicate to the students the quality they must strive for. Make sure that the objective challenges the students to achieve; it should define the *desired* performance.

The criterion might refer to speed (the amount of time within which the student must complete the task) or to accuracy. Examples:

To the nearest minute/whole number/hundredth
With no more than two errors

Within 80% accuracy
With no misspellings
With no repetition

Another type of criterion is quality. Of the three types of criteria, quality is the most difficult to include in an objective. Because communicating the desired quality of the performance may appear subjective and arbitrary, Robert Mager recommends defining the "amount of acceptable deviation from perfection or from some other standard" (p. 83). He describes "acceptable roundness," for example, as "no more than one-eighth inch deviation from a standard template."

At times, a criterion may not be explicitly described in an objective. In these instances, it is appropriate to "point" to a document, an evaluation checklist, or even a film or photo that shows how something is done. For example:

Given a model, the student will demonstrate the sequence of CPR techniques *according to the Red Cross guidelines.*

If the criterion is external to the objective, both teacher and student should have access to the materials that represent or describe the criterion.

The previous examples have been rewritten below to include the criterion component:

Given a box of eight crayons, the students will select the three primary colors *on their first try.*

Without referring to the emergency map and directions, the students will walk in single file, silently, to the correct exit and wait in line by the school fence. *The students will line up in the correct spot within sixty seconds of the sounding of the fire alarm.*

Using the tools in the trunk, the students will follow the procedure for replacing a flat tire with an inflated tire on the Driver Education car *according to the car's Owner's Manual.*

The students will circle the compound words on the sports page of the morning newspaper *without omitting more than one compound word per article.*

Use the following planning sheet to help prepare for your lesson plans. For each assignment you plan, write an objective. Be sure to include conditions and criteria.

Planning Sheet: Objectives

Duplicate this sheet for each objective you write.

Performance objective: _____
_____
_____
_____

Conditions: _____
_____
_____
_____

Criterion: _____
_____
_____
_____

Preparation/materials: _____
_____
_____
_____

Presentation: _____
_____
_____
_____
_____
_____
_____
_____
_____
_____

Reflection and Evaluation: Behavioral Objectives

In this chapter you learned (or reviewed) the components of a well-constructed behavioral objective. How do you think this information has helped you in terms of identifying the objectives and purposes of the work you assign to your class?

_____

_____

_____

_____

How do you think this information will help you in your future planning? _____

_____

_____

_____

How has this chapter helped you relate your assignments and lessons to a specific unit, to the subject area, or to broad curriculum goals?

_____

_____

_____

How has this information helped you in connecting the assignments and lessons to the students needs?

_____

_____

_____

How has this chapter helped you in matching activities and materials to your planned objectives? _____

_____

_____

_____

How have your objectives helped in evaluating student performance? _____

_____

_____

_____

_____

_____

Chapter 9

Diagnosis

CHOOSING appropriate and effective instructional materials is one of the most important tasks for successful teaching. Resources other than textbooks and curriculum guides are often valuable sources for creative teaching when they are connected with curricular goals. And the goals that lead to the most effective teaching are those that fulfill students' needs. When these goals can be achieved through exciting and enjoyable activities, so much the better. Yet, remember that effective teaching begins with an objective determined by an observed, measured, or expressed need—an objective for which activities and materials are planned. While any activity may fit somewhere into the curriculum, instruction will probably be most effective when it logically relates to your established objectives.

This chapter is not intended to destroy the spontaneity of those magic moments inspired by student interest and curiosity, but to help you establish a sense of purpose for the ideas, activities, games, books, and resources you bring to class. You should be able to explain the purpose of anything that goes on in your classroom. Diagnosis will help you determine your students' needs so you can choose instructional materials and activities wisely.

The Purpose of Diagnosis

Diagnosis is the process of evaluating the condition of the learner, of determining what he or she has learned prior to your instruction. The process is most effective as an ongoing exchange between teacher and student and is especially important before you introduce new material.

This chapter presents procedures for diagnosing content knowledge—the facts, concepts, and skills the students have already acquired—to help you tailor your instruction to the needs of each student. This form of diagnosis is directly related to your content selection and content objectives.

Once you have selected the content that you plan to teach and have arranged it in some logical sequence, you are ready to determine which elements, if any, in that sequence need to be taught.

Remember that students differ in their previous experiences, learning needs, and inclinations, so it is unrealistic to expect that any group of students will be equally prepared to learn a new skill.

Diagnosis not only provides an assessment of the student's ability to perform a particular task, but also allows you to examine the student's understanding of prerequisite content. In addition, it provides evidence to back up your decision to place students in a particular group or assign them certain tasks or materials. Diagnostic testing is not intended to provide numbers for your grade book, but to answer the question: "What do I teach next?"

The Diagnostic Process

As an ongoing process, diagnosis may take several forms. You may not need to prepare a formal exam to diagnose a student's knowledge of a particular fact or process. Simply *asking* a student for the information may tell you all you need to know. Examples:

"Point to the blue crayon."

"Show me how you would do this problem."

"Which book tells about horses?"

"Tell me a word that rhymes with 'hat.'"

"Write down three compound words."

This process is useful for gathering information before you introduce new content and for checking students' progress. Asking students to perform a particular task is quick, informal, and effective. You may conduct this process with or without paper and pencil, but be sure to keep a written, dated record of all diagnostic results and observations.

Although you may use this process with individuals, small groups, or large groups, most large group assessments require the students to produce some product, usually written, regardless of how brief or simple the diagnosis.

Keep in mind that many areas of the curriculum do not break down quite as easily as math operations or language arts skills. There are many ways to assess a student's entry level, including general surveys ("Write down/Tell me everything you know about the Civil War."); predictions ("What do you think will happen if we add water?"); and tests that cover the material. You may wish to use a portion of a posttest as a pretest to determine what the students know prior to instruction.

Formal diagnostic instruments usually require writing or problem solving, and may assess several skills at the same time. They may be used to determine entry level, to check progress, or to see if students have mastered the material. The instruments are only diagnostic if they are used to identify student needs for further instruction.

Preparing a Diagnostic Instrument

The following suggestions are provided to help you design a diagnostic instrument:

1. If you have never worked with the students before and do not know their background in a particular content area, consider diagnosing prerequisite skills. For example, rather that starting with multiplication, you may want to check the students' ability to add and subtract or determine how well they understand place value or the concept of multiplication. This will identify students who still require instruction on prerequisite skills and give the other students an opportunity to demonstrate their skills.

2. Test and evaluate performance on each skill separately. Multiple skills may be assessed with the same instrument, but keep items separate. You are not looking for an overall percentage, but the level of competence at each skill level.

3. Test the skills in a sequence, putting the simplest items first and then testing each subsequent skill. Do not label or identify skills with words such as "adding with regrouping" or "subtraction facts"; label by *code* only.

4. Include an adequate number of items for each skill to assess the students' performance and understanding, but keep the number to a minimum. If the student cannot do one two-digit multiplier with a regrouping-type problem, he or she will not be able to do twenty. Three or four problems of one type will give you enough information for placement, particularly if your skill categories are fairly specific.

5. If the skill is broad, as in "multiplication facts," break it down into its components. For example, use "multiplication facts to 6" and "multiplica-

tion facts to 12 (tables)." Skills that include some subtle variations should have the variations included as well.

6. Make sure the item tests the skill. For example, if you want to know if the students can count from one to ten, simply ask them individually to count aloud to ten. Asking them to write the numbers or fill in the blanks on a test requires skills that are somewhat different from "counting from one to ten."

7. If you are diagnosing a process skill, require that the student show how he or she obtained the answers. Evaluate the process as well as the product. This is especially important for math operations and problem solving.

8. Do not give any rules, hints, or examples in your directions.

Diagnosis and Teaching

Pretests provide information to help you plan a new unit or to introduce new content. Intermittent diagnosis can alert you to students who need remediation, or to students who have mastered the material and need to move on.

When you encounter students who cannot do what the curriculum guides say they should be able to do, you have, essentially, two alternatives: teach the concept anyway, or find out what the students know and plan instruction to prepare them for the subject matter you want to teach.

The middle school math teacher whose students can't grasp factors and multiples may have to return to simple addition. From there, the teacher can build knowledge and accomplish more than the teacher who barrels through the curriculum, exposing unprepared students to one failure after another.

When your diagnosis reveals that certain students have already mastered the skill you are about to teach, you have three alternatives:

1. Teach the skill—they may need practice.

2. Teach the next skills in the sequence.

3. Allow the students opportunities to use their knowledge in more abstract applications of the same skill by having them work with enrichment activities not required of other students. As with students requiring remediation, capable students need to work with appropriate materials.

Practice Sheet: Diagnosis

For each situation listed below, think of one or more questions you might ask yourself in order to determine ways to help the student.

Example:

Helen cannot regroup in a subtraction problem that has a zero in the minuend.

A. Can Helen regroup if there are no zeros in the minuend?

B. Can Helen subtract without regrouping?

C. Does Helen know her subtraction facts?

D. Does she understand the concept of subtraction?

Becky cannot solve simple multiplication word problems.

_____

_____

_____

_____

Jose cannot do long division.

_____

_____

_____

Marie cannot read a calendar.

_____

_____

_____

Lamont cannot copy a simple sentence from the board.

_____

_____

_____

_____

Fred cannot tell the difference between short *e* and short *i* words.

_____

_____

_____

_____

Nicole cannot sound out simple rhyming words.

_____

_____

_____

_____

Donya cannot alphabetize to the third letter.

_____

_____

_____

_____

Dwayne cannot measure to the nearest ¼ inch.

_____

_____

_____

_____

Patrice cannot multiply by a two-digit number.

_____

_____

_____

_____

One of my own students cannot _____

_____

_____

_____

Each question you have written should represent a prerequisite skill or concept. For each, develop one or more questions or problems you can assign to see if the student has mastered that skill or concept.

Example:

Helen:

A. 647   B. 859   C.   7   11   8 - 3 = _____
    -359   -628   -4   -8   15 - 9 = _____

D. Ask Helen to demonstrate "six minus two" using manipulatives.

Ask Helen to demonstrate "nine take away four" using manipulatives.

Becky:

Jose:

Marie:

Lamont:

Fred:

Nicole:

Donya:

Dwayne:

Patrice:

One of my own students:

Imagine that, through diagnosis, you have found that the answers to your questions are all "no." Now what? Consider each student's problem individually.

Example:

Helen:

Since Helen cannot do any *type of subtraction problems and does not seem to understand that the concept of subtraction involves "taking away," I will try to determine if she has an understanding of the concept and process of addition before introducing subtraction.*

Becky: _____
_____
_____
_____
_____
_____

Jose: _____
_____
_____
_____
_____
_____

Marie: _____
_____
_____
_____
_____
_____

Lamont: _____
_____
_____
_____
_____
_____
_____

Fred: _____
_____
_____
_____
_____

Nicole: _____
_____
_____
_____
_____

Donya: _____
_____
_____
_____
_____

Dwayne: _____
_____
_____
_____
_____

Patrice: _____
_____
_____
_____
_____

One of my own students: _____
_____
_____
_____
_____
_____

Planning Sheet: Diagnosis

Look again at the skill sequences you developed in Chapter 7. Using the guidelines for preparing diagnostic instruments (page 73), develop a diagnostic test for that skill area.

_____

_____

_____

_____

_____

_____

_____

_____

_____

_____

_____

_____

_____

_____

_____

_____

_____

_____

_____

_____

_____

_____

_____

Administer the test to the students in your class (or to the students who have mastered the skills prerequisite to those in your diagnostic instrument).

Reflection and Evaluation: Diagnosis

In what ways was your skills list helpful in developing the diagnostic instrument? _____
_____
_____
_____

What changes did or would you make in the skills list? For what purpose? _____
_____
_____
_____

What did you learn from administering this assessment? _____
_____
_____
_____

What do you intend to do with this information? _____
_____
_____
_____

How adequate were the questions on your diagnostic instrument? _____
_____
_____
_____

What changes would you make in the instrument for future use? _____
_____
_____
_____

What changes would you make in your administration procedures? _____
_____
_____
_____
_____
_____

Chapter 10

Paper Grading and Record Keeping

BEFORE CONSIDERING the methods and purposes of paper grading and record keeping discussed in this chapter, complete the questionnaire below to examine your practices and attitudes.

Self-Evaluation Questionnaire

How frequently do you check students' papers?

☐ Daily (including weekends)

☐ 1–2 days per week

☐ 5–6 days per week

☐ less than 3 times per month

☐ 3–4 days per week

Do you check papers on weekends?

☐ Frequently ☐ Occasionally ☐ Seldom or never

Do you check papers during unassigned (prep) time in school?

☐ Frequently ☐ Occasionally ☐ Seldom or never

Do you check papers at home?

☐ Frequently ☐ Occasionally ☐ Seldom or never

How many hours per week do you spend grading papers?

☐ More than 15 ☐ 5–9 hours ☐ Less than 2

☐ 10–15 hours ☐ 2–4 hours

What types of feedback do you give students on their papers?

Letter grades

☐ Frequently ☐ Occasionally ☐ Seldom or never

Percentage grades

☐ Frequently ☐ Occasionally ☐ Seldom or never

Good, fair, poor

☐ Frequently ☐ Occasionally ☐ Seldom or never

$\checkmark + \checkmark \checkmark -$

☐ Frequently ☐ Occasionally ☐ Seldom or never

☺ ☺ ☹ ☹

☐ Frequently ☐ Occasionally ☐ Seldom or never

Rubber stamps or stickers

☐ Frequently ☐ Occasionally ☐ Seldom or never

Written comments

☐ Frequently ☐ Occasionally ☐ Seldom or never

X on incorrect items; and no mark on correct items

☐ Frequently ☐ Occasionally ☐ Seldom or never

X on incorrect items; and C on correct items

☐ Frequently ☐ Occasionally ☐ Seldom or never

Other: _____

☐ Frequently ☐ Occasionally ☐ Seldom or never

What information do you record from your evaluation of your students' work?

Grades (letters, checks, percentages)

☐ Frequently   ☐ Occasionally   ☐ Seldom or never

Comments in anecdotal records

☐ Frequently   ☐ Occasionally   ☐ Seldom or never

Checks for work completion

☐ Frequently   ☐ Occasionally   ☐ Seldom or never

Other: _____

☐ Frequently   ☐ Occasionally   ☐ Seldom or never

From what types of assignments do you record information? (Check all that apply.)

☐ Quizzes or tests   ☐ Some homework
☐ All class work   ☐ All group work
☐ Some class work   ☐ Some group work
☐ All homework   ☐ Other: _____

How much of the students' work do you check?

☐ All items on all assignments
☐ Some items on all assignments
☐ All items on some assignments
☐ Some items on some assignments
☐ Other: _____

What other ways do you have of checking students' work?

_____

_____

_____

_____

For what reasons do you check your students' work?

_____

_____

_____

_____

What do you do with the information you gain from evaluating students' work? Be specific and give examples:

_____

_____

_____

_____

_____

Paper Grading and Record Keeping

What teacher who has sat up late meticulously checking papers and writing extensive comments has not been frustrated to discover these returned papers squashed in the back of a desk or tossed in the trash unexamined? The paperwork involved in teaching can be rather overwhelming and often comes high on any list of teacher complaints, particularly at the elementary level.

Perhaps because the red pencil and grade book are such time-honored traditions in education, most people in the field simply accept the task as a fact of life. To be sure, teaching without evaluation is only a job half-done, but paper grading sometimes has little to do with evaluation. Paper checking can serve a number of purposes, and papers can be checked in a variety of ways. Nonetheless, many teachers would be willing to admit that they spend far more time grading papers than they would like.

Cutting down on the time that paper grading consumes is not simply a matter of devoting fewer hours or accidentally "losing" piles of assignments here and there. Managing the task requires rethinking the purpose of evaluating student work.

What's in It for You?

Teachers check papers for a variety of reasons, among them power, obligation, and information. Associating the grade with a reward or punishment is often assumed to be a powerful motivator for students, although this may have been more true in the past than it is today. Teachers who feel that they have the fewest options in motivating students to achieve or in correcting negative student behaviors are most likely to rely on grades as a source of power and control. Other strategies for encouraging cooperation from students are available, however, and the use of grades to achieve such ends is neither recommended nor particularly effective.

You may believe that paper grading is something that simply comes with the territory or that you owe it to the students and their parents. If you have been putting a lot of time into paper grading, you will certainly want to think you have had a good reason for doing so. Believing that you *should* spend the time may be somewhat reassuring. Yet, in terms of paper grading, what do you owe your students?

Certainly you must give attention to their work. However, is checking each item, each word, each problem, and then commenting on the paper the most effective attention you can give them? How well do they scrutinize your comments? Do they use the written feedback to correct errors and improve performance? Checking papers to provide feedback and acknowledgment is a legitimate purpose, but it is valuable *only to the extent that it actually reinforces or teaches something.* If your students use and respond to your comments, then your time may have been well spent. If not, perhaps your feedback would have more impact in a small group or one-to-one review of the assignment.

Yes, it is important to acknowledge students' work. Yet, if you simply want to acknowledge the fact that they did the work and not evaluate it for future placement or planning, isn't it appropriate to simply put a check or stamp a smiling face on the top of the paper? If children expect some mark indicating that you have seen their work, it is likely that they will be satisfied with even minimal acknowledgment. Likewise, if parents understand your methods and purposes for checking student assignments, they are less likely to be critical of the symbols and strategies you use, particularly if they are aware that you are monitoring their children's progress and responding to their needs.

Grading papers may allow you to feel that you are fulfilling a commitment. It may motivate students to achieve, and it will certainly give you data to fill the little boxes in your record book. Yet, in terms of teaching in response to student needs, *the most valid purpose for looking at a child's work is to determine what you need to teach next.* Regardless of any other purpose this task serves, if you are not using the information you obtain from checking or evaluating your students' work for planning and instruction, you may be wasting a lot of time.

Your record keeping should be consistent with school policy and understandable to parents and administrators. Fortunately, you can translate your evaluation into various terms regardless of the purpose. The presentation of the symbols is not, in itself, a purpose for grading. As long as you are looking at what your students produce, you may as well use the information to see if they are placed at the appropriate skill level, if they need further practice or instruction, or if they need to move on to more challenging work. Then, however you record this information, you also have a basis for future planning.

Guidelines for Checking Papers

Below are some suggestions for checking your students' work. The guidelines are designed to help you make the most of the time you put into evaluating their work and are arranged according to the purpose of the grading. If the purpose is to see if the students understand a concept or to keep track of their progress:

▶ you will probably need to check the entire exercise when there are several skills or concepts in an assignment. Note which areas have been mastered and which still need work.

▶ check a few problems or questions. If, for example, a child has done twenty-five similar subtraction problems, or written fifty long *a* words, you can tell by checking 10% to 20% of the answers whether the child understands the concept.

▶ ask the child to perform a task for you. Watching a student write a capital *F* or set up and answer a multiplication problem will tell you a great deal about how well the child can perform.

▶ ask the student to explain a process. This alternative demands higher-level functioning than the previous suggestion, for it is more difficult to explain a process than to perform it. This alternative will give you information about the child's understanding of the process, or at least of his or her ability to verbalize it. (See Chapter 9 for additional suggestions on diagnosis.)

▶ record descriptive information as anecdotal records. Record language, examples, processes, format, or any related behavior observed. (See Chapter 12 for additional suggestions on keeping anecdotal records.)

▸ file work samples in individual students files.

If the purpose is to give feedback and acknowledgment:

▸ check each item. Mark errors. Expect the student to correct the errors and resubmit the paper. This alternative might be especially valuable if the errors included occasional misspellings, or careless errors on a math paper, when the student clearly understood the concept. If the errors indicate a need for reteaching, set the paper aside until you (or an aide or tutor) can help the student make the corrections.

▸ check a few items and write a comment based on your observations, such as, "You seem to understand this assignment," "I checked the first five and they were all correct," "Your handwriting is excellent," "Where are your capital letters?" "I agree with your ideas," or "Let's go over these together."

▸ let the students grade their own papers. They can receive feedback directly from the answer key.

▸ go over the assignment with each student individually. In addition to verbal feedback about what the student has already done, you may ask the child to perform a task for you again. As you observe, your comments will reinforce what the student is doing correctly. You will be there to correct errors and model the correct performance.

▸ go over the assignment with students in a small group. Small groups are preferable to large groups because you are better able to maintain maximum contact with each student. Allow each child to check his or her own paper and respond. Giving additional examples and having the students work out new problems can give you more opportunities to observe and give feedback and instruction as needed.

▸ check each paper for some particular quality, such as neatness or spelling.

If the purpose is to check for work completion:

▸ use a check or some other symbol to acknowledge that an assignment is complete. This alternative is particularly valuable when you are checking homework assignments, self-checking math problems, or practice and review work such as math drills.

Whatever your purpose, be sure to let the students know in advance. In other words, if you plan to check spelling, or if neatness counts, let students know what you'll be looking for.

Record-Keeping Systems

By checking students' work, you will obtain information about the students' performance on given assignments. Remembering who did what well and who needs work on what skills is impossible without the aid of some system of recording the information you have obtained.

There are many systems, symbols, and methods used for recording pupil progress. A number of them are described below.

Letter grades:

▸ can be written: A, B, C, D, F; or G (good), F (fair), P (poor); or $\sqrt{+}$ $\sqrt{}$ $\sqrt{-}$

▸ are designed to show quality of work done; are often very general, that is, not skill- or concept-specific.

▸ can be very subjective and are usually based on comparing a students' performance with the performance of others in the class.

▸ are often used on a whole group; do not readily show progress of individual students.

▸ do not readily show instruction needs of individual students.

Percentages:

▸ are most often a numerical representation of a percent of correct items out of the total number of items on a given assignment or test.

▸ are designed to show quality of work done.

▸ are often very general, that is, not skill-or concept-specific.

▸ focus on the whole assignment.

▸ are less subjective than letter grades.

- are time-consuming because they require grading each item on each paper.

- are often used on a whole group; do not readily show progress of individual students.

- do not readily show instructional needs of individual students.

Mastery records:

- indicate mastery, partial mastery, or no mastery (no degree of acquisition of a particular skill or concept). May also show amount of work completed.

- are skill- and/or concept-specific; focus on individual performance on specific content and performance objectives.

- show specific achievement and instructional needs of individual students.

- are useful for individualization and skill grouping; performance relative to the group is also clearly shown.

- are simple; data can be collected by grading each item or random items, or through observation.

- show progress readily.

Work completion checklists:

- use symbols to represent work completed, work not done at all, incomplete assignments, and incomplete assignments completed at a later time.

- verify only whether or not the assignment was done, regardless of quality.

- show the amount of work completed.

- are generally used for the whole class.

- are easy to obtain and record.

- can provide data for part of a grade and document work/study habits.

Anecdotal records:

- can document teacher-observed behaviors in a student's performance of a task.

- can document specific language used, processes followed, or topics chosen that indicate related interests, attitudes, strengths, or weaknesses.

- are excellent for collecting support data.

- are more descriptive than symbols.

- are easily understood by parents and support staff.

- need no decoding or computation.

- are very personal and individual; do not necessarily show student's performance in reference to the rest of the class.

- may be time-consuming because they require some reading and sorting.

- can validate progress in many areas.

Checking for Mastery

Your regular grade book will probably not serve you well in recording your students' mastery of various skills. To record student progress, you will need an ongoing record-keeping chart that shows entry skills (pretest results) and progress (acquisition of skills).

An effective record-keeping chart requires somewhat larger boxes after each student's name. Each box represents a specific skill or objective and requires space for marking pretest results, assignments completed, and mastery. The chart lists the students' names in the left-hand column and the skills in the column headings at the top. You will probably want to include the codes that correspond to the specific skills, columns showing the dates of the pretest and posttest, and a heading naming the skill area across the top of the page.

Your record-keeping chart might look something like this:

Skill Area 5: Multiplication of Whole Numbers								
		5-A	5-B	5-C	5-D	5-E	5-F *	
	Pretest Date	Mult. facts to 6 tables	Mult. facts to 12 tables	1-digit mult.	2-digit mult. w/o regroup.	2-digit mult. with regroup.	3-digit mult.	Posttest date
Andrew								
Brittany								
Carlos								

*F is an enrichment skill, not necessarily required of all students.

Checking for mastery is somewhat different from grading for an overall percentage or grade. Instead of grading all items to determine an overall grade based on the ratio of correct items to total items, you determine an achievement or performance level for each separate skill, and evaluate each skill accordingly.

Three performance levels are listed below, along with ways to determine and record that performance level. The implications for teaching are also described.

Mastery Level

Definition: Mastery refers to an achievement level reached when a student demonstrates understanding of a particular concept and/or process. Mastery would indicate that the student needs no further instruction in that skill/concept, and may need no further practice other than an occasional skill maintenance assignment.

Determination: Mastery may be determined by percentage, and if so, is usually set at 85% to 90% or above. More likely, the teacher will decide if a student has achieved mastery when the student's answers reflect an understanding of that type of problem. For example, if three to six problems are given on a diagnostic pretest and all are correct—product and process—then it is probably safe to assume that the student has mastered that particular skill.

Recorded: Indicate mastery by placing an *X* (in blue ink) in the box next to the student's name under the particular skill mastered.

Remediation Level

Definition: Remediation level implies partial understanding of the skill. Remediation level means that, after some clarification and practice, the student should be able to demonstrate mastery.

Determination: Remediation level may be indicated by a lower percentage than mastery, perhaps between 70% and 85%, or by inconsistencies in the student's performance. If, out of three to six diagnostic items, the student misses one or two because of an error in process, the student's understanding of the skill may be weak and in some need of review. Frequent careless errors despite an apparent understanding of the process may also indicate remedial placement in that skill for that student.

Recorded: Indicate remediation level on the chart by placing a diagonal line (/) in the box next to the student's name under the particular skill (in blue ink).

Instructional Level

Definition: Instructional level implies either that the student has *no* understanding of that skill or that he or she has a *mis*understanding of that skill. Instructional level means that the student requires instruction in that skill before he or she attempts to do any work or practice at that skill level independently.

Determination: Instructional level may be indicated by a performance of, for example, less than 70% on a particular set of items for one skill, or any answers, products, processes, or behaviors that reflect a lack of understanding on the student's part. In determining whether the student is at the remediation level or the instruction level, the deciding factor is the amount of instruction needed. At the remediation level, the skill requires strengthening or clarifying; at the instructional level, a more thorough presentation of the content is necessary.

Recorded: Indicate instructional level on the chart by leaving the box that represents the skill blank (that is, no blue marks).

Please note that the use of blue ink has been suggested so that future entries regarding work completion can be marked in a contrasting color. Black ink may be used in place of blue ink when you are recording the results of diagnostic instruments.

Using Your Skill Mastery Chart

Once students have been placed in skill groups, have received instruction, and have completed prescribed tasks, you will need to use the chart to maintain records of progress.

After completing a prescription or assignment, each student will meet with you, either in a conference or small group, or will turn in some kind of work to be evaluated. At that time, you will record any assignments the student has completed on the chart. Using a red pen, indicate with a diagonal line (/) in the appropriate skill box, the completion of each task at that skill level. If the student had demonstrated an understanding of that skill at the remediation level on the diagnostic test, there will already be a blue diagonal line in that box. The red line can be made under the blue line, going in the same direction. If more than one assignment

has been completed before the skill has been mastered, mark the box with adjacent diagonals, representing the various tasks completed.
    Sample:

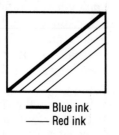

——— Blue ink
——— Red ink

When the skill is mastered, mark the box with a red diagonal line in the opposite direction, creating an *X* in the box.
    Sample:

——— Blue ink
——— Red ink

You can use this chart to record the progress of all students in that skill area. The chart will be "active" as long as any students remain at the remediation or instructional levels in that skill area. As you add new skill areas and skills to the sequence, you will extend your chart to include these additional skills.

Reflection and Evaluation: Paper Grading and Record Keeping

Describe and evaluate the various paper-grading and record-keeping systems you use.

	To see if the students understand a concept and to keep track of progress	To give feedback/ acknowledgment	To check for work completion
System			
Strengths			
Weaknesses			
Proposed changes			

Planning Sheet: Skill Mastery Chart

Step 1

In Chapter 7 you developed a sequence of skills to be used in the development of a diagnostic instrument in Chapter 9. Develop a chart to record the results of this or some other diagnostic, skill-specific instrument.

Step 2

Following the assignment of the diagnostic instrument, record the results according to the procedure described on pages 86–88. Mark the chart to indicate the performance level for each student on each skill tested.

Step 3

Use this chart to record progress once you start instruction and evaluation on those skills. As you add new skill areas and skills to the sequence, expand your record chart to accommodate these additional skills.

Reflection and Evaluation: Using the Skill Mastery Chart

After you have been using your skill mastery chart for a while, answer the following questions:

To what degree has this record-keeping system been helpful in terms of:

monitoring student progress? _____

giving students feedback? _____

matching instruction to student needs? _____

reporting student achievement? _____

personal time management? _____

What changes have you made (or do you propose to make) in using this system of record keeping?

_____

_____

What other types of record-keeping systems are you still using? What changes, if any, have you made in those systems?

_____

_____

_____

UNIT III

Getting to Know Your Students

Chapter 11

Interest Inventories

WHAT DO YOU KNOW about your students? How well have you become acquainted with each child in your class? With all the demands of teaching, you may find it difficult to get to know each student as well as you'd like—or as quickly as you'd like. In many cases, your grade book, along with a permanent record file, provides the bulk of the information you have on your students. Unfortunately, these two resources offer only a limited profile of the individuals in your class. Students are multidimensional people, whose interests and experiences, as you get to know them, provide a wealth of information that can help in your planning and selection of content, activities, and materials.

Knowing, for example, that one of your students has a new pet, has been overseas, helps cook dinner, or loves space movies can give you points of reference in your discussions that will help you relate new information to personal experience. Likewise, discovering that a student is interested in sharks might inspire you in your search for books or films to share with that student or the entire class. One first grade teacher decided to capitalize on her students' interest in reptiles and designed her entire instructional program around that interest. Her students wrote reptile stories, made huge stuffed creatures for art projects, studied a spelling list made up of reptile names, practiced addition facts written on reptile "eggs," and did an entire unit on reptiles for science. Another teacher discovered that none of her students had library cards and planned a trip to the local library to help them establish a relationship with that institution.

Obviously, you discover many facets of your students' lives through your contact and conversation with them. But how much time do you really have to chat? And how can you be sure you haven't missed anyone? Interest inventories offer a systematic means of discovering all sorts of things about your students that can help you understand their backgrounds and habits. The inventory results will also help you plan your lessons and motivate your students.

Questions on the inventory may explore any of a variety of topics, such as:

▶ the student's world in general (siblings, pets, prized possessions).

▶ privileges, responsibilities.

▶ hobbies, interests, collections, or special abilities.

▶ television habits (viewing frequency, favorite shows, inquiries about particular shows).

▶ reading habits (frequency, types of materials, use of library, last book read).

▶ personal experiences (general preferences or specific inquiries).

▶ personal perception of strengths and weaknesses.

▶ personal goals and wishes.

▶ subject area or topic preferences.

▶ personal feelings or reactions to situations.

Please note that interest inventories are *not* intended to be invasive. Consider your questions carefully so that the information you secure is actually useful, not only in getting a better sense of who your students are, but also in your teaching.

The form and administration of your interest inventories will depend on the type of information you would like to obtain, the students' ages and reading abilities, and the size of your class. Two types of inventory formats are presented in this chapter: fill-in and checklist.

Fill-in Questionnaires

Fill-in questionnaires provide the student with the beginning of a sentence or paragraph they need to complete. A fill-in survey might include questions such as:

I like to _____ on Saturday.
I collect _____.
My favorite story is _____.
I like to _____ in school.
I really wish I could _____.
I like to read the _____ section of the newspaper first.
My best subject is _____.
Sometimes I feel sad when _____.
My best memory from last year/summer is ___ _____.
I wish I could be better at _____.
If I had $1000, I would _____.
If I were principal of this school I would _____ _____.

This type of inventory may be given to the entire class as a written assignment or presented orally, to individuals or to the group. In the case of young children or disabled readers, you can ask student questions in an interview fashion and record his or her answers. Students who are capable of completing the inventory independently may be encouraged to do so.

Checklist Inventories

The checklist inventory provides a series of questions with specific answer categories for students to check. The format will vary according to the age of the students and the types of information you are seeking. Sample questions:

How many books did you read last summer?
☐ None   ☐ 1   ☐ 2-4   ☐ 5 or more

Do you have a library card? ☐ Yes   ☐ No

Do you like to read:

adventure stories? ☐ Yes ☐ Sometimes ☐ No
love stories?   ☐ Yes ☐ Sometimes ☐ No
about horses?   ☐ Yes ☐ Sometimes ☐ No
comic books?   ☐ Yes ☐ Sometimes ☐ No

the newspaper's:

sports page?   ☐ Yes ☐ Sometimes ☐ No
front page?   ☐ Yes ☐ Sometimes ☐ No
want ads?   ☐ Yes ☐ Sometimes ☐ No
advice column?   ☐ Yes ☐ Sometimes ☐ No

Have you ever:

traveled to another state?
☐ Many times   ☐ Once or twice   ☐ Never did
played football?
☐ Many times   ☐ Once or twice   ☐ Never did
been to a rodeo?
☐ Many times   ☐ Once or twice   ☐ Never did
made cookies?
☐ Many times   ☐ Once or twice   ☐ Never did
played with a computer?
☐ Many times   ☐ Once or twice   ☐ Never did
taken books out of the library?
☐ Many times   ☐ Once or twice   ☐ Never did
touched a snake?
☐ Many times   ☐ Once or twice   ☐ Never did
written a poem?
☐ Many times   ☐ Once or twice   ☐ Never did
sent away for anything in the mail?
☐ Many times   ☐ Once or twice   ☐ Never did

How many television shows do you watch every night?
☐ None ☐ 1 ☐ 2 ☐ 3 ☐ 4 ☐ 5 ☐ More than 5

	Agree ☺	Sometimes True 😐	Disagree ☹
I would like to learn French.	◯	◯	◯
I've always done well in Math.	◯	◯	◯
I read a little bit every day.	◯	◯	◯
I can control my temper.	◯	◯	◯

I enjoy getting
good grades
in school.

◯   ◯   ◯

I enjoy helping
at home.

◯   ◯   ◯

I'm a great
cook!

◯   ◯   ◯

This type of inventory can be administered orally to individuals or to a group. A checklist format eliminates the need for students to write out their answers. As with the fill-in questionnaire, students who can complete the checklist independently should be allowed to do so.

One advantage of the checklist type of inventory is that it permits systematic data collection and analysis. For example, you can determine a percentage or graph the number of students who have library cards, who have played football, or who watch television every night, and gain an overview of your class' interests and experience.

Using the Information

Students generally enjoy filling out inventories that ask about aspects of their lives, which makes the exercise valuable as a good way to occupy your students for a little while. The questionnaires can also provide some insights and enjoyable reading. Yet the true value of interest inventories comes in applying the information.

Your greatest benefits will result from using the information in your planning, motivation strategies, materials selection, and day-to-day conversation. If possible, try to discuss the students' responses with them. Every reference you make to information you receive from the inventories tells your students that you are interested in them and are paying attention.

Interest inventories tell you about strengths you can build on and gaps you may need to fill. And every time you connect something new or unfamiliar to something the students have actually experienced, something that is real or enjoyable for them, they are much more likely to understand the new material.

Once you have obtained the information you need, you may want to store the inventories in individual student files for future reference, or to share with parents or support staff at a later date.

Planning Sheet: Interest Inventories

What sort of information are you after? _____

_____

_____

_____

Which format do you plan to use? _____

How do you plan to administer this inventory to your students? _____

_____

_____

In the space below, list questions or topics that will be useful in learning about your class: _____

_____

_____

_____

_____

_____

_____

_____

_____

_____

_____

_____

_____

_____

_____

_____

_____

_____

_____

Reflection and Evaluation: Interest Inventories

PURPOSE/CONTENT

Did the inventory help you achieve the goal you stated on the planning sheet? _____

How would you broaden or narrow your purpose for future inventories? _____

_____

_____

What changes would you make in the content if you were to give this inventory again? _____

_____

_____

_____

_____

_____

_____

_____

_____

FORMAT/ADMINISTRATION

Did the format or design work as intended? _____ What changes might you make in the format or design of future inventories?

_____

_____

_____

_____

Did the administration go as planned? _____ How might you administer the inventory differently in the future?

_____

_____

_____

_____

RESULTS

What was the overall response of the students to the inventory? _____

_____

_____

What did you learn about your class as a whole? _____

_____

_____

What are some of the significant findings about the individuals in the class? _____

_____

_____

_____

How will the results of this activity affect your planning, content selection, and expectations, if at all?

_____

_____

_____

How will this activity help you in understanding, diagnosing, and providing for the needs of individuals in your class?

_____

_____

_____

_____

_____

_____

_____

_____

_____

_____

_____

_____

_____

_____

_____

Chapter 12

Anecdotal Records

MANY TEACHERS rely on test scores and evaluations of work performances as the primary sources of data for assessing their students' needs. While extremely valuable, the information from these sources tends to be rather one-dimensional in comparison with the insights children can provide about themselves through their language and behavior. Even interest inventories, which can provide important perceptions and excellent overviews, are almost always a one-shot investigation.

Anecdotal records provide a systematic, ongoing journal of student behavior that will help you understand who your students really are. These records can lead to valuable insights about your students because they hold information that is not evident from test scores or daily work checks: information about the students' personalities, interests, attitudes, abilities, interactions, behaviors, and so on. Unlike interest inventories, in which the information is supplied exclusively by the student, anecdotal records are records based on *your* observations and interactions.

Benefits of Anecdotal Record Keeping

Anecdotal records contribute toward teacher effectiveness because they:

- ▶ help you see, study, and know the child as a whole person.

- ▶ allow you to focus on a broad spectrum of student behaviors.

- ▶ supply information helpful for planning and selecting books, materials, and content for instruction.

- ▶ help you remember significant student language, interactions, and behaviors.

- ▶ increase the likelihood that you will address specific student needs and capitalize on student interests and strengths.

Anecdotal records contribute to effective reporting because they:

- ▶ present a multidimensional picture of a student, as an individual and as a member of the class.

- ▶ help you track a student's social and emotional growth.

- ▶ capture moments in the school life of the student, which support grades and other classroom records in describing the student's growth and progress.

- ▶ give you a tool for documenting student behavior, performance, attitudes, and interactions to support evaluations, placements, planning, or referrals. As such, the records can protect the student (and the teacher) in a conflict situation.

Anecdotal records contribute to teacher professionalism because they:

- ▶ provide concrete examples of patterns in student behavior.

- ▶ reduce the necessity of relying on your memory of details and events.

- ▶ indicate a concern for and interest in the student as a whole person.

- ▶ are far more likely to generate parent and staff support than verbal reports or opinions.

Keeping records on your students helps to make processes such as observing and recording more systematic and automatic parts of your teaching behavior.

What to Record

What kind of information is valuable? Just about anything that tells you something about the student can go into his or her anecdotal record file. Focusing observations on a student's relationships, attitudes, interests, needs, and strengths offers information that can help shape your perception of that student. A better understanding of the student will help you create a learning situation which adequately responds to the student's needs.

You may also wish to record a student's ability to perform certain responsible learning behaviors or describe his or her behavior during a class activity. Some examples might include a student's:

- ability to take care of materials.

- independent work habits.

- participation in group activities.

- completion of assignments.

- attention during a filmstrip.

- ability to share materials or work cooperatively in a group.

- choices of activities or playmates during unstructured time or recess.

- behavior during an independent reading period.

You may also need to document evidence of special needs, particularly when you suspect that parents or outside resource people may need to be consulted. Consider incidents in which the student is:

- distracted from work, not participating, or not paying attention.

- interfering with someone else's work.

- unable to do some task.

- resistant to a particular activity or class.

- not challenged by the regular classroom work.

- involved in some conflict with another student.

- involved in some conflict with a teacher or other adult.

- not interacting well with other students or is choosing to be socially isolated.

- not getting much work done during the course of the school day.

- particularly or unusually distraught, anxious, listless, or depressed.

- continually unprepared.

Depending on your goal and purpose for observing, it may also be useful to note details such as the time of day, subject or activity, grouping or organization during which the behavior occurred, names of other students involved, or special circumstances. For example:

> LAURA
>
> 9/8   Hit Mark, who was working on a puzzle.
>
> She said she did not know why she did it.
>
> (10:00 a.m., Independent Work)

> LAURA
>
> 9/10 Ms. Johnson reported her for fighting on the playground. (10:25 a.m.)
>
> Accused Patty of "looking at me." Crying. (2:00 p.m., Committees)

> LAURA
>
> 9/14 Selected Louise as partner. Played well together.
>
> (2:25 p.m., Self-selection)

```
LAURA

9/21 Fighting with Mark over a library
book during Independent Reading.

Mark wanted to read her book.
Settled the problem themselves. (1:15 p.m.)
```

Follow-up and Application

Observing students and recording their behavior will seem tedious and pointless unless you are able to use the information in some constructive way. In most instances you will simply store your anecdotal notes in a student record folder and review them before a parent conference, a referral meeting, a student conference, or before issuing report cards. Whatever management system you choose, be sure to look over your notes from time to time, particularly those which suggest or require a follow-up. You may even want to note any follow-up you plan to do. For example:

```
JACKIE

Dec. 4- During sharing time, she talked
about special she saw on TV about gorillas.

Dec. 5- Brought in Great Apes book from home.

Dec. 8- *Remember to order film on gorillas
for the end of the week!
```

Guidelines and Management

In observing and recording student behavior, keep the following guidelines in mind:

1. Get the facts! Record only *observable* behaviors and *direct* language. Do not interpret student behavior. For example: *"Threw pencil and stomped feet* when not called first" is preferable to *"Got angry* when not called first."

2. Be honest. Record positive and negative behaviors that you may need to respond to.

3. It is probably best if your students are not aware of the times they are being observed and recorded, whatever the occasion. You may wish to share the records with the students from time to time, or make each student's records available for him or her to look through.

4. Do not use these records as punishment. Anecdotal records are not intended as a way to "get" the students, but are designed to help you record the students' growth and needs. Students should also perceive these records as indications of your concern—not as evidence against them.

5. In addition to "incidents," which you may wish to record for the students' protection as well as your own, try to establish a weekly focus for your observations. The focus may be on those comments and behaviors that reflect the students' interests, participation, social interaction, or strengths.

6. Attempt to add at least one entry to each student's anecdotal record file every week. To avoid overlooking your less visible students, use a weekly checklist to make certain that all students are observed.

7. If you document problem behaviors, attempt to record the times when the behavior does *not* seem to occur.

Anecdotal records can be designed and managed in a number of ways. To begin, each student should have a separate file for documentation. A 3″ × 5″ file box may be useful, but a separate manila file folder for each student allows you to include other data about the student that may not fit on a 3″ × 5″ card.

To be sure that you observe each class member during a given time period, prepare a lined record sheet with the name of each student on one side of each line and a blank space for notes after each name. For example:

| ADRIAN |
| BILL |
| CINDY |
| DAWN |

A prepared sheet divided into boxes will serve the same purpose.

As behaviors occur, simply jot down your observations in the space next to the name of the student performing the behavior. At the end of the time period, you may want to write or stamp the date on each line or in each box, cut the sheet along the lines, and file the observations.

Another method, or one you may use with the one suggested above, involves recording behaviors on slips of paper. The only materials you need (in addition to a storage system) are blank slips of paper, at least 3″ × 5″. Leftover dittos torn into four sections work fine. Keep some slips handy, at your desk and in easy-to-reach places around the room, so that they will be available when you see something you want to record.

While the above method is probably the easiest to manage, you will probably want to use some form of a checklist, in addition, to make sure you are recording for each student. Because you are not working from a list, you may find yourself in the habit of making a lot of notes about a handful of students. At the end of the day, before filing the slips, simply check the names of the students who have been observed to get a better sense of who you've missed. The checklist can also help you identify specific students to observe the following day.

You can also make a 3″ × 5″ card for each student, put all the cards in alphabetical order, and put them on a clip ring. You may then keep the entire pack in a pocket. In this way, the recording materials will always be with you, and you can make notations at any time. You may also wish to include a few blank cards in the pack each week, in case observations of a particular student require more than one card.

Look through the cards from time to time to make sure you are observing everyone. File the cards at the end of the week and make a new pack for the following week.

The most important step in anecdotal record keeping is to find a management system you can live with. A program or strategy that is too much work or trouble will not serve the teacher who does not bother to use it. So, as with any other teaching program, keep it simple. Use one of the three systems suggested above, modify the suggestions to fit your program, or develop something unique to fit your own style and needs.

Commit yourself to working out your management system, modifying or trying more than one, and using the records on a regular basis. The benefits will be more and more evident as you continue to record and use your anecdotal records. You will be able to leaf through the records of a particular child and perceive his or her growth and your responses. Your own growth will then be reflected by your success in the classroom.

Planning Sheet: Anecdotal Records

What type of anecdotal record-keeping system do you propose to design and implement? What materials will you need? Where will these materials be kept?

_____

_____

_____

_____

How will you check to be sure you are observing all of your students? How frequently do you plan to observe each one?

_____

_____

_____

Where and how will you store your notations? What additional materials, if any, will you need for storage?

_____

_____

_____

What type of information do you intend to record? How do you intend to use this information?

_____

_____

_____

_____

_____

_____

_____

_____

_____

_____

Reflection and Evaluation: Anecdotal Records

How has your anecdotal record-keeping system been working? _____

_____

_____

_____

_____

_____

What changes have you made in your system during the time you have been using it? _____

_____

_____

_____

_____

_____

How frequently are you making anecdotal entries:

    during the day/week? _____

_____

    for each student? _____

_____

What types of information have you been recording? _____

_____

_____

_____

_____

_____

_____

_____

_____

_____

What patterns, if any, have you observed with:

individual students? _____

_____

_____

_____

_____

_____

the class in general? _____

_____

_____

_____

_____

_____

your observation habits and record-keeping skills? _____

_____

_____

_____

_____

_____

In what ways have you followed up on or used the information you have recorded? _____

_____

_____

_____

What impact has your observing and recording had on your perceptions of the students, on your interactions with the students, and on your teaching behavior (in terms of planning, responding, meeting various student needs)?

_____

_____

_____

_____

_____

_____

_____

_____

_____

Chapter 13

Learning Styles Inventory

THE LEARNING STYLES INVENTORY (Dunn & Dunn, 1975) included in this chapter has been designed to assess specific needs and preferences for various stimuli that affect students' learning.

About the Inventory

Four categories of stimuli are assessed:

▶ *Environmental,* which includes the student's response to sound, light, temperature, and design.

▶ *Emotional,* which includes the student's motivation toward school work, persistence, responsibility, and need for structure.

▶ *Social,* which includes the student's preference for working alone, with one peer, with several peers, with adults, or some combination.

▶ *Physical,* which includes the student's perceptual preferences, needs for food intake or mobility, and time preferences.

Information is elicited by a series of true/false questions in each category. In many instances, there are mulitple versions of the same questions to allow you to check the consistency of the answers.

Purpose and Application

Scoring the inventory produces a percentage (or, in some cases, a pair of percentages) that helps determine the degree to which a student needs or prefers certain stimuli. For example, the "sound"

category in the "Environmental Stimuli" section is broken down into two subcategories: "needs silent or quiet areas" and "sound is acceptable or desirable." A student whose percentage is 20% in "needs silent or quiet areas" probably does *not* need silence in order to work or study. If the percentage in the next subcategory, "sound is acceptable or desirable," is high, then the student may work better with music or noise in the environment, or at least may not be particularly affected by it. Likewise, if both percentages are low, then sound in the environment may not be a factor in the student's learning.

In each category, the percentages will indicate the effect of various stimuli on your students' learning. This information may shape your decisions about your teaching behavior, scheduling, environment, materials, routine, management, and grouping. For example, one teacher who discovered that a number of her students preferred working in pairs, started letting students select partners for certain assignments as long as the partners agreed to stay with the task. A middle school teacher, tired of the fact that her students weren't understanding her explanations, provided visual aids and hands-on experiences for her students when she realized that few of them were auditory learners. Both of these teachers noted a significant improvement in student performance following these changes.

Another teacher, who was having difficulty with his class during the independent silent reading period, found that the majority of his students required or preferred an informal design in the learning environment. After adding a few carpet pieces and pillows to the environment, he allowed his students to choose where they wanted to read, as long as they followed the class rules for the activity. Few children chose to stay at their desks. Perhaps because of the novelty, or because of their involvement in the decision, the students became far more involved and cooperative during this time. Whether they were on the floor, propped up in a corner against a pillow, with a friend, or even under their desks, the children were reading—and that was this teacher's main objective.

Even when you discover preferences that will be difficult to meet, knowing your students' learning styles can help you make adjustments to accommodate more and more of their needs. Most elementary teachers present their reading instruction in the morning. One teacher was having difficulties with a group of students who seemed to be getting farther and farther behind. After administering this inventory, she learned that almost every person in the reading group showed a strong preference for afternoons and evenings. While she wasn't about to reconvene the group after dinner each night, she found that the students performed much better when she taught them reading in the afternoons and scheduled less demanding activities in the morning.

Cabinets, shelves, and room dividers can help you change the atmosphere and lighting of the classroom in response to students' needs. Study carrels can reduce distraction, and activities can be presented with varying degrees of structure. Before making changes, first determine the needs and preferences of your students.

Administering the Inventory

The inventory can be administered to individuals or to the entire class. It may be completed independently or checked by students as each item is read to them by the teacher, a helper, or a tape. The length of the inventory may require that you administer sections of it at separate times.

Scoring Procedures

In addition to a copy of the inventory, you will also need a scoring sheet and profile sheet for each student.

Examine the scoring sheet (pages 117–120) that follows the copy of the inventory. Note that the numbers on the scoring sheet refer to the questions on the inventory (student response sheet). For example, a sample scoring-sheet section and a set of student responses are shown below.

Student Responses
1. T
2. T
3. F
4. T
5. F
6. F
7. F
8. F
9. F
10. F
11. F
12. T
13. T

Sample Scoring Sheet Section 1–A: Environmental Stimuli: Sound

Needs silent or quiet areas

True ① ② ④ 5 8 ⑫ ⑬
False ③ ⑤ ⑥ ⑦ ⑨ ⑩ ⑪

Note that *certain* numbers on the scoring sheet follow the word "true" and others follow the word "false" (some other categories have "true" items listed only). When an item whose number appears after the word "true" is marked "true" by the student, you circle the number on the scoring sheet. If that item is marked "false," circle the number *if it comes after the word "false"* on the scoring sheet.

In the example above, the numbers 1, 2, 4, 12, and 13 have been circled because of the seven numbers listed after the word "true," those are the five that the student marked "true." All of the numbers after "false" were circled because the student answered "false" to each of those questions. (In most categories, you will check only the "true" answers).

Once you have circled the numbers on the scoring sheet that correspond to the students' answers, the next step is to determine the percentages. Look at the example below.

True ① ② ④ 5 8 ⑫ ⑬ True _5_
False ③ ⑤ ⑥ ⑦ ⑨ ⑩ ⑪ False _7_

Total T + F _12_ / 14 = _86_ %

To the right of the numbers circled, in the blank next to the word "true," indicate the number of questions circled (in this case, 5). Then count the number of "false" questions circled (7) and write in that number. Next to "Total T + F," write the total number of questions circled in both "true" and "false" categories (5 true + 7 false = 12).

To find the percentage, divide the number of "total true + false" (12) by the total number of questions (14). In this case, the high percentage

(86%) indicates a strong preference for silence or quiet when working.

In most cases, you will only have answers in the "true" category to consider in determining the percentage. To do so, simply divide the number of "true" answers circled by the total number of "true" questions listed. For example:

True ③ 7 ⑧ ⑨   True _3_/4 = _15_ %

The Learning Style Profile

The scoring sheet allows you to determine percentages for each category. The Learning Style Profile on page 121 allows you to make some generalizations based on the percentages you have determined. The profile sheet is divided, by category, into two columns. The first column is for comments based on the student's responses. For example, consider the following student's Sociological Stimuli scores:

Prefers learning, working, studying, or doing things:

Alone	*0%*
With one peer	*50%*
With two peers	*100%*
With several peers	*67%*
With adults	*33%*
Combined	*50%*

According to these scores, putting this student in an isolated study environment could be disastrous. Your comment would indicate the preference for working with peers, probably in a small group. You might also note that any arrangement is preferable to working alone.

You may simply want to write the subcategory with the highest percentage, and information such as, "Requires a great deal of light—100%" or "Needs a warm environment—80%." You may wish to clarify with other subcategories and percentages. "Early morning, 90%; late morning, 70%; others, below 30%." Or you may just want a few key words such as "quiet" in the sound category, "adult" in the motivation category, and "visual" in the perceptual preferences category. The profile allows you to translate the student's responses into a clear and useable form.

The second column is included for comments based on your observations. Your personal experiences and the ideas you have about a particular stu-dent may be somewhat different from the information revealed by the student's survey results. It may be important to note your observations as a reminder to double-check your opinion. For example, if a student claims to be persistent and responsible and you have reason to believe otherwise, is it possible that the student really is persistent but that you've been bailing him or her out? Is the student indeed responsible when given an opportunity and a reason to be? Is the student persistent and responsible in other classes or at home? Or did he or she simply answer the questions the way he or she thought was "right"? Discrepancies may also occur if you are operating on assumptions about what your students would prefer, or if you have never offered your students opportunities to work, for example, with one peer, with greater mobility, or in another management structure.

You may also wish to develop a chart or list of students grouped according to similar preferences, or draw up a *class* profile that indicates overall preferences. Once these profiles have been completed, you will have a handy source of information that will facilitate planning for particular students as well as for classroom development, materials selection, and activity groups.

Learning Styles Inventory [1]

Name _____ Date _____

Check true or false.

		True	False
I. Environmental Stimuli			
A.	1. I can study best when it is quiet.	___	___
	2. I can work with a little noise.	___	___
	3. I can block out noise when I work.	___	___
	4. Noise usually keeps me from concentrating.	___	___
	5. Most of the time I like to work with soft music.	___	___
	6. I can work with any kind of music.	___	___
	7. I often like to work with rock music playing.	___	___
	8. Music makes it difficult for me to work.	___	___
	9. I can work if people talk quietly.	___	___
	10. I can study when people talk.	___	___
	11. I can block out most sound when I study.	___	___
	12. It's difficult to block out TV when I work.	___	___
	13. Noise bothers me when I am studying.	___	___
B.	1. I like studying with lots of light.	___	___
	2. I study best when the lights are low.	___	___
	3. I like to read outdoors.	___	___
	4. I can study for a short time if the lights are low.	___	___
	5. When I study I put all the lights on.	___	___
	6. I often read in dim light.	___	___
	7. I usually study under a shaded lamp while the rest of the room is dim.	___	___
C.	1. I can concentrate if I'm warm.	___	___
	2. I can concentrate if I'm cold.	___	___

[1] From the book *Educator's Self-Teaching Guide to Individualizing Instructional Programs* by Rita Dunn and Kenneth Dunn © 1975. Used by permission of the publisher, Parker Publishing Company, Inc., Englewood Cliffs, N.J. 07632.

3. I usually feel colder than most people. ____ ____

4. I usually feel warmer than most people. ____ ____

5. I like the summer. ____ ____

6. When it's cold outside, I like to stay in. ____ ____

7. When it's hot outside, I like to stay in. ____ ____

8. When it's hot outside, I go out to play. ____ ____

9. When it's cold outside, I go out to play. ____ ____

10. I find extreme heat or cold uncomfortable. ____ ____

11. I like the winter. ____ ____

D. 1. When I study I like to sit on the floor. ____ ____

2. When I study I like to sit on a soft chair or couch. ____ ____

3. When I study I feel sleepy unless I sit on a hard chair. ____ ____

4. I find it difficult to study at school. ____ ____

5. I finish all my homework at home. ____ ____

6. I always study for tests at home. ____ ____

7. I finish all my homework in school. ____ ____

8. I find it difficult to concentrate on my studies at home. ____ ____

9. I work best in a library. ____ ____

10. I can study almost anywhere. ____ ____

11. I like to study in bed. ____ ____

12. I like to study on carpeting or rugs. ____ ____

13. I can study on the floor, in a chair, on a couch, and at my desk. ____ ____

14. I often study in the bathroom. ____ ____

II. Emotional Stimuli

A. 1. I feel good when I do well in school. ____ ____

2. I feel good making my mother or father proud of me when I do well in school. ____ ____

3. My teacher feels good when I do well in school. ____ ____

4. Grown-ups are pleased if I bring home good reports. ____ ____

	True	False

5. Grown-ups are pleased when I do well in school. _____ _____

6. I like making someone feel proud of me. _____ _____

7. I am embarrassed when my grades are poor. _____ _____

8. It is more important to me to do well in things that happen out of school than in my school work. _____ _____

9. I like making my teacher proud of me. _____ _____

10. Nobody really cares if I do well in school. _____ _____

11. My teacher cares about me. _____ _____

12. My mother cares about my grades. _____ _____

13. My father cares about my grades. _____ _____

14. My teacher cares about my grades. _____ _____

15. Somebody cares about my grades in school. _____ _____

16. I want to get good grades for me! _____ _____

17. I am happy when I do well in school. _____ _____

18. I feel bad and work less when my grades are bad. _____ _____

19. I feel happy and proud when my marks are good. _____ _____

20. There are many things I like doing better than going to school. _____ _____

21. I love to learn new things. _____ _____

22. A good education will help me to get a good job. _____ _____

B.　1. I try to finish what I start. _____ _____

2. I usually finish what I start. _____ _____

3. I sometimes lose interest in things I began to do and then stop doing them. _____ _____

4. I rarely finish things that I start. _____ _____

5. I usually remember to finish my homework. _____ _____

6. I often have to be reminded to do my homework. _____ _____

7. I often forget to do or finish my homework. _____ _____

8. I often get tired of doing things and want to start something new. _____ _____

9. I usually like to finish things that I start. _____ _____

		True	False

10. My teacher is always telling me to finish what I'm supposed to do. _____ _____

11. My parent(s) remind me to finish things I have been told to do. _____ _____

12. Other grown-ups tell me to finish things that I have started. _____ _____

13. Somebody's always reminding me to do something! _____ _____

14. I often get tired of doing things. _____ _____

15. I often want help in finishing things. _____ _____

16. I like getting things done! _____ _____

17. I like to get things done so I can start something new. _____ _____

18. I remember on my own to get things done. _____ _____

C. 1. I think I am responsible. _____ _____

2. People tell me that I am responsible. _____ _____

3. I always do what I promise to do. _____ _____

4. People say that I do what I said I would do. _____ _____

5. I do keep my promises most of the time. _____ _____

6. I have to be reminded over and over again to do the things I've been told to do. _____ _____

7. If my teacher tells me to do something I try to do it. _____ _____

8. I keep forgetting to do the things I've been told to do. _____ _____

9. I remember to do what I'm told. _____ _____

10. People keep reminding me to do things. _____ _____

11. I like doing what I'm supposed to do. _____ _____

12. Promises have to be kept. _____ _____

13. I have to be reminded often to do something. _____ _____

D. 1. I like to be told exactly what to do. _____ _____

2. I like to be able to do things my own way. _____ _____

3. I like to be given choices of how I can do things. _____ _____

4. I like to be able to work things out for myself. _____ _____

5. I like other people to tell me how to do things. _____ _____

	True	False

6. I do better if I know my work is going to be checked.   _____ _____

7. I do the best I can whether or not the teacher will check my work.   _____ _____

8. I hate working hard on something that isn't checked by the teacher.   _____ _____

9. I like to be given clear directions when starting on new projects.   _____ _____

III. Sociological Stimuli

   A. When I really have a lot of studying to do:

      1. I like to work alone.   _____ _____

      2. I like to work with my good friend.   _____ _____

      3. I like to work with a couple of my friends.   _____ _____

      4. I like to work in a group of five or six classmates.   _____ _____

      5. I like to work with an adult.   _____ _____

      6. I like to work with a friend but to have an adult nearby.   _____ _____

      7. I like to work with a couple of friends but have an adult nearby.   _____ _____

      8. I like adults nearby when I'm working alone or with a friend.   _____ _____

      9. I like adults to stay away until my friends and I complete our work.   _____ _____

   B. The things I like doing best, I do:

      1. alone.   _____ _____

      2. with one friend.   _____ _____

      3. with a couple of friends.   _____ _____

      4. with a group of friends.   _____ _____

      5. with a grown-up.   _____ _____

      6. with several grown-ups.   _____ _____

      7. with friends and grown-ups.   _____ _____

      8. with a member of my family who is not a grown-up.   _____ _____

	True	False

IV. Physical Stimuli

  A. 1. If I have to learn something new, I like to learn about it by:

      a. reading a book. _____ _____

      b. hearing a record. _____ _____

      c. hearing a tape. _____ _____

      d. seeing a filmstrip. _____ _____

      e. seeing and hearing a movie. _____ _____

      f. looking at pictures and having someone explain them. _____ _____

      g. hearing my teacher tell me. _____ _____

      h. playing games. _____ _____

      i. going someplace and seeing for myself. _____ _____

      j. having someone show me. _____ _____

    2. The things I remember best are things:

      a. my teacher tells me. _____ _____

      b. someone other than my teacher tells me. _____ _____

      c. someone shows me. _____ _____

      d. I learned about on trips. _____ _____

      e. I read. _____ _____

      f. I heard on records. _____ _____

      g. I heard on the radio. _____ _____

      h. I saw on television. _____ _____

      i. I wrote stories about. _____ _____

      j. I saw in a movie. _____ _____

      k. I tried or worked on. _____ _____

      l. my friends and I talked about. _____ _____

    3. I really like to:

      a. read books, magazines, or newspapers. _____ _____

      b. see movies. _____ _____

      c. listen to records. _____ _____

	True	False
d. make tapes on a tape recorder.	____	____
e. draw.	____	____
f. look at pictures.	____	____
g. play games.	____	____
h. talk to people.	____	____
i. listen to people talk.	____	____
j. listen to the radio.	____	____
k. watch television.	____	____
l. go on trips.	____	____
m. learn new things.	____	____
n. study with friends.	____	____
o. build things.	____	____
p. do experiments.	____	____
q. take pictures or movies.	____	____
r. use typewriters, computers, calculators, or other machines.	____	____
s. go to the library.	____	____
t. trace things in sand.	____	____
u. mold things with my hands.	____	____

B.
1. I like to eat or drink while I study.   ____ ____

2. I dislike eating or drinking or chewing while I study.   ____ ____

3. While I'm studying I like to:

   a. eat.   ____ ____

   b. drink.   ____ ____

   c. chew gum.   ____ ____

   d. nibble on snacks.   ____ ____

   e. suck on candy.   ____ ____

4. I can eat, drink, or chew only after I finish studying.   ____ ____

5. I usually eat or drink when I'm nervous or upset.   ____ ____

6. I hardly ever eat when I'm nervous or upset.   ____ ____

	True	False

7. I could study better if I could eat while I'm learning. ____ ____

8. While I'm learning, eating something would distract me. ____ ____

9. I often catch myself chewing on a pencil as I study. ____ ____

C. 1. I hate to get up in the morning. ____ ____

2. I hate to go to sleep at night. ____ ____

3. I could sleep all morning. ____ ____

4. I stay awake for a long time after I get into bed. ____ ____

5. I feel wide awake after 10:00 in the morning. ____ ____

6. If I stay up very late at night I get too sleepy to remember anything. ____ ____

7. I feel sleepy after lunch. ____ ____

8. When I have homework to do, I like to get up early in the morning to do it. ____ ____

9. When I can, I do my homework in the afternoon. ____ ____

10. I usually start my homework after dinner. ____ ____

11. I could stay up all night. ____ ____

12. I wish school would start near lunchtime. ____ ____

13. I wish I could stay home during the day and go to school at night. ____ ____

14. I like going to school in the morning. ____ ____

15. I can remember things when I study them:

    a. in the morning. ____ ____

    b. at lunchtime. ____ ____

    c. in the afternoon. ____ ____

    d. before dinner. ____ ____

    e. after dinner. ____ ____

    f. late at night. ____ ____

D. 1. When I study I often get up to do something (like take a drink, get a cookie, etc.) and then return to work. ____ ____

2. When I study I stay with it until I am finished and then I get up. ____ ____

	True	False

3. It's difficult for me to sit in one place for a long time. ____ ____

4. I often change my position in my chair. ____ ____

5. I can sit in one place for a long time. ____ ____

6. I constantly change position in my chair. ____ ____

7. I can work best for short amounts of time with breaks in between. ____ ____

8. I like getting my work done and over with. ____ ____

9. I like to work a little, stop, return to the work, stop, return to it again, and so forth. ____ ____

10. I like to stick to a job and finish it in one sitting if I can. ____ ____

11. I leave most jobs for the last minute and then have to work on them from beginning to end. ____ ____

12. I do most of my jobs a little at a time and eventually get them done. ____ ____

13. I enjoy doing something over and over again when I know how to do it well. ____ ____

14. I like familiar friends and places. ____ ____

15. New jobs and subjects make me nervous. ____ ____

Scoring Sheet

Part I: Environmental Stimuli

A. Sound

Needs silent or quiet areas.

True	1 2 4 5 8 12 13		True_____	Total
False	3 5 6 7 9 10 11		False_____	T + F _____ / 14 = _____ %

Sound is acceptable or desirable.

True	2 3 5 6 7 9 10 11		True_____	Total
False	1 4 8 12 13		False_____	T + F _____ / 13 = _____ %

B. Light

Requires a great deal of light.

True	1 3 4 5		True_____ / 4 = _____ %

Requires low light.

True	2 6 7		True_____ / 3 = _____ %

Light is probably not a factor if 6 or 7 of the questions are marked either all true or all false.

C. Temperature

Needs cool environment.

True	2 4 7 9 11		True_____ / 5 = _____ %

Needs warm environment.

True	1 3 5 6 8		True_____ / 5 = _____ %

Temperature not a factor (only extremes).

True	3–4, 6–7, 10		True_____ / 5 = _____ %

Divided or paired (3–4, 6–7) answers may indicate that temperature is not a factor.

D. Design

Requires formality

True	3 7 8 9		True_____ / 4 = _____ %

Requires informality

True	1 2 4 5 6 10 12 14		True_____ / 9 = _____ %

Design not important

True	10 13		True_____ / 2 = _____ %

Scoring Sheet, continued

Part II: Emotional Stimuli

A. Motivation Toward School Work

    Self-motivated

    True   1 16 17 19 21 22   True_____ / 6 = _____ %

    Adult-motivated

    True   2 4 5 6 7 12 13 15   True_____ / 8 = _____ %

    Teacher-motivated

    True   3 6 7 9 11 14 15   True_____ / 7 = _____ %

    Unmotivated

    True   8 10 18 20   True_____ / 4 = _____ %

B. Persistence

    Persistent

    True   1 2 5 9 16 17 18   True_____ / 7 = _____ %

    Not persistent

    True   3 4 6 7 8 10 11 12

                    13 14 15   True_____ / 11 = _____ %

C. Responsibility

    Responsible

    True   1 2 3 4 5 7 9 11 12   True_____ / 9 = _____ %

    Not very responsible

    True   6 8 10 13   True_____ / 4 = _____ %

D. Structure

    Needs structure

    True   1 5 6 8 9   True_____ / 5 = _____ %

    Needs little structure

    True   2 3 4 7 8   True_____ / 5 = _____ %

Scoring Sheet, continued

Part III: Sociological Stimuli

Prefers learning, working, studying, or doing things:

Alone

True   A1   A8   B1   True_____ / 3 = _____ %

With one peer

True   A2   A8   B2   B8   True_____ / 4 = _____ %

With two peers

True   A3   A9   B3   True_____ / 3 = _____ %

With several peers

True   A4   A9   B4   True_____ / 3 = _____ %

With adults

True   A5   B5   B6   True_____ / 3 = _____ %

Combined

True   A6   A7   A8   B7   True_____ / 4 = _____ %

Part IV: Physical Stimuli

A. Perceptual Preferences

Auditory

True   1b   1c   1e   1f   1g

               2a   2b   2f   2g   2h   2l

               3c   3h   3i   3j   3n   True_____ / 16 = _____ %

Visual

True   1a   1d   1e   1f   1h   1j

               2c   2e   2h   2j

               3a   3b   3f   3k   3s   True_____ / 15 = _____ %

Tactile

True   1h   2i   3e   3o   3t   3u   True_____ / 6 = _____ %

Kinesthetic

True   1i   2d   2k   3d   3g   3l

               3p   3q   3r   True_____ / 9 = _____ %

Scoring Sheet, continued

B. Intake

Requires intake

True   1   3a   3b   3c   3d   3e

         5   7   9   True _____ / 9 = _____ %

Does not require intake

True   2   4   6   8   True _____ / 4 = _____ %

C. Time

Early morning

True   8   14   15a   True_____   Total

False   1   3   5   10   11   12   13   False_____   T + F _____ / 10 = _____ %

Late morning

True   5   12   15b   True_____   Total

False   3   8   9   10   11   13   14   False_____   T + F _____ / 10 = _____ %

Afternoon

True   3   5   9   12   15c   15d   True_____   Total

False   7   8   11   13   14   False_____   T + F _____ / 11 = _____ %

Evening

True   2   4   5   10   11   13   15e   15f   True_____   Total

False   6   8   14   False_____   T + F _____ / 11 = _____ %

D. Mobility

Needs mobility

True   1   3   4   6   7   9   12   True _____ / 7 = _____ %

Does not need mobility

True   2   5   8   10   11   13   14   15   True _____ / 8 = _____ %

Learning Style Profile

Student: _____ Grade: _____ Date: _____

Stimuli	Comments based on highest percentages noted on the survey	Comments based on observations and other information
I. Environmental:		
Sound		
Light		
Temperature		
Design		
II. Emotional:		
Motivation		
Persistence		
Responsibility		
Structure		
III. Sociological:		
Appears to work best with		
IV. Physical:		
Perceptual		
Intake		
Time		
Mobility		

Reflection and Evaluation: Learning Styles Inventory

How did the administration of the learning styles inventory go? What changes would you make in administering this instrument in the future?

_____

_____

_____

_____

What impact do you think these findings will have on your planning and management for the whole group?

_____

_____

_____

_____

_____

_____

What impact do you think these findings will have on your planning and management for particular students?

_____

_____

_____

_____

_____

_____

How do you intend to use this information? _____

_____

_____

_____

_____

_____

_____

_____

_____

Chapter 14

Time-on-Task Studies

D O YOU HAVE a student who doesn't disrupt the class, but never seems to get anything done? Have you ever wondered why some students manage to take hours to complete something that should take only a few minutes? Time-on-task studies enable an observer to account for what a student does with his or her time in class. This type of observation is especially valuable in analyzing and documenting the behavior of students who don't complete their work or make the best use of their time. When a student seems to be spending a good deal of time off-task, observation can help you discover patterns in his or her attention span, mobility, and distractibility. Observation can also reveal what the student is doing during work time.

Specifically, a time-on-task study is conducted by an observer who describes and records a student's behavior at regular intervals (for example, every twenty seconds) for a given period of time, perhaps ten to fifteen minutes. Although students are usually observed as they work independently at their seats, records of behavior in reading, small groups, or play groups may be useful and appropriate. The intervals and duration of the observations will depend on the activity and the student being observed.

Your observations may be difficult or impractical until the students have developed adequate independent work skills. Nonetheless, the act of focusing on a particular student for a specified purpose can greatly aid in your understanding of that student.

Observation Guidelines

If you have decided to conduct a time-on-task study, consider the following suggestions:

1. In order to conduct a time-on-task study in your own classroom, be sure to have all your students occupied and declare yourself "off-limits" except for an emergency.

2. Be sure that the activity corresponds to your objective. For example, if you set out to examine the child's use of time during independent work sessions, do not observe the child during inter-active activities.

3. Record observations for one student at a time.

4. Note the day of the week, time of the day, sequence of activities, and any other information you feel will be helpful or relevant (previous activities, weather, materials used, changes in environment, movement or interaction required, or special rules assigned for the completion of the activity).

5. Observe at a routine time, such as during daily morning seat work.

6. Record at regular intervals. Use a stopwatch or a wristwatch with a second hand to mark intervals.

7. Record observable behaviors. Do not record assumptions about a student's feelings. For example:

   Turning pages in reading book
   Coloring science picture
   Playing with glue
   Hitting pencil on chair; singing
   Head on arms as if asleep
   Copying problems from the chalkboard

   Do not attempt to interpret the student's behavior or guess his or her purpose.

8. Record behavior as it occurs *at specified observation intervals only*. Use the time between intervals to record what you have observed. If possible, avoid looking at the student except at specified times.

9. Record the behavior of the observed student only. If behavior involves other students, state your observation in terms of the subject's behavior. For example:

Listening to J. and D. talking

Asked P. for a crayon

Watching G. work

Talking to S.

10. Observe discreetly. Your students should not be aware of your observations or at least should not know who is being observed.

Interpreting Time-on-Task Observations

Your time-on-task observations can provide you with different kinds of information, and there are many ways to approach the records you have obtained. One method is to follow the procedure below:

1. Determine whether the observation (description of the student's behavior) indicates on- or off-task behavior. On-task behaviors might include working (reading, writing, interacting with materials), preparing to work (getting materials without distraction, opening book), or work-related interactions.

2. Indicate on-task behavior by any of the following methods:
   ▶ Mark the line (observation of on-task behavior) with a highlighting marker.
   ▶ Draw a vertical solid line between the interval markers (seconds) and the on-task behavior described.
   ▶ Circle the on-task behavior.
   These markings help visually distinguish on- and off-task behaviors and show patterns in the frequency and duration of such behaviors.

3. Determine overall percentages of on- and off-task behaviors using the following formula:

$$\frac{\text{Number of on-task observations}}{\text{Total number of observations}} = \text{\% of } on\text{-task behavior}$$

100% – (% of *on*-task behavior) = % of *off*-task behavior

4. Look for patterns in work behavior such as:
   ▶ longest uninterrupted time-on-task.
   ▶ number of brief on-task periods (one minute or less).
   ▶ average length of on-task periods.
   ▶ average length of off-task periods.
   ▶ frequency and number of interruptions (off-task behaviors).
   ▶ nature of interruptions or distractions.
   ▶ types of off-task behavior (passive, aggressive, interactive, and so forth).

5. Record patterns, comments, and recommendations on the reproducible "Time-on-Task Observation Form" (pages 125–126).

You are now able to make some generalizations and develop a statement based on the information obtained in the steps above. This statement can help you determine strategies for minimizing off-task behaviors and maintaining on-task behaviors. For example, if the student is occupied with toys or materials at his desk, you might ask him to store the materials in a locker or cubby. If the student is distracted by other students, you may be able to provide a more private or isolated work space, such as a study carrel or private desk. This suggestion may be particularly valuable for students who are unable to stay on task for more than a minute or two at a time.

You can even use this information as you would an interest inventory. Students' off-task behavior usually indicates preferences that you may want to consider in providing motivation and rewards. The distracting toys or materials mentioned above might be provided *after* the student completes the assigned tasks (or a specified portion of the assignment). If the student has a tendency to wander around the room, you might make this movement contingent on completion of a specified amount of work. Be sure the student has plenty of materials on hand before he or she starts to work.

Using the time-on-task study in conjunction with information gained from other instruments mentioned in this unit can help you make adjustments to meet a particular student's needs. For example, if you have learned that the student is not a "morning person," and that he or she likes to draw, works best with a partner, or requires structure, you may be able to provide some of these options. If you make changes after analyzing the time-on-task study, be sure to follow up with subsequent observations and compare your new findings with the previous ones.

Use the observation form to record your observations and analyze the results.

Time-on-Task Observation Form

Student observed: _____ Date: _____

Day: _____ Time: _____ Special Conditions: _____

_____

Assignment: _____

Observer: _____

Min :Sec	Observation:	Min :Sec	Observation:
____ :00	_____	____ :00	_____
:20	_____	:20	_____
:40	_____	:40	_____
____ :00	_____	____ :00	_____
:20	_____	:20	_____
:40	_____	:40	_____
____ :00	_____	____ :00	_____
:20	_____	:20	_____
:40	_____	:40	_____
____ :00	_____	____ :00	_____
:20	_____	:20	_____
:40	_____	:40	_____
____ :00	_____	____ :00	_____
:20	_____	:20	_____
:40	_____	:40	_____
____ :00	_____	____ :00	_____
:20	_____	:20	_____
:40	_____	:40	_____
____ :00	_____	____ :00	_____
:20	_____	:20	_____
:40	_____	:40	_____
____ :00	_____	____ :00	_____
:20	_____	:20	_____
:40	_____	:40	_____

_____ % *on* task   _____ % *off* task

Patterns: _____
_____
_____
_____
_____
_____
_____
_____
_____

Comments: _____
_____
_____
_____
_____
_____
_____
_____
_____

Recommendations: _____
_____
_____
_____
_____
_____
_____
_____
_____
_____

Reflection and Evaluation: Time-on-Task Studies

Why did you select the student you observed? _____

_____

How sucessful were you at observing without interruptions? _____

_____

Is there anything you might do differently next time? _____

_____

How successful were your attempts to observe unnoticed? _____

_____

How successful were your attempts at objective recording during specified time intervals? _____

_____

_____

What did you learn while you were observing? _____

_____

_____

_____

What did you learn from analyzing the findings of the survey? _____

_____

_____

_____

What do you intend to do with the information you obtained? _____

_____

_____

How do you feel this process has helped (or will help) you in understanding this particular student and in identifying needs and possible means to help this student?

_____

_____

_____

Do you plan to use this survey with this same student? If yes, at what point? _____

_____

With other students? _____

_____

Chapter 15

Sociograms

▶ Ms. Adams is having a hard time keeping her third graders' attention because everyone is excited about a pajama party one of the girls is planning.

▶ Donald has been crying all morning because the children at the sand table made fun of his haircut.

▶ Sandy has a hard time getting along with anyone and often ends up working and playing alone.

▶ Martin, one of the most popular kids in the school, seems to set the tone for how the other students in class behave.

LIKE IT OR NOT, social factors influence your classroom climate, however task-oriented you or your management strategies may be. While many of these factors remain outside your control, the more information you have about the social dynamics of your class, the more you are able to use that information in your teaching.

Sociograms visually represent the relationships among the members of a group. When completed, the sociogram reflects patterns in the dynamics of the group that may be helpful in providing information about the social relationships of the individuals in that group. The underlying assumptions of this chapter are that social skills are important components of the "whole child," and that teachers can play an important role in the child's social development.

Social skills are among the interdependent variables that make up a student's self-image and affect a student's performance in school. Social status can also have a tremendous influence on the

degree of success a student experiences in a particular learning situation.

While sociograms may be valuable for identifying social leaders and groups, they are probably best suited for identifying socially isolated children. These students often have limited opportunities to learn social skills and are more likely to have problems in their school careers and later in life. With the information provided by the sociogram, you may be able to encourage social development in your students. Particularly with students who are having behavioral problems or who are socially isolated, problems such as low peer acceptance, poor social skills, and lack of self-esteem will probably continue without some teacher intervention.

Providing interactive activities at which a student will succeed can build a student's self-esteem. By putting a student in a helping role, as a peer tutor or committee chairperson, for example, you can also reinforce a student's belief in his own social competence.

Finally, a sociogram can provide information to help you in grouping students. For heterogeneous groups, you may want to distribute students according to variables such as leadership capabilities and social desirability. Pairing students who might not have chosen to work together can benefit everyone involved.

Collecting Data for the Sociogram

In many instances, you will be able to spot the most obvious leaders or isolated students by simply observing the day-to-day interactions of your class. This process is especially valuable in identifying children who tend to get lost in the shuffle, and in revealing some of the subtle social forces you may not have noticed.

In order to obtain information for this particular sociogram, you will have to ask each student the following: "If we were going on a field trip, pick the person from this class with whom you would want to sit." Each student then indicates a first, second, and third choice. They can provide this information by writing their choices on a slip of paper (their name must also be on the paper),

Name _Joe B._

1st Choice _Pete_

2nd Choice _Manuel_

3rd Choice _Roneice_

or by checking first, second, and third choices on individual class lists,

Name _Elizabeth_

_____ Allen

___3___ Barry

___1___ Caroline

_____ Ann

_____ Elizabeth

___2___ Francine

_____ Gary

or by naming their choices in a face-to-face interview during which you record their responses.

Whatever your method, sociograms bring up some sensitive issues and you should stress confidentiality. For counselors and other professionals devoted to identifying and meeting the needs of a particular student, a sociogram can provide important information, but under normal circumstances, the data does not need to be shared with anyone. Written responses, when complete, should be folded and collected immediately. A skillful teacher will minimize the importance of who is choosing whom and shift the focus of the activity to something else.

Organizing the Data

To draw the sociogram, start with one student's response.

Name _Joe B._

1st Choice _Pete_

2nd Choice _Manuel_

3rd Choice _Roneice_

Begin a rough draft by drawing a box or a circle with the student's name in it.

Then draw boxes or circles with the names of the student's choices in them.

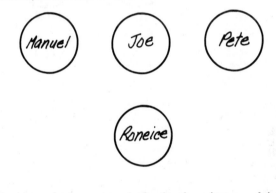

Connect the boxes or circles by drawing a *red (or unbroken)* arrow from the student to his or her first choice: ————⟶ . Draw a *blue (or broken)* arrow from the student to the second choice: — — —⟶. Finally, indicate the third choices with a *green (or dotted)* arrow: ·····⟶.

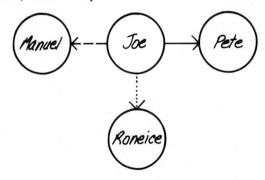

Select another student, perhaps one of the first student's choices.

Name _Pete L._

1st Choice _Carlos_

2nd Choice _Roneice_

3rd Choice _Joe_

Add circles (or boxes) and arrows as needed.

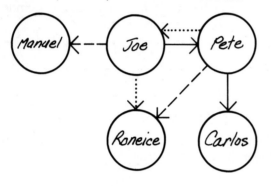

Continue and complete the draft. You may need to redraw to provide greater clarity in layout and connections.

In addition to the drawing described above, consider making a list that includes each student and marking it according to the number of times each one is chosen as a first, second, or third choice. While this list will not show the connections, you will still get a sense of each student's social standing in the class.

Reflection and Evaluation: Sociograms

In planning the sociogram, what were your primary considerations? _____
_____
_____

How well were you able to get information from the students? _____
_____

How would you change your method of getting information, if at all? _____
_____
_____

Reflect on the process of constructing the sociogram: _____
_____
_____
_____

What did you learn about your class (and/or individuals) from constructing and analyzing the sociogram?
_____
_____
_____
_____
_____

What needs have you become aware of? _____
_____
_____
_____

How will this experience help you meet the needs of your students? _____
_____
_____
_____
_____
_____
_____
_____

UNIT IV

Behavior Management

Chapter 16

Problem-Solving Strategies

WHEN YOU are faced with problems in the classroom, how do you begin to solve them? So many factors are involved in running a classroom, and so many things can go wrong, that even little problems can sometimes appear impossible and overwhelming. This chapter provides a process by which these challenges can become manageable.

If you're feeling overwhelmed by the challenges of teaching, the more concrete and specific you make them, the easier they are to approach and solve. Just as an enormous house cleaning job becomes much less threatening when you break it down into smaller, separate tasks in individual rooms, so the job of teaching becomes more manageable when you divide it into separate tasks.

To begin, you may want to separate what you want to work on into "interactive" and "noninteractive" categories. Other chapters in the book address issues of organization, instructional management, and professionalism. This unit examines problems in teacher-student interactions, usually called "student behavior problems." The process described in this chapter is designed to help you isolate—and approach—one specific problem with one specific student. Eventually, you may wish to apply the process to solving problems with other students or to problems that are not specifically related to students.

The process involves isolating a problem, defining and documenting it, and then implementing and evaluating various solutions. Working through the process has several advantages, including the fact that you are likely to remedy a problematic situation. Along the way, you may feel better about the fact that you are at least trying to solve the problem. If you then discover that the problem is beyond what you are capable of dealing with in the classroom, you have solid documentation to support a decision to enlist outside help. Consider the following steps for problem solving.

Step 1

Try to define exactly what the problem is. For example, "Michael always seems to be out of his seat," is far more specific, and therefore easier to work with, than "Michael is driving me crazy." Although Michael may have a number of other problems, start with the one that is most disruptive or annoying.

Try to focus on what you can observe in the classroom. Dealing with disruptive behavior that occurs in your classroom is important even when it may be caused by things outside of your classroom, such as the birth of a new sibling or a divorce. Understanding outside influences will be helpful, yet they do not excuse unacceptable behavior, nor will they change the fact that the behavior is disturbing your classroom.

Step 2

Now that you have identified a specific problem, begin collecting data to document its existence and describe its depth, dimensions, frequency, and impact on other students. Do your data collecting before you make any changes in your behavior; you simply want to determine how bad the problem is. For example, Ms. Montoya, a first grade teacher, determined, simply by making marks on a piece of scratch paper, that a student she was observing was at her side with a question or interruption more than forty times between the morning bell and the first recess.

By collecting data, you may discover that what had seemed to be a big problem either has improved or wasn't as big as you had originally thought. Is Gloria *always* difficult, or just when she tries to work with art supplies? Is Ron always noisy, or just after physical education? How long has it been since Danita was in a fight? Although the student will probably be the primary source of data, you may wish to examine other sources, such as parents, support staff, former teachers, or cumulative folders.

Use various strategies to collect data about the student's performance, behavior, and attitudes. Select strategies that will give you the most useful information about the problem you have identified. Depending on the problem you are studying, you may compile anecdotal records; collect work samples and results of diagnostic or placement assessments; or administer student interviews and inventories, time-on-task studies, or sociometric assessments.

You may want to use the same strategy at different times, or for several days, to determine consistency. Ms. Montoya, for example, might observe her student's behavior during the next few mornings, in other classes, or between lunch and dismissal. As you collect data about a particular student, file the materials in a separate folder for that individual.

Keep in mind that the purpose of data collection is not to produce a weapon against the student. The only reason you are collecting data is to help determine the best strategy for changing negative behavior—not to punish the student.

Step 3

Use the collected data to formulate a summary statement that documents the problem and describes it in some detail. This step will help you integrate the information you have obtained and move toward a solution.

Step 4

Brainstorm some possible solutions to this problem based on the information in your statement. Note anything that sounds good, whether or not you plan to implement it. For each solution you propose, also indicate the outcome you expect.

Return for a moment to the example in Step Two. To deal with the student, Ms. Montoya might consider ignoring him unless he's in his seat (which would probably only make him more persistent), calling on him more often (which might meet his need for attention), allowing him specified conference time (which would probably only work during that specified time), or gluing him to his chair (which would probably get her fired from her job). Noting the probable outcomes will help you decide which solutions to implement.

Step 5

Select one or more proposed solutions to implement. Record the outcomes and, if possible, reassess the situation with the data collection strategies you selected in Step Two.

Ms. Montoya decided to "sell" conference time, and gave the student five paper clips which he placed on his belt. Each paper clip could "buy" her attention when she was working with another student or group. According to the rules, he could interrupt her at any time he needed her, as long as he had one of his paper clips, which he surrendered, one by one, each time he came up to talk to her. She warned him that he would have to decide when it was really important for her to help him, as she would not answer him unless he had a paper clip left. He could ask other class members for help if he wanted. She also made a point of stopping by his desk when he was working independently and reinforcing his positive choices.

Ms. Montoya started giving the student five paper clips for the morning and another five for the afternoon. Within days, he was down to five for the entire day, and then three. Within two weeks, the problem was solved.

Continue testing other possible solutions if your first attempts do not produce satisfactory results. When you test your ideas, you will be making some changes in your behavior, in the environment of the classroom, or in interactive patterns. Keep track of the impact the changes have on the student—good and bad—and evaluate the proposed solution. When necessary, go back to Step Four and think through some more ideas. If you feel stuck, you may want to share the file with your principal, the school counselor, a trusted colleague, or even the student's parents, for additional suggestions.

Step 6

Describe your plans for maintenance and follow-up. You may need to collect more data and implement new solutions from time to time.

Use the reproducible Problem-Solving Case Study worksheets (pages 136–140) to record your progress through these six steps.

Worksheet: Problem-Solving Case Study

STEP 1   DATE: _____

Identify the problem you plan to study and would like to solve. Be specific in your description.

_____

_____

_____

_____

_____

STEP 2   DATE: _____

What data sources do you plan to use? _____

_____

_____

_____

How do you plan to document the problem described in Step 1? _____

_____

_____

_____

_____

_____

_____

_____

_____

_____

_____

_____

Implement the strategies you described above. File the results in a separate folder.

STEP 3   DATE: _____

Write a summary statement of the problem based on the data you collected in Step 2.

_____

_____

_____

_____

_____

_____

_____

_____

_____

_____

_____

_____

_____

_____

_____

_____

_____

_____

_____

_____

_____

_____

_____

_____

_____

_____

_____

_____

_____

_____

STEP 4   DATE: _____

Use the chart below to brainstorm possible solutions. Note the probable outcomes (impact, needs addressed, and direct change in student behavior).

Proposed solution   Probable outcome

1. _____   _____

   _____   _____

   _____   _____

2. _____   _____

   _____   _____

   _____   _____

3. _____   _____

   _____   _____

   _____   _____

4. _____   _____

   _____   _____

   _____   _____

5. _____   _____

   _____   _____

   _____   _____

6. _____   _____

   _____   _____

   _____   _____

7. _____   _____

   _____   _____

   _____   _____

8. _____   _____

   _____   _____

   _____   _____

9. _____   _____

   _____   _____

   _____   _____

   _____   _____

STEP 5   DATE: _____

Test your proposed solutions. Use the form below for each solution you test:

Proposed solution _____

_____

_____

_____

Reason for implementing _____

_____

_____

_____

Implementation strategy _____

_____

_____

_____

Observed outcomes with support data _____

_____

_____

_____

_____

_____

_____

_____

_____

Evaluation _____

_____

_____

Date(s) implemented _____

_____

_____

STEP 6   DATE: _____

Describe your plans for maintenance and follow-up: _____

_____

_____

_____

_____

_____

_____

_____

_____

_____

_____

_____

_____

_____

_____

_____

_____

_____

_____

_____

_____

_____

_____

_____

_____

_____

_____

_____

Reflection and Evaluation: Problem-Solving Case Study

Describe the impact and value of each of the following steps in this problem-solving project:

Specifically identifying the problem _____
_____
_____

Collecting data _____
_____
_____

Brainstorming solutions _____
_____
_____

Testing proposed solutions _____
_____
_____

Following up on solutions _____
_____
_____

How was this process helpful to you? _____
_____
_____
_____
_____

Did you have a need to share the data you collected or the results of the changes you implemented with the administration, support staff, and/or parents? If so, how was your experience (and the information) helpful?
_____
_____
_____

How do you plan to use this process in the future? _____
_____
_____
_____

Chapter 17

. . . .

Encouraging Student Responsibility

IF ASKED how they would change their students, most teachers would make them more self-managing and responsible. Few teachers mind filling the cognitive gaps, yet teaching students self-management skills often takes up valuable instructional time.

Some teachers condition their students to act irresponsibly by not recognizing the self-management skills they do have. These teachers assume that students are unable to handle responsibility and that adults must take on much of that responsibility for them. In this way, well-meaning teachers may trap themselves into doing things students could do, or learn to do, thereby preventing the students from experiencing opportunities for growth in these areas.

On the other hand, some teachers are amazed when a lesson fails because the students did not have the self-management skills necessary to complete the task. Student success is often undermined when the activity requires decision making, interactive competence, or other forms of self-management that the students have not yet acquired. Quite naturally, these disasters tend to occur during independent, small-group activities or activities that require students to independently select a task and work alone.

This chapter is based upon the following assumptions:

▶ Students need certain responsible learning (self-management) behaviors to succeed in school.

▶ Students have not necessarily learned these behaviors and may not know how to apply them when they come to your classroom.

▶ Students can be taught responsible learning behaviors. As with any set of behaviors, these are more effectively achieved gradually and with practice.

In an informal survey I made, several elementary teachers identified a variety of skills and behaviors as necessary for effective learning. Below is the list of behaviors which the teachers in the survey considered important:

INTRAPERSONAL SKILLS AND BEHAVIORS

Pays attention

Exercises self-control

Listens

Uses time constructively

Does work and assignments

Stays with task until complete

Follows directions

Sets personal goals

Reviews work

Takes care of materials

Has command of the language

Works independently

Has pride in progress

Has desire for achievement and success

Meets class standards and teacher expectations

Gives best of self

INTERPERSONAL SKILLS AND BEHAVIORS

Gets along with others

Shares information

Verbalizes with peers and teachers

Asks questions

Helps others

Cooperates; works well in a group

Participates

Respects the rights and property of others

The rest of this chapter will focus on how to help students develop these behaviors and the decision-making skills that are necessary in most learning situations.

Expectations and Abilities

Many proponents of the open classroom concept in the 1960s and 1970s insisted that students had the ability to select meaningful learning experiences. The validity of this viewpoint came under question when teachers experienced the problems that arose from simply turning students loose on a roomful of exciting and stimulating materials. Unfortunately, creativity and curiosity cannot compensate for a lack of self-management skills, and students who were not able to choose activities, care for materials, or work independently were often lost, overwhelmed, and distracted. Most teachers would recognize the futility of assigning algebraic word problems to students who cannot add or subtract, yet how often are teachers tempted to assign complex work contracts to students who fall apart trying to decide which pencil to use?

Sadly, many students come to a classroom from previous experiences—home or school—in which they were offered few opportunities to make decisions that would have any impact on their lives. Conditioned dependency can contribute significantly to failures and frustrations in school, for both the student and the teacher. When adults offer students instruction and opportunities to become responsible, students become more self-reliant.

Encouraging Decision-Making Skills

The ability to make decisions is fundamental to becoming a responsible person. The classroom offers an array of opportunities for students to make decisions and experience the consequences of those decisions.

If your students are exceptionally responsible, and if you are equipped and well organized, then asking the students to select meaningful learning experiences within the parameters of certain rules may be a realistic objective for your particular class. However, if your students have difficulty deciding between two books for independent reading, don't despair. By starting with simple decisions, you can build your students' confidence in their ability to function independently. Eventually, even the most flustered child can learn to become truly self-managing.

Help students who have difficulty in making decisions by offering assistance, setting time limits, or allowing them to change their minds. If their choices will be final for a certain activity or time period, let them know ahead of time. You can build choices into just about any assignment.

The following activities can help you encourage student responsibility. These activities are fairly simple and are designed to give the students confidence in decision making. Some ideas are more appropriate for older children, a few of whom may require practice at even easier decision-making tasks.

Opportunities for Decision Making

You may wish to offer some of these decision-making choices:

▶ Decide which of two dittos to do first.

▶ Decide which two crayons to use in a drawing.

▶ Decide which two of the three language puzzles to complete.

▶ Decide which ten math problems to do.

▶ Decide where to sit for independent reading when given no option to leave once that location has been selected.

▶ Decide whether to stop talking or to leave the room.

▶ Decide, in a group, how to share two cookies between three people so that all three people are satisfied with the decision.

▶ Decide how to arrange certain materials in a display.

▶ Decide whether to take a one-minute break now or a three-minute break in ten minutes.

▶ Decide which learning center to visit during self-selection activity time.

▶ Decide whether to display a drawing or to take it home to share with the family.

▶ Decide whether or not a skill requires more practice.

Reflection and Evaluation: Encouraging Student Responsibility

List responsible learning behaviors you have observed in your classroom: _____

_____

_____

_____

_____

What opportunities for decision making are available to your students on a daily basis? _____

_____

_____

_____

_____

_____

_____

What other opportunities have you provided to encourage the development of responsible student behavior?

_____

_____

_____

_____

_____

_____

_____

_____

In what ways do the students handle these opportunities successfully? _____

_____

_____

_____

_____

_____

_____

_____

In what ways do they experience difficulty? _____

_____

_____

_____

_____

_____

What decisions do you feel your students should ideally be able to make in your classroom? Which responsible learning behaviors would you like to see exhibited (or exhibited more consistently)?

_____

_____

_____

_____

_____

_____

What plans do you have to help your students achieve these goals? _____

_____

_____

_____

_____

_____

_____

_____

_____

_____

_____

_____

_____

_____

_____

_____

_____

Chapter 18

Reinforcing Positive Behavior

WHEN ADDRESSING behavior management, teacher training programs tend to emphasize using praise as positive reinforcement and as a means of maintaining discipline. This emphasis discourages negative practices such as yelling, criticizing, or humiliating students. While research has proven the value of positive reinforcement, teachers need to examine how and why they use it.

Several types of positive reinforcement are possible. Activity reinforcement—rewarding a student with a desirable activity—is discussed in detail in the following chapter. Social reinforcement and token reinforcement are presented in this chapter.

Social Reinforcement

Reinforcement is the foundation of operant conditioning, through which individuals gradually develop a particular behavior. The improvement in performing the behavior comes about as a result of reinforcement. A reinforcer can be anything that encourages a behavior to occur again. Social reinforcers include praise, compliments, or attention to a behavior. They may be verbal or nonverbal.

One of the problems with operant conditioning is that the student must give the desired response or action spontaneously before conditioning can begin. Teachers often try to use praise, one type of social reinforcer, in the hope of *eliciting* responses. However, a statement such as, "I like the way Bobby is sitting quietly," is more likely to prolong Bobby's good behavior than get the other students to settle down and imitate Bobby. Positive reinforcement is most effective when used to recognize and reinforce positive behavior. It is not a means of *eliciting* a positive response.

When a teacher uses praise as a way of controlling behavior, students will probably perceive it as dishonest and insincere. Be sure to praise students for their accomplishments.

Using praise can have negative effects on students, particularly in conflict situations. It can block teacher-student communication when it is used to make a student feel better or to deny a problem. When a student does something poorly, a teacher's praise will not improve the behavior. The student will probably feel that the teacher simply does not understand him or her. Praise may also encourage student dependence on the teacher.

Public praise of one student may be interpreted by other students as criticism of them. Students may also become so accustomed to praise that they perceive an absence of praise as criticism. Recognizing a *particular* achievement may be more successful for encouraging self-management than offering general praise.

Reinforcement with Tokens

Another form of positive reinforcement involves the use of tokens. Some tangible reward is offered for the performance of a desired behavior. The reward may be a piece of candy, a sticker, a marble, a poker chip, a gold star, or any item that the student considers valuable. While using tokens can change student behavior quickly, it may not be the most effective long-term strategy. As with incorrect use or overuse of social reinforcers, several dangers exist in using tokens.

One danger is that teachers may be tempted to increase the rewards, causing "token inflation" to occur. Teachers can get caught up in devoting too much time to distributing, recording, and cashing in tokens. Also, students may become dependent on tokens and perceive the absence of a reward as criticism or failure. Dependence on tokens discourages students from working for intrinsic rewards.

Reinforcement with tokens is usually unnecessary under regular classroom conditions. If you use tokens, do so sparingly, decreasing the rewards over time. Tokens can be useful rewards for nighttime reading, returning weekly progress reports, bringing in news clippings, or completing a weekly assignment. They are not recommended for modifying in-class, off-task student behavior, which may be best accomplished through social and activity reinforcement. Candy and gum are not recommended as token reinforcers.

Reflection and Evaluation: Reinforcing Positive Behavior

What types of social reinforcement do you currently use in your classroom (verbal and nonverbal)? What are your actions intended to reinforce?

_____

_____

_____

_____

_____

When you acknowledge student achievement, to what degree do you specifically recognize performance (as opposed to praising compliance)?

_____

_____

_____

_____

_____

What responses do you elicit from your students as a result of your social reinforcers? _____

_____

_____

_____

_____

What are your plans for the future use of social reinforcers? _____

_____

_____

_____

_____

_____

_____

Are you currently using any system of reinforcement with tokens? If so, please describe:

Token _____

Desired behavior _____

Criteria for reward _____

_____

Frequency of reward _____

_____

How long have you been using this system? _____

_____

How has the amount and/or frequency of your rewards changed over the time you have been using this system?

_____

_____

_____

To what extent has this system worked to help you maintain the desired behavior? _____

_____

_____

_____

_____

_____

What plans do you have for future use of reinforcement with tokens (this system or another)? _____

_____

_____

_____

_____

_____

_____

_____

Chapter 19

. . . .

Contingency Management

I N AN EFFORT to keep things under control, many teachers, particularly beginning teachers, start the year with a list of rules and a commitment to be firm. The fear of losing control often leads to a belief in the necessity of continual policing. Intervening when students misbehave will occasionally be necessary, but spending the year watching for and responding to negative behaviors won't leave much time for teaching. In addition, such a role will probably leave you feeling that teaching isn't much fun for you or your students.

This chapter examines a positive approach to getting students to do what you want them to do. The strategies rely on the assumption that promising students a positive outcome for completing work, for example, is more effective—and certainly more pleasant—than threatening them with a negative consequence for not doing so. This approach is called *contingency contracting* [1] and is based on the principle that a desired behavior is more likely to occur if it is followed by a reward each time it occurs. The type of reward suggested by contingency management is a form of positive reinforcement called activity reinforcement.

In contingency management, the rewards for a student's positive behavior are activities or events desired by the student. Contingency contracting uses the principles of operant conditioning, which suggest reinforcing "low probability behaviors" (usually what the teacher wants) with "high probability behaviors" (what the student wants).

The critical element in this process is the reinforcer. Since the value of any reinforcer varies from one person to the next, you may want to observe students to discover which activities or materials they select most frequently when given the choice. Interest inventories might also help you select appropriate reinforcers.

[1]L. Homme, *How to Use Contingency Contracting in the Classroom*, 1973.

Activity Reinforcers

Activity reinforcers might include working in a favorite center, running an errand, reading with a friend, playing with a favorite toy or game, or doing some helping work like filing or grading papers. Regardless of the reinforcer you offer, the student will only be motivated by those that are personally meaningful and worth cooperating for. The object is to make the students' access to the reinforcer contingent upon their completion of a particular task. In this way you are getting the students to do what you require without the use of threats or authority.

Management Guidelines

Lloyd Homme suggests the following guidelines regarding the use of reinforcement in contingency management:

▶ The contract payoff (reward) should be immediate.

▶ Initial contracts should call for and reward small approximations (request small, specific, and simple tasks at first). Work toward the ultimately desired performance gradually.

▶ Reward frequently with small reinforcements; they are far more effective than a few large ones.

▶ The contract should call for and reward accomplishments rather than obedience. . . . Reward for accomplishment leads to independence. Reward for obedience leads only to continued dependence on the person to whom the child learns to be obedient.

▶ Reward the performance after it occurs. Present the reinforcer upon the adequate performance of the behavior (pp. 18–19).

The following guidelines describe the characteristics of proper contracting:

▶ The contract must be fair. Try to relate the amount of reward to the amount of performance.

▶ The terms of the contract must be clear. The child must always know *how much* performance is expected of him and *what he can expect as a payoff.*

▶ The contract must be carried out immediately, according to the terms specified in it.

▶ The contract must be positive. The terms of the contract should *contribute* something to the child's experience, rather than take something away from him.

▶ Contracting as a method must be used systematically. The laws of contingency go on working all the time, whether one pays any attention to them or not. Once contracting has been established as a motivation-management procedure, it should be maintained (pp. 19–21).

What about the "morality" of this reward system? Homme explains that although "teachers (and parents) sometimes feel uncomfortable with rewarding students 'for what they should be doing anyhow,' . . . the fact is that children learn better, and more willingly, if reinforcers follow difficult activities" (p. 20).

Motivating with Positive Contingencies

Alex is having a hard time paying attention to his work. He is not disturbing anyone, but he should have been finished a long time ago. What do you do to encourage Alex to do his work? Without considering the possibility of ignoring or accepting Alex's off-task behavior, you have two choices: to offer a reward or a threat. The negative response might be:

"If you're not done in ten minutes, you can't go out for recess."

"If you don't get busy, I'll have to call your mother tonight."

"That does it! You're going to the principal's office right now!"

On the other hand, you might simply turn the first example around and say:

"If you're done in ten minutes, you can go out for recess."

You're saying the same thing, yet in a far more positive way. Now if Alex isn't a big fan of recess, neither statement is likely to work very well. What else do you have to offer?

"Alex, would you run this message to the office as soon as you're done?"

"Why don't you finish up so you can play 'Battleships' with Joshua?"

"If you can finish before the bell, you can use the Teacher's Guide to check your own paper."

The motivation you offer will depend upon the preference of the individual student. Selecting effective reinforcers is easier to do when you have collected data, observed, and interacted with students to learn their preferences.

While the negative response might get Alex back to work, would you rather have him finish his assignment to avoid going to the principal's office or to check his own paper? Clearly, the positive reinforcers are geared more toward developing self-management skills.

Practice Sheet: Contingency Management

What are some threats you have used or been tempted to use with your students? In the spaces below, write the threat ("If you don't . . . [I'll]/you won't . . . ") and then write two or three positive alternatives.

Threat: _____

Alternatives: _____

_____

_____

_____

_____

Threat: _____

Alternatives: _____

_____

_____

_____

_____

Threat: _____

Alternatives: _____

_____

_____

_____

_____

Threat: _____

Alternatives: _____

_____

_____

_____

_____

Threat: _____

Alternatives: _____

_____

_____

_____

Below are several examples of student behavior. Some may be familiar to you. For each, identify the desired or preferred behavior and imagine positive reinforcers the students might desire. Write each as a statement you might make to the student.

Student: *Petra*
Problem: *Her desk/work area is a mess.*

Desired behavior: _____

_____

_____

Possible reinforcers: _____

_____

_____

_____

_____

Student: *Jeanine*
Problem: *She is a pest. She wants you to check her work every few minutes.*

Desired behavior: _____

_____

_____

Possible reinforcers: _____

_____

_____

_____

_____

Student: *Angelo*
Problem: *He keeps forgetting to bring in materials and assignments from home.*

Desired behavior: _____

_____

_____

Possible reinforcers: _____

_____

_____

_____

_____

Student: *Vaughn*
Problem: *His talking to Anthony is keeping both of them from doing their work.*

Desired behavior: _____

_____

_____

Possible reinforcers: _____

_____

_____

_____

_____

Student: *Sherri*
Problem: *She is 32 pages behind in her Reading workbook.*

Desired behavior: _____

_____

_____

Possible reinforcers: _____

_____

_____

_____

_____

Planning Sheet: Contingency Management

In the space below, identify students in your own classroom and specific problems they are having that might be remedied with positive contingencies.

Student: _____

Problem: _____

_____

Desired behavior: _____

_____

Possible reinforcers: _____

_____

_____

_____

Student: _____

Problem: _____

_____

Desired behavior: _____

_____

Possible reinforcers: _____

_____

_____

_____

Student: _____

Problem: _____

_____

Desired behavior: _____

_____

Possible reinforcers: _____

_____

_____

_____

_____

Reflection and Evaluation: Contingency Management

To what degree have you been able to use positive contingencies instead of threats? _____

_____

_____

_____

To what degree has the use of contingency management been successful? In what instances has it worked best?

_____

_____

_____

_____

Which reinforcers seem to be the most motivating? _____

_____

_____

_____

How successful have you been in following the suggestions in the guidelines regarding:

immediate payoff? _____

_____

small approximations at first? _____

_____

frequent, small rewards? _____

_____

rewarding accomplishment rather than obedience? _____

_____

clarifying expected behavior (criteria for receiving reward)? _____

_____

clarifying the reward (what the student gets, and when)? _____

_____

offering positive outcomes? _____

_____

_____

_____

What information sources have you used to identify meaningful reinforcers? _____

_____

_____

_____

What are your plans for gathering additional information? _____

_____

_____

_____

What impact, if any, has the contingency management had on:

the general behavior of your students? _____

_____

_____

_____

your relationship with your students? _____

_____

_____

_____

the general climate of the classroom? _____

_____

_____

_____

What are your plans for the future use of contingency management? What other contingencies would you like to offer?

_____

_____

_____

_____

_____

_____

_____

_____

_____

Chapter 20

Student Behavior and Consequences

THE THREE behavior management techniques presented in this chapter are similar in that they are nonpunitive and nonjudgmental. They are intended to help students see the connection between their behavior and the outcome of their behavior. All three strategies encourage mutual respect between student and teacher and are based on the assumption that students have the right to make independent decisions. Strategies involving *public criteria, I-messages,* and *logical consequences* are nonauthoritarian and often more effective than "power trips," which can be the cause of much disruption.

Like contingency contracting, these strategies deal with consequences. However, rather than focusing on a student reward which will be given upon the completion of a particular task, these strategies involve helping students see the impact of their behavior on another person, on the class, or on themselves. While useful for eliciting positive behavior, they are also appropriate for intervening in negative student behavior.

Public Criteria

Getting students to cooperate with the dozens of management rules necessary to run a classroom can occupy a large portion of a teacher's time. There are good reasons for the rules and considerations. While it may seem obvious to you why the students need to return reference books in a certain order, put the lids back on the paste jars, put the marbles away when they're done playing, or keep their hands out of the fish tanks, these are often the very behaviors you have to state and explain.

Public criteria are statements made by the teacher that explain why students should behave in a certain way. The reasons for the requested behavior are clearly stated and often explained in terms of consequence on the group, environment, or

some object in the environment, rather than being stated as an accusation.

Study the two sets of statements below. Notice how the ones on the left are preferable to those on the right:

"Please put the books back in alphabetical order so they will be easier to find the next time we use them."	*"These books are a mess! Put them back in alphabetical order."*
"Please cover the paste when you are finished so that it will not be dried up when we need to use it again."	*"I told you to put the covers on the paste jars."*
"Please pick up the marbles so that no one slips on them and gets hurt."	*"Please put those marbles away for me."*
"If you take the fish out of the fish tank, they won't be able to breathe."	*"Don't touch the fish tank."*

Note that the examples on the left are not commands. This fact alone may contribute to their effectiveness. In addition, when students cooperate with requests stated as in the examples on the left—those stated in terms of a cause and effect—they are doing so for the benefit of the class, the fish, or themselves. When students cooperate with statements such as those on the right, they are doing so to please the teacher or as a result of the teacher's power.

Public criteria offer a logical reason for doing something, which encourages the development of independence and self-management. Likewise, the likelihood of the student maintaining and repeating the positive behavior without instruction or threats from the teacher is increased.

I-Messages

Public criteria may sometimes be stated in the form of *I-messages*.[1] I-messages tell the student what is happening to the teacher as a result of the student's behavior and are offered as strong alternatives to the accusation of a you-message. Consider the differences in the statements below:

"I can't hear my reading group with all this noise."

"You are making too much noise."

"I don't enjoy reading a story when no one seems to be listening."

"You are being extremely rude."

Note that the statements on the left do not hold the judgments and negative evaluations that are present in the statements on the right. For this reason, the I-message is less likely to generate a negative response from the student.

Because they focus on the needs of the teacher, I-messages seem to work most effectively when a generally positive relationship already exists between the teacher and student. Stating that something is bothering you won't have much impact unless your students care, at least to a certain degree, about how you feel. This technique provides an excellent alternative to accusing or attacking your students, and is especially effective when stated in terms of the best interest of the group. While I-messages can also foster a positive, open relationship between you and your students, be careful that you are not simply using this technique to manipulate your students.

Logical Consequences

Logical consequences also show the connection between the student's behavior and the outcome of that behavior.[2] As with public criteria, logical

[1] T. Gordon, *T.E.T., Teacher Effectiveness Training*, 1974.

[2] R. Dreikurs and L. Grey, *Logical Consequences: A New Approach to Discipline*, 1968.

consequences are based on rules of order which operate to protect and benefit the group; they are not simply the results of arbitrary, individual decisions.

Stating the logical consequence is helpful particularly when a student is exhibiting some negative behavior.

Because of your devotion to your job, the time you put into planning and preparing, and the fact that you generally care about your students, you may find it difficult not to react emotionally to problems that arise, either out of frustration for having to deal with situations you wish wouldn't occur, or because of a tendency to take conflicts personally (especially when materials you care about are being abused or when you are criticized or verbally attacked). One feature of stating logical consequences is that it allows you to disengage from the emotionalism of a conflict. You can withdraw from the conflict and the child's provocation without withdrawing from the child. Require that the child take responsibility for the consequences of his or her behavior.

Adult disengagement does not mean accepting or ignoring negative behavior. It does, however, preclude fighting with the child, preaching, nagging, threatening, or criticizing, and it also precludes giving in. Disengagement releases you from the role of the punisher, a power role in which you may be angry and judgmental.

Your involvement, then, is limited to arranging the consequences by offering choices and helping the student understand the connection between what he or she did and what happened, or will happen, as a result. Imagine that Justin has forgotten his library book. Patrice has been bothering the other students at her table. Maria and Eddie are arguing over a book. Mark just called you "stupid." How do you respond to these situations? You might say:

"I'm sorry, Justin. You can take that book out as soon as you return the last one you borrowed."

"Patrice, will you please find a place to work alone until lunchtime. You're welcome to work at your table this afternoon if you can do so quietly."

"I don't want this book to get damaged. I'll take it until you two resolve the problem of who gets it first."

"Mark, we don't call names in this classroom. I'll be happy to talk with you as long as you don't call names."

In each example, the consequence results from the student's behavior. Explaining the logical consequences puts the responsibility for the problem back on the shoulders of the student who created it. You are able to stand back, without getting angry or involved in the problem, and without solving the problem for the student. You also demonstrate that, while the behavior is unacceptable, the student is still accepted. By doing this, you assume the role of an encourager, one who helps students to grow and realize their potential through successful performance and social integration. You also help your students recognize and select available options, thus fostering their ability to make decisions and predict outcomes.

Whenever possible, let students know ahead of time what the consequences of their actions will be. If you have told Justin that he needs to return his library book by tomorrow in order to sign out another book, then Justin's responsibility for the book is reinforced. Although the students are responsible for their behavior, the logical consequences are arranged by the adult. Your role in arranging the consequences is one of giving choices. Without preaching or moralizing, you are telling the students what they *could* do—not what they should do. With that knowledge, the student becomes responsible for the decision he makes as well as the *immediate* outcome of his choice.

Planning Sheet: Public Criteria

In the first column on this page, identify several specific behaviors you have asked, or plan to ask, of your students. For each, create a statement that requests that behavior in terms of public criteria—a logical reason that is in the best interest of the group, not a request based on your authority. Write that statement in the second column.

Behavior requested	Public criteria	Outcome

Apply some of the explanations you have suggested. In the final column, record the outcomes of using the public criteria with your students.

Practice Sheet: Logical Consequences

Several classroom situations are presented below. Develop at least one logical consequence of the behavior described in each that, expressed, might eliminate or change the undesired behavior. Make sure each consequence is nonpunitive, nonjudgmental, and directly related to the student's behavior.

Nick says that he does not understand your directions, no matter how clearly or slowly they are expressed. He frequently requests that you repeat the instructions for him.

_____

_____

_____

_____

_____

You are showing the class your slides from your trip to Italy. Some students begin talking and soon the class is quite noisy.

_____

_____

_____

_____

_____

Marlene has forgotten to bring in her lunch money for the past two weeks. Despite frequent reminders, she has not paid for this week's lunches. You know that Marlene has not brought her lunch. You also know that she is no longer able to buy her lunch on credit.

_____

_____

_____

_____

The class has learned how to write in cursive script. You've required that the class complete their stories in cursive. Everyone has complied except Donnie, who has printed his.

_____

_____

_____

_____

_____

In the spaces below, record situations that actually take place in your classroom.

Student(s)	Situation	Logical consequence	Outcome

Reflection and Evaluation: Student Behavior and Consequences

In what instances have you incorporated the use of public criteria and logical consequences in your classroom?

_____

_____

_____

_____

_____

_____

_____

_____

_____

What was the effect in terms of encouraging cooperative student behavior? _____

_____

_____

_____

_____

_____

_____

_____

_____

_____

_____

What was the effect in terms of building a positive classroom climate and avoiding the abuse of power?

_____

_____

_____

_____

_____

_____

_____

_____

_____

Chapter 21

Using Support Staff

THIS MANUAL provides strategies for making the most of your teaching experiences. Still, on occasion, you may need the resources and skills of support personnel such as a principal, counselor, psychologist, social worker, nurse, or resource specialist to help solve problems you encounter in working with your students. These support people can provide valuable assistance for those students who have problems or needs that would be better met with help from outside the classroom. Requesting support is easily justifiable when it is for the benefit of the student rather than for the convenience of the teacher. Asking for assistance is not considered an admission of failure or inadequacy on the part of the teacher.

Support staff can help by:

▶ collecting data or documenting special needs.

▶ making parent contacts or assisting with parent contacts.

▶ working with individual students or groups of students outside the classroom.

▶ suggesting materials and/or strategies for working with particular students or problems.

▶ helping to solve problems that occur outside the classroom but that might affect student behavior in the classroom, such as absenteeism, disease, injury, neglect, or abuse.

Preparing a Referral

Requesting help from support staff may involve formal or informal processes that require certain procedural considerations and interpersonal and professional courtesies. The first question to consider is whether you actually need help and how you would benefit from outside assistance. If you have a student who doesn't respond to anything you have tried, or one who appears to have many outside problems that you cannot address sufficiently, you need to decide who, among the resource personnel available in your school or district, would be the most effective source of support.

Once you have identified the problem and the potential resources for help, consider the approach that will generate the greatest support and the quickest solution. Defining the problem and providing strong documentation of its existence, frequency, and impact is far more likely to attract assistance than simply grabbing the counselor or principal in the hall and saying, "This student is making me crazy."

Before contacting a support person, it is most helpful for all concerned if you have the specific needs defined and present a clear picture of the problem. This information may include:

▶ anecdotal records, time-on-task observations, or sociographs (see Unit III).

▶ work samples.

▶ records of parental contacts.

Keep the data together in a file. Make sure the material you present is relevant to the problem you are documenting. In a meeting with support staff or a general conference with parents, your data file will provide the backbone for discussions and decisions, and may make the difference between action or inaction. In many instances, the quantity and quality of the data you collect and present will determine the future placements of or services available to that particular student.

Make a copy of your records to keep on hand if you release the data file to a resource person. Maintain confidentiality by restricting the visibility of your records, unless everyone present is directly involved with the welfare of the child. This information should not be the subject of casual teachers' lounge chatter.

A final precaution: In some states, it is required that parents sign a consent form prior to the involvement of certain specialists. Determine what, if any, conditions or restrictions apply in your district and follow the procedures prescribed.

Making a Referral

Once you have your documentation in order, you are ready to approach the resource people who will be most helpful. Except in cases of emergencies, request assistance at the resource person's convenience. Request a time to meet, preferably in writing. Briefly state your need and, if necessary, the urgency of your request. Be prepared to explain your reasons for requesting help in terms of the kind of assistance this person can give you.

When you meet with the resource person, describe the problem, using the support data you have gathered. Be objective. Describe your observations and experiences. Avoid opinions, interpretations, and personal feelings (unless your personal feelings are requested or are particularly relevant to the problem). Maintain your professionalism and focus on the needs of the student.

Plan a course of action with the resource person. This plan may include additional information-gathering tasks on your part. Be sure to follow up. Remember that the support staff exists to help you and your students. Cooperation and effective, high-quality service can be inspired by the groundwork you prepare in your data collection and presentation, your willingness to do your part, and your consideration for the schedule, needs, and limitations of the support staff with whom you are working.

The chart on the following page may be duplicated for planning and executing referrals for individual students.

Planning Sheet: Referral to Support Staff

Student: _____

Reason for referral: _____

_____

_____

Support data assembled: _____

_____

_____

_____

Resource person: _____

Task: _____

_____

_____

Resource person: _____

Task: _____

_____

_____

Resource person: _____

Task: _____

_____

_____

Action: _____

_____

_____

Outcome: _____

_____

_____

Follow-up: _____

_____

_____

_____

Chapter 22

Weekly Progress Reports

TYPICALLY, the first formal evaluation a student's parents receive is a report card. Unless the school requires and schedules time for parent conferences or an Open House, the report card may be the first contact the parent has with the teacher. And even though you give students regular feedback with grades and comments on class work and homework, there is something much more serious about the grades on the report card. Although report cards are an important means of communication between the home and the school, they are extremely limited as a source of feedback for both parents and students.

Unit I presented newsletters, conferences, home visits, and telephone calls as valuable means of building positive relationships with parents. All of these methods are important and effective, but they are rarely employed with consistency. While these communications may be useful in encouraging positive student behavior, they are most often used to deal with specific incidents.

This chapter presents support and guidelines for establishing a practice of regularly issuing progress reports that identify and reinforce, for students and parents, the desirable in-class behaviors that may or may not be evaluated on the report card. Too much happens between report card periods to allow teacher-parent contacts to depend entirely on quarterly grades.

Benefits of Weekly Progress Reports

▶ Weekly progress reports assess, on a regular basis, student behaviors that affect learning.

▶ Regular and frequent feedback reinforces student behavior and emphasizes that these behaviors are essential to success in school.

▶ Progress reports help break the pattern of the "bad note" or the "bad phone call," as well as perceptions of teacher-parent contacts as punitive.

▶ Weekly feedback can protect you in the event of a learning problem requiring referral. Regular contact can help you avoid being placed in the embarrassing situation in which a parent comes in at report card time asking, "Why didn't you tell me before this?"

▶ The reports focus on the positive. Since they are intended as "good notes," they are usually not threatening to students. In most instances, students and parents look forward to receiving these reports.

▶ The reports indicate progress in social and emotional development. They can acknowledge small increments of growth and alert parents to weaknesses that may have an impact on their children's learning.

▶ Weekly contacts assure parents and students of your interest in and commitment to the students' success. The parents will also see that you want to include them in reinforcing their children's progress.

▶ Your administrator may be especially appreciative of your efforts.

▶ The reports are flexible, take only minutes to complete, and can change as the students master various learning skills.

Developing and Using Weekly Progress Reports

The progress reports communicate what you feel are important behaviors and learning skills in your classroom. To begin, you need to list the behaviors you want to reinforce. Observable behaviors are easiest to evaluate and are most effective as reinforcers when stated positively.

Keep your form simple and brief, listing the five or six most important behaviors you have specified. As the students build competence in these behaviors, the skills can be replaced with others still to be mastered.

Consider the following sample formats. This report might be used in a primary classroom:

Weekly Progress Report

for _____

I take care of materials.	
I raise my hand to talk.	
I can work independently.	
I finish my work in class.	
I keep my cubby neat.	

Note:

This report might be used in the upper elementary grades or middle school:

Weekly Progress Report

for _____

	Most of the time	Has shown improvement
Comes to class on time.		
Comes to class prepared.		
Turns homework in on time.		
Works cooperatively in groups.		
Gets to work quickly.		
Participates in class.		

Note:

Determine a way of rating the students for each behavior. The most positive approach involves marking, with a check, a star, or a "smiley face," only those skills that the student performed well that week. Make sure that every student gets at least one or two marks. You may also choose to use a rating scale, with symbols indicating "most of the time," "sometimes," and "rarely." Marking improve-

ment, whether or not the student has exhibited the behavior "most of the time," is another option.

Try to judge each student against his or her own previous performance, rather than comparing students to the best example of each behavior in the class. This will enable even your least-skilled students to improve and excel at some things each week.

The space for your comments can be used to highlight a particular strength or area of improvement. You may also wish to leave space for the parent's comments and signature, or request that they use the back of the report for these purposes.

Determine a day of the week you will regularly distribute the reports. Because the reports evaluate the behaviors for the week, Friday is a logical choice, but distributing the reports on Thursday may prevent the reports from being lost or forgotten over the weekend. Filling in the information should not take more than ten to twenty minutes, depending on the size of your class. You may wish to have the students help by having them write their own names on the reports and return them to you to complete.

Before you begin sending the reports, compose a letter to the parents explaining the purpose of the progress reports and the importance of the behaviors you are evaluating. Tell them how often you plan to issue the reports and on what days they can expect to receive them. Invite them to reinforce and encourage their children. Ask them to help by signing the reports and having the children return them to school.

Encourage students to bring the reports back, signed, by a certain day. You may wish to offer stickers or check marks to encourage the students to remember, perhaps attaching a special privilege to each sticker or group of stickers. If a student does not return his progress report with a signature, follow up, if possible, by calling or visiting the parents. After the first few weeks, the pattern will be established, and any problems with returns should diminish.

Keep the returned reports in the students' files. When returns are particularly erratic because of limited cooperation from the parents, you may wish to keep copies of the reports you've sent home on file, as well as a note verifying your attempts to encourage the parents' participation. All in all, you should find the parents supportive and the students enthusiastic. You should also see growth in the skills you report each week.

Planning Sheet: Weekly Progress Reports

1. Develop a list of behaviors you consider desirable and necessary in order for students to function and learn successfully in your class. State the behaviors positively and objectively, and be sure that they are observable.

_____

_____

_____

_____

_____

_____

_____

_____

_____

_____

_____

_____

_____

_____

_____

_____

_____

_____

_____

_____

2. Select five or six of the statements above to use in your progress report. Establish a rating system. Construct a progress report appropriate for your class and attach a copy of it to this page for future reference.

3. Following the guidelines in the previous section, compose a letter to the parents explaining the progress reports and their role. Attach a copy of the letter to this page for future reference.

4. Add other important skills to the list as you think of them. These behaviors can be used in future versions of your progress reports.

5. Send progress reports home each week for at least six to eight weeks before completing the reflection and evaluation activity that follows.

Reflection and Evaluation: Weekly Progress Reports

How is the form/design working out? _____

_____

_____

_____

What changes have you made in the form/design since you started using it? _____

_____

_____

What changes in the format, rating system, or list of behaviors do you anticipate in future weeks? _____

_____

_____

_____

When do you send the progress reports home? _____

_____

How consistent have you been in doing so? _____

_____

How have the students responded to these progress reports? _____

_____

_____

_____

_____

Have you noticed any changes in the students' behavior that you might attribute to their having received these reports on a regular basis for the past few weeks? If so, describe:

_____

_____

_____

_____

_____

_____

_____

How have the parents responded? _____
_____
_____

Regarding their comments (if any):

    Questions you've received _____
    _____
    _____

    Comments about the progress reports themselves _____
    _____
    _____

    Comments about the evaluation and/or your comments _____
    _____
    _____

How frequently have you had to follow up on unreturned progress reports? _____
_____
_____

To what degree has your follow-up been effective? _____
_____
_____

What do you do with the signed, returned progress reports? _____
_____

How does your principal (or other support staff members) feel about your efforts? _____
_____
_____
_____

What are your plans for continuing to use the progress reports? _____
_____
_____
_____
_____
_____

UNIT V

Instructional Management

Chapter 23

Routine Management

AMONG THE NUMEROUS concerns of running a classroom are the decisions you face regarding the use and management of instructional time. In addition to managing the students' work load and arranging groups, you have dozens of routines to organize on a daily basis.

Without careful planning, your management of daily routines may be ineffective. And yet most of the routines practiced in classrooms can provide excellent opportunities for students to develop responsibility and independence. The less you have to attend to simple routines, the more time you have to devote to instruction. Involving the students, providing clear and simple guidelines, and conducting the routines with regularity and consistency will reduce the amount of time and energy the routines consume.

This chapter suggests management strategies for a number of daily routines that are common in many classrooms. Although based on observations in self-contained elementary classrooms, many of the strategies will be useful in other settings and with older students.

Taking Attendance

Few routines are more common or simple than taking attendance, but the following suggestions are offered to make this particular routine even simpler.

Attendance Chart

If your school provides individual attendance cards for each student: Construct an attendance chart or board with library pockets for each student. Write the students' names on the pockets. File the attendance cards in the individual pockets. When the students enter the room, they pull their cards and place them in one large envelope or basket at the bottom of the chart. A student monitor can check to make sure the remaining cards actually represent absent students (and were not simply forgotten). The monitor then pulls the remaining cards for you to mark before sending them to the office. At the end of the day, have a student refile the attendance cards in the individual pockets.

If you mark a single attendance sheet: Construct an attendance chart with library pockets as described above. For each pocket, construct a card that is green on one side and red on the other. Mark the green sides with the word "present" and the red sides with the word "absent." When the students enter the room, they turn the card so that the green side shows. A simple glance will enable you to mark your attendance records. At the end of the day, the cards are all turned over so that the red side shows.

Daily Sign-in Sheet

Type or print the names of your students down the left side of a page. Draw lines to the right of their names. Duplicate this sign-in sheet and have students sign in next to their names, either as they enter the room, or as the sheet is passed around.

Monthly Attendance Grid

Construct a grid on a large piece of paper or poster board with the students' names listed on the left and a series of boxes after each name. Mark the date above each column of boxes and have the students initial the appropriate box as they enter the room.

Attendance Clothesline

String a short clothesline near the entrance to the room and place a small basket nearby. Mark each student's name on a wooden clothespin and place the clothespins on the line. When the students enter the room, they remove their clothespins and put them in the basket.

Calling Attendance

Assign a student monitor to call the names of the students and mark the appropriate attendance records.

Sharing

Sharing, or show-and-tell, offers students valuable opportunities to speak to an audience as they present some item or story of personal value. The experience also provides opportunities to use language, develop confidence in speaking in front of peers, and develop skills as a listener. Because sharing demands the attention of an audience, the student also has a chance to experience and identify with the teacher's role by encouraging the other students to listen politely.

In conducting a daily sharing time, consider the following guidelines:

1. Allow sharing time for two to four students. If more than that number of students bring in items or stories to share, reserve some time later in the day for them, if possible.

2. Let sharing be voluntary. Don't require sharing, but encourage everyone who wishes to participate.

3. Unless there is a problem with the content, setting criteria for content is probably not necessary. Sharing is very individual; students will most often share items or experiences that have a special meaning for them. Sharing, however, should never hurt or embarrass anyone.

4. Instruct students to wait for the attention of their audience. Require that sharing be contingent on the sharer's having everyone's attention.

5. Help students keep sharing time brief. Help them encourage questions and feedback from the audience.

6. Try to become less directive and increasingly more a part of the audience.

Lining Up

You may need to move your students from one area in the school to another several times a day. Probably the most orderly way to do this is to have the students assemble and walk in a line. The two

biggest problems of moving students in line are *keeping* them in line and keeping them *quiet* in line. Therefore, to avoid anxiety attacks at line-up time, a few guidelines might help:

1. Use public criteria (Chapter 20) to establish line-up rules. Examples:

    "In order that we do not disturb any of the other classes going on . . . ."
    "For safety's sake . . . ."

2. Use contingency managing (Chapter 19) to control line-up behavior:

    "As soon as you are all in a straight, quiet line, we will go out for recess."

3. Use logical consequences (Chapter 20) if students do not follow set criteria:

    "I'm sorry, but you are not ready to leave for recess yet. You will leave when everyone is in line."
    "We are making too much noise to remain in the hall. Let's go back to the room and try again.

    Make sure you follow up. Do not threaten, but indicate the consequence that will logically follow the behavior.

4. Do not be tempted to permit a disorderly line simply to avoid having to line students up again, or to prevent them from missing a minute or two of an activity. You will find the lining-up practice and the waiting time well invested.

The Bathroom Pass

Lining students up to go to the bathroom as a group at specified times makes sense only if everyone has to go at the same time. To avoid using potential instructional time for this activity and to develop students' self-management skills, provide a pass that students can use to excuse themselves as needed. This pass system does require some management considerations:

1. Having one pass is usually enough. This allows only one student at a time to leave the room.

2. To avoid having students interrupt for permission to use the pass, make it available as needed.

3. Define the uses for the pass. Allow students to go to the bathroom, get a drink, or even just take a break from the classroom if necessary. As

long as the students follow the criteria for using the pass, there should be no problem.

4. You may wish to restrict the pass to only those students not receiving direct instruction (students working independently, for example, while you are teaching a reading group). If you are working with the whole group, students should not be able to get up and walk out until you have finished speaking.

5. You may wish to limit pass privileges to two times in the morning and again in the afternoon.

6. Set a reasonable time limit on the use of the pass, but only to the extent that you notice that a student has been out of the room for more than a few minutes.

7. Students should be able to use the pass independently, without causing any disruption. If the pass creates commotion in the classroom, put it away for a time. Announce that the class can try again in a half hour, for example.

8. If a student abuses his or her pass privileges, particularly if the student's use of the pass interferes with the completion of the student's work or creates a disturbance, you may wish to withdraw that student's pass privileges for a short period of time.

9. Expect the pass to be used too often at first, particularly if your students have never used a hall pass before. Within the limits you set, allow a bit of time for them to test and enjoy their freedom.

10. If a student is ill or has an emergency, you may not want to wait for the pass if it is out. If required by the school, write a brief note, if only the word "pass," for the student to take out of the room.

11. Should you or the students need a break during the day, use a brief game or stretching exercise instead of marching everyone down to the bathroom.

Getting Attention

Have you ever found yourself talking to a *part* of your class when everyone was supposed to be listening? Do you ever notice that your voice is getting louder and louder in an attempt to maintain the attention of those who are listening or to get the attention of those who do not appear to be? Since

you will be speaking with your class frequently, you will want them to listen while you are talking, demonstrating, or giving directions. At such times, the following strategies might be useful:

▶ If the students are involved in work and you need their attention, some signal, such as flicking the lights, ringing a bell, giving a verbal cue, or even standing still and holding up your hand until you have their attention may be helpful in alerting them to the fact that you have something to say to them.

▶ Do not begin talking until you have everyone's attention. If necessary, ask the students to look at you and wait until it is quiet and each pair of eyes is turned your way.

▶ Once you get the students' attention, get to the point. If you start losing their attention, simply stop talking. Wait until it gets quiet before starting again. Say thank you when it gets quiet.

▶ If you need to wait more than a few seconds, glance at your watch. You may wish to make a statement about their behavior preventing you from getting to a particular activity.

▶ If you are in the middle of an activity that demands students' attention, you may wish to excuse inattentive students from the activity, making sure that they have something else to do at a specific location away from the rest of the group.

▶ If you are in the middle of an activity which demands students' attention and the entire class—or a large portion of the class—is having difficulty sustaining their attention, you may wish to discontinue the activity until another time. Describe your decision as a logical consequence: "Since you are having difficulty staying quiet, we'll stop for today. Perhaps it will be better tomorrow." Once the statement is made, you are committed to it; do not be tempted to resume the activity.

Independent Reading

Independent reading (also called Sustained Silent Reading, or S.S.R.) is such a valuable classroom activity at any grade level that it could warrant an entire chapter to itself. This activity is most effective when conducted as a part of the daily routine.

Consider the following management guidelines for independent reading:

1. Sell the idea of independent reading. Your enthusiasm along with a variety of materials are prerequisite to successfully conducting this activity.

2. Stock your room with reading materials such as:
   ▸ books from the school library.
   ▸ books from series not adopted for your district or building.
   ▸ books from commercial "classroom library" kits.
   ▸ old textbooks and readers.
   ▸ books and materials you pick up at garage sales or flea markets.
   ▸ your own books that might interest your students or relate to topics you are covering in other areas of instruction.
   ▸ books the students bring in.
   ▸ magazines, catalogs, cookbooks, travelogs, sales and promotional materials, or even old calendars.

3. Allow students to supply their own reading material, including books they have selected from the school or public library.

4. Conduct independent reading time, if possible, at approximately the same time each day.

5. Use a timer, preferably with a bell, to indicate the end of the independent reading period.

6. Limit the period to a few minutes at first. Once the students get used to the routine and criteria, gradually extend the reading period.

7. Allow the students one book each for that day's independent reading selection to avoid having them spend the entire time selecting and exchanging books.

8. Although you might require that students remain in their own seats for independent reading, many people prefer a more relaxed posture for reading than sitting at a table or desk. If you have the appropriate furniture (or pillows, for example) and the floor space, you may wish to allow the students to select a reading space for the duration of the reading period. Make it clear to students that the privilege of selecting a reading space will depend on their ability to manage their behavior during the reading period.

9. Restrict the students' talking, writing, doing other classwork, leaving their seats or reading spaces, and the use of the bathroom pass. Emphasize that this time is for reading.

10. Students who do not wish to read may be allowed to sit quietly at their desks.

11. Model the type of behavior you expect from students. Spend the period reading one of your own books rather than working on lesson plans or grading papers.

12. Do not allow students to come up to talk to you (that is, disturb your reading) or behave in any way that takes your attention from your reading. Although you will want to maintain some awareness of your students, make it clear that your role during that time is not to watch, warn, or reprimand.

Cleaning Up

A messy environment can be a distraction, a deterrent to organization, and a health or safety hazard. If cleanup is an automatic part of *your* routine, your students may eventually develop an awareness of the crayon on the floor, or the tissue in the fish tank, and learn to pick up after themselves. At the very least, you want to avoid being in a position of playing the maid at the end of the day or making a permanent enemy of the custodial staff of your school. There is no reason for any teacher to be left with papers on the floor, or games, materials, and supplies jammed into the wrong places.

Once you have set the room up in a neat and orderly fashion, there are several strategies you can employ to maintain your environment.

1. Label shelves or storage units where materials are kept. Cover table tops or shelves with adhesive paper, trace the shapes of the items stored on them, and label the shapes.

2. Model neatness in the maintenance of your own area and in the initial setup of the environment for students.

3. Allow adequate space for storage. Avoid stacking or piling materials on top of one another for storage.

4. Encourage the proper care of materials. If necessary, remove the materials if students do not take care of them.

5. Take time to practice getting materials and putting them back properly. Make sure students can, for example:
   - screw lids back on paint jars securely.
   - put reference books back in alphabetical order.
   - replace cards and other materials from commercial kits in the correct places.
   - put math counters back in the box.
   - put materials back on shelves in their correct places.

6. Make dismissal contingent on a neat environment. For example:
   - dismiss students in rows or tables if their work space, including the floor around them, is tidy and the materials they were using have been put away.
   - wait until general work areas are straightened up before dismissing anyone in the class. These areas might include the seats in the reading circle, the books in the class library, or the materials in the art center.
   - if the floor is a mess, demand that each student have one or two "tickets," or scraps from the floor, in order to get out of the room. When dismissing students, have them deposit their scraps in the trash can on the way out the door.

Dismissal

Sometimes by the end of the day you may be so worn out that you are anxious only to get the students out of the room. However, a whole-group dismissal can be disorderly and even dangerous. Therefore, dismissal is another routine that requires some management considerations.

1. Use a predismissal time to get everyone's attention for last-minute announcements, or instructions, or to pass out notes or papers to go home that evening.

2. If students need to get coats or books from a closet or locker, let them do so in small groups. The students can be dismissed individually or in groups, by table or row, when their floor spaces and desks are cleaned up.

3. If you dismiss the class as a whole group, have them line up first. Students can line up individually or in groups, by table or row, when their floor spaces and desks are cleaned up.

4. Rather than dismissing by tables or rows, you can dismiss students according to certain categories: students whose names start with *M,* students wearing yellow, or students whose birthdays are in April, for example.

5. If dismissal becomes disorderly, call the students back to their seats and wait for them to settle down again.

6. Use similar dismissal procedures for releasing students for recess, lunch, or special subjects.

Reflection and Evaluation: Routine Management

A number of routines have been described in this chapter. In what ways are your management systems similar to those described? In what ways do you plan to change your current management systems?

TAKING ATTENDANCE

Similarities: _____

_____

Plans for change: _____

_____

_____

SHARING

Similarities: _____

_____

Plans for change: _____

_____

_____

LINING UP

Similarities: _____

_____

Plans for change: _____

_____

_____

BATHROOM PASS

Similarities: _____

_____

Plans for change: _____

_____

GETTING ATTENTION

Similarities: _____

_____

Plans for change: _____

_____

_____

INDEPENDENT READING

Similarities: _____

_____

Plans for change: _____

_____

_____

CLEANING UP

Similarities: _____

_____

Plans for change: _____

_____

_____

DISMISSAL

Similarities: _____

_____

Plans for change: _____

_____

_____

How have the suggestions in this chapter helped you to manage your classroom routines?

_____

_____

Chapter 24
. . . .

Whole-Group and Small-Group Management

NOW THAT YOUR ROUTINES are running smoothly, how will you organize the rest of the day? When do you do whole-group activities? When are your reading groups scheduled? How do you manage independent work? This chapter examines the purpose and management of the different instructional phases in each teaching day.

The Daily Schedule

With the exception of departmentalized programs, most elementary teachers have a good bit of flexibility in their daily planning and scheduling. Schedules usually include the following phases.

Orientation Phase

Most often conducted with the whole group, this phase may include activities and procedures such as attendance, announcements, sharing, or brief daily drills. Often the day's schedule and assignments are presented and discussed before the class moves into the next phase of the day. The orientation phase may run approximately five to forty minutes, depending on the teacher's goals and needs. The routine, content, and length of time are usually fairly consistent from one day to the next in any given classroom.

Small-Group/Independent Work Phase

During this time the teacher usually meets with reading groups, or skill groups in math or language arts. At times, the teacher may meet with students for individual conferences. During this time, students not meeting with the teacher are involved in independent work assignments. This

phase generally lasts the entire morning and sometimes may continue after lunch. The phase may be broken up by a recess period or a brief whole-group activity.

Whole-Group Phase

During this time, the teacher may shift from working with skills groups to introducing conceptual or process-oriented curriculum such as social studies or science. This phase often involves whole-group discussions or a number of small groups working on the same material. Because of the usual shift in content during this time of day, the groups are often more sociologically heterogeneous than the ability groups and skill groups of the morning small-group phase. Individualization in these subjects may be based on personal interest rather than on skills or content knowledge.

Please note these descriptions are broad generalizations; any number of phase variations may appear in any classroom on any day. Some teachers may choose to reverse or extend the phases or may tend toward different variations of one phase only. Make your scheduling responsive to the needs of your students and the other teachers with whom you work. If, for example, you have one group of students for reading who are not available (or very awake) in the morning, you may need to schedule some time for small-group work later in the day. Suggestions for conducting each phase of the day are offered below.

Managing the Orientation Phase

In conducting the orientation phase, consider the following suggestions:

1. Do orientation activities with the total group.

2. Be fairly consistent about starting time, content, sequence, and length of time.

3. Involve students in orientation routines.

4. Keep routines short and the schedule tight. Use orientation time efficiently.

5. Orientation routines might include:

   ▸ taking attendance (or having students mark their own attendance).

   ▸ calendar or weather activities.

   ▸ announcements.

   ▸ attention to door messages or new features in the environment.

   ▸ language or math drills.

   ▸ student sharing (show-and-tell).

   ▸ follow-up on homework calendar assignments.

   ▸ graphing or survey activities.

   ▸ introduction of new materials or routines.

   ▸ schedule and/or assignments for the day.

6. To ease the transition into the small-group phase (or the next part of your day), plan for the last orientation activity or routine to tie into the morning work.

7. Dismiss the students in small, arbitrary groups (such as by reading group, by table, alphabetically, or by features of their clothing).

Managing the Small-Group/ Independent Work Phase

During this part of the schedule, the teacher typically works with one group of children while the rest of the class works independently until their group is called. In order for this phase to run smoothly, you will need to be able to work without constant interruptions from students outside the group you're working with. In other words, the success of the small-group phase requires the following:

1. Your students should know how to work, whether alone or with a partner, without constant help or supervision from you.

2. You need to provide an adequate amount of work to keep students busy, and identify specific alternatives for them to select if they complete their assignments early.

3. Your students should have the flexibility, when confronted with something they do not understand, to ask someone else for help (another student or an aide) or to go on to something else until you are available to assist them.

4. Your students should know where to get the materials they'll need and how to obtain them without your assistance.

5. Your assignments, instruction, and record keeping should be easy for you to manage.

6. Your management system should be simple for students to follow, requiring a minimum of decision-making or self-management skills at first and gradually becoming more demanding as students' skills improve.

7. The students should practice using the responsible learning behaviors they will need for working independently (such as getting, using, and returning materials; moving around the room without disturbing others; and working alone, in pairs, or in small groups) and demonstrate competence under your supervision before they are required to work independently.

8. Once established, the basic management system, including the types of assignments done, where to get materials, and where to put finished work, should be maintained with consistency.

9. Changes should be implemented gradually and, if possible, only one at a time.

Ability Groups and Skill Groups

The small-group/independent work phase is usually skill-oriented. Although not necessarily the exclusive focus, instruction and evaluation are frequently based on the students' understanding, performance, practice, and integration of skills—most often in reading and language arts, and sometimes in math. For this reason, the groups you call during this phase will either be ability groups or skill groups.

Ability groups are formed on the basis of the students' general ability in a particular subject area. Reading groups are the most common example of ability groups. Within the ability group will be a range of specific capabilities, experiences, and knowledge. Students within a particular ability group are generally expected to make about the same progress. When students move outside the group's range, however, they may be held back or moved ahead into another group. Otherwise, ability groups tend to be fairly enduring.

Skill groups focus on a specific skill and are usually temporary. A skill group is comprised of students who have been identified as deficient in a particular skill or concept. Skill groups rarely involve the entire class. Only students who have not mastered a skill are called to the skill group, and only that skill is taught. Once students have mastered the particular skill, they no longer are called to that group, although they will probably participate in a skill group that addresses a different skill.

Both types of groups are designed to help you better meet your students' needs and provide instruction at appropriate levels. In either case, you will be working with small groups of students, usually for five to forty minutes each, depending on the nature of the group, the content you are teaching, and the age of your students. The rest of the class will have time to practice on their own the content they have learned in the groups.

Ideally, the system you develop for managing this phase of your instruction should become increasingly individualized and varied, without sacrificing quality and consistency. Some specific suggestions for management:

1. Prepare a file folder for each student's finished work. This technique helps to focus on the individual student rather than the particular assignment.

2. Determine how much time you will need for your small-group phase. The time consideration is important in planning for independent work activities.

3. In planning the independent work activities, be careful not to overwhelm the students with too much work. Provide a set of alternative materials for students to select if they finish early.

4. Independent work activities might include:

   ▸ story starter or creative writing activities.

   ▸ handwriting assignments or prescriptions.

   ▸ reading or language skills worksheets or activities.

▸ math skills worksheets or activities.

▸ spelling exercises.

▸ games, puzzles, or concrete manipulatives.

▸ newspaper, or audiovisual activities.

▸ independent workbook pages.

▸ exercises in a text or on the blackboard.

▸ cards or materials in a commercial kit.

5. Keep independent work very simple at first, providing opportunities for initial student success. Allow the students to concentrate on mastering the management system by:

   ▸ using materials and processes that the students are already familiar with.

   ▸ assigning content that the students will be able to handle.

   ▸ assigning work that at first will require a minimum of movement (out-of-seat), interaction, and decision making.

   ▸ assigning the same work (or nearly the same work) for all students at first.

   ▸ planning to diversify assignments (content and quantity) after the students—and you—get the system down.

6. Introduce new materials, kits, processes, and instructional routines one at a time. Present the new materials at other times, such as during morning orientation, before requiring independent use of the materials.

Assigning Independent Work

There are many methods for assigning independent work to students. Several possible methods are described below.

Method 1: List assignments on the board and distribute materials to the students before starting. Characteristics:

   ▸ It is a good initial management system.

   ▸ It is simple, requiring little preparation.

   ▸ It requires a minimum of movement from students.

   ▸ Students can make decisions about the order in which they do their work, unless activities are listed in a required sequence.

▶ It does not lend itself well to individualization, but if the class is divided into smaller groups for different subjects or activities, assignments for various groups may be listed on the board.

Method 2: Put assignments in individual student folders. Characteristics:

▶ It is suitable for a variety of assignments.

▶ It requires a minimum of movement from students.

▶ It allows the students to make decisions about the order in which they do their work.

▶ It makes correction and follow-up convenient for focusing on individual needs.

▶ The preparation is time-consuming.

Method 3: Prepare a prescription or work contract for each student. Characteristics:

▶ It is suitable for a variety of assignments.

▶ It makes correction and follow-up convenient for focusing on individual needs.

▶ You may use a mimeographed prescription form and specify page, card, problems, or lessons to meet each student's needs.

▶ Students must get their own materials.

▶ Students can use materials already in the room, or you can leave duplicated materials in a central location. This eliminates the time spent on distributing materials to students and minimizes preparation of daily student materials other than the prescription itself.

▶ The preparation is generally less time-consuming than stuffing individual folders, although follow-up is similar.

▶ Students can check off work as they do the assignments.

▶ Daily prescriptions can be sent home.

Method 4: Put assignments in numbered baskets, folders, bags, or cans. Students work in sequence, taking materials from the containers. Characteristics:

▶ It allows students to pace themselves.

▶ The preparation is less time-consuming than stuffing individual folders.

▶ It is possible to individualize the quantity of work required by assigning different minimums to individual students. By putting the "core" assignments at the front of the sequence, and the more complex or enrichment assignments later in the sequence, you can require that all students do the first six baskets, while specifying which students must finish eight, ten, and so on. If a student completes the minimum assigned, he or she can continue in the sequence.

▶ You may individualize content by assigning specific baskets to specific students.

▶ It will be difficult to meet the specific skill needs of individual students.

Method 5: Put assignments and materials in different learning centers around the room. Characteristics:

▶ It requires movement around the room.

▶ It usually requires specifying a maximum number of students who may work at a center at any given time unless students simply go to the center to get materials.

▶ The preparation time will vary according to the complexity of the centers.

▶ The activities at the learning centers will probably not be sequenced. Students can decide which activities to do first.

▶ You may individualize content by assigning students to specific centers.

▶ You may individualize content by having different assignments or levels of work at a given center. For example, you can color code the different folders or task cards, or label them with the names of students assigned to that activity.

Begin with one method, and eventually combine several methods. This process will increase the flexibility of your instructional program. For example, you may end up with a management system that offers a general list of independent work assignments on the board, assigns specific tasks on individual prescriptions, and allows students to select materials from containers at various centers in the room. In building your management system, take into account the needs, abilities, and work habits of your students. Select methods that will encourage students to develop self-management skills.

Managing the Whole-Group Phase

The whole-group phase is distinguished from the small-group phase by differences in content and management. In this phase, all students may be working in the same subject area or on the same topics. Subjects might include art, music, values education, physical education, science, social studies, interdisciplinary content, math, or language concepts. During the small-group phase, the teacher calls students to ability groups or skill groups while the rest of the students work independently. During the whole-group phase, the teacher usually works with the entire group or supervises individual or group projects. When students are separated into groups during this time, the grouping is more likely to be social and heterogeneous than based on similar abilities.

Instruction during the whole-group phase may take the form of a lecture, a guest visit, a teacher-led discussion, a research and work session, or integrated small-group activities. Because teacher-directed instruction is the most common form of whole-group instruction, this chapter examines it in detail.

Teacher-Led Whole-Group Activities

The image of the teacher standing in front of a group of students is a common one at any grade level. Even in elementary classrooms, where a great deal of instructional time is devoted to small-group activity, teacher-directed whole-group instruction is a fact of life.

Yet whole-group arrangements often become lectures during which the teacher does most, if not all, of the talking. Participation, when it is requested, may relate more to the content than to the students' personal experiences. While a good lecturer may hold an audience's attention, the younger the audience and the more impersonal the topic, the more difficult it will probably be for them to listen for extended periods.

Although some teachers and administrators insist that whole groups are easier to manage, the usual lack of active or personal involvement and the lack of intimacy caused by the diffusion of the teacher's attention can often create behavior problems. To decrease the likelihood of losing an audience, consider the following:

▶ Try to keep lectures brief, interspersing "teacher talk" with a student activity such as working on a problem.

▶ Enhance lectures with visual aids, music, or filmstrips.

▶ Whatever the age of your students, try to tie your explanations and questions to student experiences as much as possible. Keep the discussion concrete and personal.

▶ Avoid standing in one spot while you talk; circulate among the students, if possible.

▶ Rather than simply calling on students for answers, encourage them to participate by sharing experiences, asking questions, and giving feedback.

In addition to lectures, the following types of activities are likely to be conducted in a whole-group setting:

▶ an announcement that affects everyone or nearly everyone.

▶ an activity of general interest, such as a slide presentation.

▶ an activity that can be individually interpreted, such as creative writing based on a single story starter, or a drawing-to-music exercise.

▶ an activity such as listening to a story, singing, or movement that involves group participation.

▶ a sharing activity, such as show-and-tell.

▶ a presentation of tasks or materials that will be encountered at some point later in the day.

Students can participate in most of these activities with a high degree of success without the individual attention provided in smaller-group settings.

Individualizing Whole-Group Assignments

Although whole-group instruction does not usually provide for individual differences among students, it is possible to include some flexibility in whole-group assignments to at least accommodate individual preferences and interests. The following assignments are examples of how a teacher might individualize whole-group activities:

- ▶ Given a page with twenty similar multiplication problems, each student can choose any ten problems to do.

- ▶ Each student can demonstrate letter-writing competence by writing a letter to a public figure of his or her choice (musician, actor, athlete, and so on).

- ▶ Given twenty geography questions, each student can choose a country to investigate.

- ▶ Each student can present or describe the use of a simple machine.

- ▶ Each student can create a monochromatic drawing in the color of his or her choice.

- ▶ Each student can practice addition facts with any two of the following: a math board game, flash cards, a coloring ditto, a dot-to-dot puzzle, a page in the textbook, a card from the math lab kit, or a worksheet.

- ▶ Each student can design a science research problem related to the human body.

Reflection and Evaluation: Orientation Phase

Do you have an orientation phase in your daily schedule? If so, what sorts of activities or procedures happen during this time?

_____

_____

_____

_____

_____

_____

In what ways are you satisfied with your use of this time? _____

_____

_____

_____

_____

_____

_____

What changes or additions would you like to implement for this time period? _____

_____

_____

_____

_____

_____

_____

_____

_____

_____

_____

_____

_____

Reflection and Evaluation: Small-Group Phase

Do you have a small-group phase in your school day? If so, what types of groups do you conduct during this time?

_____

_____

_____

What are the rest of the students doing during this time? _____

_____

_____

What skills do students need to work on under the system you have developed? _____

_____

_____

What did you do to prepare the students to work independently? _____

_____

_____

What do you still need to do, if anything, to help the students develop in this area? _____

_____

_____

How are the assignments and materials organized? _____

_____

_____

What changes do you intend to make in the management of your small-group phase? _____

_____

_____

_____

_____

_____

_____

_____

_____

_____

Reflection and Evaluation: Whole-Group Phase

Do you have a whole-group phase? If so, what do you do during that time? _____

_____

_____

_____

In what ways do you encourage student interest and participation during whole-group activities? _____

_____

_____

_____

_____

In what ways do your whole-group activities account for individual interests, preferences, and abilities?

_____

_____

_____

_____

In what ways do you plan to change or expand your whole-group phase? _____

_____

_____

_____

_____

_____

_____

_____

_____

_____

_____

_____

_____

_____

Chapter 25

. . . .

Integrated Small-Group Activities

NOT ALL SMALL GROUPS are based on similar skill needs or abilities. At times you may want to group together students who have different cognitive and social skills. Heterogeneous or social grouping enables students to work together in a cooperative setting in which each person is able to make a valuable contribution, build interactive skills, and assume a leadership role.

To arrange for these small-group activities, divide the entire class into four to six heterogeneous groups and assign each group a different task or set of tasks. All of the groups can work on their projects at the same time in different locations. Usually all groups work in the classroom, although at times one of the activities may require the students to visit the library or collect materials outside the classroom. During the course of an activity cycle, the students stay in the same groups, and each group rotates from one activity to another over a period of time.

All of the activities assigned to the groups can be built around a particular concept or theme. Activities may explore specific topics, such as "teeth" or "corn"; broad subjects such as "communications" or "weather"; various skills, such as "measuring" or "mapping"; or holiday and seasonal themes. All the activities developed for the groups should relate different subjects to the central theme.

For example, Valentine's Day activities traditionally lean toward arts and crafts, occasionally with some language arts included. An integrated cycle might also include a science activity about the heart and a math activity involving counting or weighing valentine candies.[1] Likewise, dinosaurs need not be exclusively taught as a science topic. You can connect different parts of the curriculum to a dinosaur theme by practicing math facts with flash cards in the shape of dinosaur eggs, making

"fossils" out of clay, writing dinosaur poems, making a prehistoric diorama or map, practicing dinosaur spelling words, making and using dinosaur puppets, working with dinosaur jigsaw (or crossword) puzzles, watching a movie about dinosaurs, or singing songs about dinosaurs.

Planning Small-Group Activities

Before developing small-group activities for your integrated learning cycle, consider the following guidelines:

1. Group the students so that there are an equal number of activities and groups.

2. You may wish to develop a general, whole-group activity to introduce the topic and launch the small-group activity cycle.

3. Acquire resources and children's literature related to the topic. For example, a cycle built on the theme of balloons might include stories, films, or records about balloons or balloon rides. These materials might be used as an introduction to the topic, as a specific group activity, or as a final activity.

4. Develop activities that represent different curricular areas.

5. Vary the types of tasks or learning behaviors required (such as writing, adding, subtracting, coloring, listening, cutting, and pasting). Activities may include a single project or a set of tasks.

6. Develop activities that do not need to be completed in a specific sequence.

7. Vary the degree of cooperation and group effort each activity requires. Activities may require the students in each group to produce a single

---

[1] T. Gerrard, *Com-Paks: Kids' Committees for Integrated Learning*, 1987.

product, to work together but produce individual products, or to work independently and then share the products they have created.

8. Only one activity may be teacher-directed, unless you have several adults available to assist the students for the entire period. Until your students are used to working independently and cooperatively in small groups, you may wish to leave yourself free to facilitate, supervise, and observe.

9. Design activities to last for approximately the same amount of time. Provide alternative activities related to the topic for those students or groups who finish early.

10. Plan time for a wrap-up activity or, at least, a final session for review, questions, and student feedback. Use this time to go over the activities, identify favorite activities, reinforce cooperative behavior and achievement, and discuss and resolve problems that arose during the activity cycle.

Constructing a Small-Group Learning Cycle

Follow the steps below to create activities and prepare the necessary materials to conduct a small-group learning cycle:

1. Identify a theme or concept for your cycle. All activities will be related to this theme.

2. List any related ideas or concepts that your theme inspires. For example, a "balloons" theme might include activities such as classifying by color and design; weaving hot air balloon gondolas; writing adventure stories; drawing bird's-eye view pictures; researching the history of balloon travel; solving a word-search puzzle with related vocabulary; playing a "balloon math" board game, or studying flying, weather, wind, heat, or molecular expansion.

3. Using the ideas you have generated, plan activities for the groups. You will need:
   ▸ an activity for introducing the cycle. Reading a story, showing a film, teaching a song, or presenting a puzzle are great warm-up ideas.

   ▸ activities for four to six groups to work on simultaneously. The number of activities you

create will depend on the size of the class, the resources and space available, and the time allotted.

   ▸ an extra activity, such as a word puzzle or coloring ditto, that can be duplicated and left in a central location for students to take if they finish early. Books, reference books, or duplicated short readings might also be made available as alternative time fillers.
   ▸ a final or wrap-up activity.

4. For each small-group activity, determine:
   ▸ the title or name of the activity.
   ▸ the concept related to the main theme.
   ▸ the curricular area or areas involved.
   ▸ the objectives of the activities.
   ▸ the materials necessary for the completion of the activity.
   ▸ the information the students will need to complete the activity.
   ▸ the location of the activity, that is, where the student will work.
   ▸ the color for coding the activity.

5. Write the directions for each activity on a separate card. To prepare the directions card for each group:
   ▸ write the title of the activity on the card.
   ▸ write the name of the theme on the back or lower corner of the directions card.
   ▸ list the materials needed.
   ▸ write clear and simple instructions for the students. Use pictures or symbols, if possible, to help young students or disabled readers.
   ▸ tell where to put the finished products at the end of the work period.
   ▸ color code the activity by writing the directions on colored construction paper or by using a colored marker to write the directions on a white index card.
   ▸ laminate each directions card.
   ▸ put each directions card and the necessary materials for each activity in separate containers. Rectangular plastic tubs or laundry baskets work very well. If students need to get additional materials from another location, include these instructions on the directions card.
   ▸ line up the containers with materials and task cards on a shelf, or keep them in a central storage location, or near where the activity will be completed.

► label each container with the name of the activity. Color code the container labels to match the directions card. Write the name of the theme or cycle on the back or lower corner of the card.

6. Schedule the activity and rotation cycle. Some options include:
   ► *Four activities:* Introduce the topic on Monday. Conduct one activity per day, Tuesday through Friday. Wrap up on Friday. *Or,* introduce the topic on Monday. Following the introduction, conduct the first activity. The other three activities can follow on Tuesday through Thursday. Wrap up on Friday.
   ► *Five activities:* Introduce the topic on Monday. Begin activities after the introduction and run one activity per day through Friday. Wrap up on Friday.
   ► *Activity Day:* If you have a self-contained classroom, you can schedule an "activity day" during which the entire day is devoted to rotating groups through the various activities. You may also wish to conduct a two-week cycle, with activities scheduled every other day.

Grouping and Rotation

Divide your class into groups so that there is one group for each activity you have planned. Groups should contain between four and seven students. If you have a very small class, you *can* have three groups, and still rotate them through five activities. You will still need five activity periods to get all three groups through the five activities. If you have a very large class, you will probably have larger groups or more activities.

In creating heterogeneous grouping arrangements, try to mix together your competent readers, independent workers, shy students, noisy or aggressive students, and so on. Groups should remain intact throughout an activity cycle.

To visually represent the grouping and rotation, follow the procedures below.

Activity Cards

1. Make a card for each activity. You may use a rectangular piece of paper (5″ × 8″ or larger) or a card cut in a shape related to the theme of the activity, such as balloons, pumpkins, or teeth.

Color code the activity card to match the other related materials.

2. On the activity card, write the name of the activity. In smaller print on the card, you may also wish to indicate where the students will be working on that activity. Write the name of the theme or cycle on the back or lower corner of the card.

3. Pin the activity cards on a bulletin board or tape them to a wall. These cards will remain in place throughout the cycle.

Group Cards

1. Make a separate card for each group. Write the names of the students in that group on the card. Do not number or color code these cards.

2. Identify a committee chairperson for each group. This person may be the chairperson throughout the cycle or only for the first activity, after which other students will take turns in the order in which their names are listed on the group cards. The chairperson's duties include: getting the container of materials, reading the directions (or appointing someone in the group to read the directions), appointing tasks for the activity where required, helping in problem solving, and directing cleanup. The chairperson may also be the only one allowed to leave the group to speak with the teacher in the event that the group cannot reach an agreement or solution if questions arise.

Try to give each student a chance to chair a committee group. The opportunity to develop some skill at leadership, to build responsibility, and to enhance one's sense of competence is particularly valuable to students who have experienced difficulty in achievement or social behaviors.

3. On the group card, mark the name of the chairperson with a star. If you plan to have a different chairperson with each rotation, mark the chairperson for the day with a colorful thumbtack, bulletin board "flag," or clothespin. Move the marker before each rotation.

4. Attach the group cards to the bulletin board or wall so that each group card is paired with an activity card. The pairing shows which students do which activity for the first activity period. In the example below, the activity cards are in the shape of hot-air balloons, and the group cards are

next to the activity cards. The name of the activity is on the balloon, and the activity location is identified in the balloon's gondola.

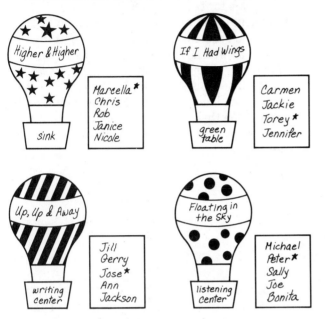

5. After each activity period, simply move each group card to the next activity card. In the example below, the group cards have been moved once, in a counterclockwise direction.

Presenting the Activity Cycle

The following guidelines are designed to help you introduce integrated small-group activities to your students, manage the groups effectively, and follow up on each activity:

1. Introduce the idea of small-group work to the students. Discuss the responsible behaviors that are necessary, including cooperation, helping, sharing, independent problem solving, following directions, and caring for materials.

2. Introduce the various activities to the entire class. Tell the students what they will be doing or making. If possible, show an example or demonstrate the process. Go over special considerations, possible difficulties, or safety reminders as needed. Explain that each group will get a chance to do each activity.

3. Tell the students where each group will be meeting and draw their attention to the containers of materials, particularly when discussing each activity. Explain where the students in each activity should put their finished projects.

4. If you will be directing an activity, announce where you will be. To avoid being continuously interrupted, emphasize the need for group problem solving.

5. Explain the duties and responsibilities of the group chairperson.

6. Explain the rotation process using the cards you have prepared. Show how the cards will be moved at the end of the activity period.

7. Identify alternative materials and activities the students can do if they finish early. Explain where they may do this work and tell them where to put the extra work when they finish.

8. Have the students practice getting into groups, going to the appointed location in the room, getting the materials, and putting the materials away, particularly if they have never engaged in independent small-group activities before. It may be useful to do this practice activity several times.

9. Take a few minutes to answer questions.

After the students have completed several rotation cycles, your introduction will focus more on the activities themselves than the mechanics of the process.

At the end of each cycle, conduct a follow-up discussion with the whole group. Use this time to go over the work the students have done, identify favorite activities, reinforce cooperative behavior and achievement, and discuss problems that arose during the activity cycle. If one of the activities was less stimulating or successful than you would have liked, ask the students to suggest how to make it better. Record their comments or the observations you have made to help you in the future.

Organizing for Next Time

One of the benefits of having prepared plans and materials for a number of activities is that you will be ready to implement the cycle again with another class with no more preparation than assembling the necessary materials and preparing new group cards.

Keep all of the prepared materials, plans, and notes for each cycle together. Keep the materials for specific activities within each cycle together. If you used materials for the activities that are not normally kept in your classroom, make a list of the materials you ordered, borrowed, or brought in from home, as well as the sources and locations of each. Make any changes in plans or materials *before* putting the materials away until next year.

Label each item, including lists and notes, with the name of the theme or cycle. Place all materials in a box, folder, or other storage container and label the container.

Planning Sheet: Integrated Small-Group Activities

Duplicate as needed.

THEME/NAME OF ACTIVITY CYCLE: _____

Related concepts/ideas	Performance objective	Curricular area(s)

Name of activity	Materials	Location
Introductory activity		
Group activity		
Group activity		
Group activity		
Group activity		
Group activity		

Name of activity	Materials	Location
Group activity		
Extra activity		
Wrap-up activity		

Related literature (include source): _____

_____

_____

_____

Related audiovisual materials (include source): _____

_____

_____

_____

Other materials/notes: _____

_____

_____

_____

_____

_____

_____

_____

Grouping: Divide the class into _____ groups.

Group	Group
Group	Group
Group	Group

Identify a chairperson for each group unless you plan to have a different chairperson each activity period.

☐ Ordered all materials not on hand.

☐ Assembled all materials available, material containers stocked and labeled.

☐ Task cards for students completed and laminated.

☐ Activity cards constructed and laminated.

☐ Group cards constructed.

☐ Be sure to mention/practice: _____.

Reflection and Evaluation: Student Behavior

In what ways were your students able to work successfully in small groups? _____

_____

_____

_____

_____

In what instances did they need your assistance or supervision? _____

_____

_____

_____

_____

What skills do your students need to practice before the next activity cycle? _____

_____

_____

_____

_____

What changes will make the next activity cycle run more smoothly? _____

_____

_____

_____

_____

_____

_____

_____

_____

Reflection and Evaluation: Activities and Materials

Duplicate as needed.

Evaluate the effectiveness of the introduction and each activity. Identify plans or proposed changes to maintain or enhance effectiveness in future implementations.

Introduction: _____   Changes: _____

_____   _____

_____   _____

_____   _____

_____   _____

_____   _____

_____   _____

Activity: _____   Changes: _____

_____   _____

_____   _____

_____   _____

_____   _____

Activity: _____   Changes: _____

_____   _____

_____   _____

_____   _____

_____   _____

Activity: _____   Changes: _____

_____   _____

_____   _____

_____   _____

_____   _____

Activity: _____   Changes: _____
_____   _____
_____   _____
_____   _____
_____   _____

Activity: _____   Changes: _____
_____   _____
_____   _____
_____   _____
_____   _____

Alternative activities: _____   Changes: _____
_____   _____
_____   _____
_____   _____
_____   _____

Follow-up activities: _____   Changes: _____
_____   _____
_____   _____
_____   _____
_____   _____

Other materials: _____   Changes: _____
_____   _____
_____   _____
_____   _____
_____   _____

Chapter 26

Prescriptive Instruction

IMAGINE THAT you have organized the content you intend to teach and have developed diagnostic instruments to assess students' needs. After reviewing the results of your diagnoses, you discover that everyone seems to have entirely different instructional needs. Lizzy doesn't know her colors, Albert can't identify compound words, and Lawrence can't remember what number comes after twelve. Even if you have some students who are weak in the same skill, how long will it be before a few of them catch on and are ready to go on to something more challenging?

The most effective way to meet specific needs of individual learners is to devise a way to assign individual instruction. To implement a program of prescriptive instruction, you will need a clear organization and sequence of content; a good sense of each student's strengths and weaknesses; a simple record-keeping and management system; and well-organized and accessible materials for the students to work with independently.

Since content organization, diagnosis, and record keeping have been covered in detail in other chapters, this chapter will focus primarily on management and materials.

How Prescriptive Instruction Works

Prescriptive instruction allows you to assign tasks to students on an individual basis. In many instances, the prescription is based on some diagnosed or observed need, although the prescription may also be determined by the student's individual pacing through a specified sequence of content. In either case, this method is based on the idea of *mastery*—once a student achieves a particular skill, he or she moves onto the next. Review and reinforcement of previously mastered skills are also important.

Prescriptive instruction begins with diagnosis, either through formal testing or informal observa-

tion. The assessment occurs *before* instruction takes place so that you can determine what needs to be taught. Preassessment will help you make a number of decisions about the instructional needs of each student. Does the student need a thorough introduction to this skill or just a review? Does he or she need to learn even easier skills first? Does the student need to move on to the next skill level? The evaluation criteria you establish will help determine the placement of the student.

Once needs are determined, your prescription should attempt to match the student with the appropriate assignment. Prescriptions may be very specific: "Do page 115, problems 3–14," for example. Or, the assignment may be more flexible: "Do any two of the worksheets in the yellow file box." In either case, the prescription assigns work at a specific skill level appropriate for the student.

Interpreting Diagnostic Records

Chapter 10 presented a record-keeping system for marking diagnostic test results skill by skill. In the example below, an *X* indicates that the student has mastered the skill, and a diagonal line shows that additional instruction or review may be needed before the student achieves mastery. A blank box indicates that the student does not appear to understand the skill and probably needs to be taught prerequisite skills.

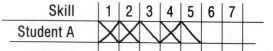

In the example above, Student A probably does not need instruction on skills 1, 2, or 4, although the lack of mastery in skills 3 and 5 indicates a need for review. The lack of any marks in the boxes under skills 6 and 7 represents an inablilty to perform those skills at any significant levels of proficiency, at least on the diagnostic test.

Skills will often be listed in sequence, with mastery of skill 2 dependent on prior mastery of skill 1. If the example above represented a sequenced set of skills, you might wonder how the student achieved mastery in skill 4 but not in skill 3. When a student displays mastery of a complex skill without mastering a simpler skill, it may be that the complex skill does not depend on mastery of the simpler skill. More often, the student does understand the concepts in both skill levels, and the lack of mastery at the lower level is due to careless errors. Sometimes a student may attempt to solve a simple type of problem with a more complex process. Further observation of the student's performance should clear up any questions or difficulties the initial diagnosis presents.

Assigning Instruction

Since skills 1, 2, and 4 appear to have been mastered according to Student A's diagnosis, no immediate instruction will probably be needed. Since skills 3 and 5 have not been completely mastered, some demonstration and instruction may be necessary to help the student understand these particular skills. The student may simply need to practice these skills.

Student A apparently has little or no understanding of skill 6. Assigning practice problems or independent work without prior instruction will very likely be a waste of time and a source of frustration for the student. If the student cannot do the problems on the diagnostic instrument, he or she will probably not be able to do them in an assignment. At this level, the student requires some form of instruction.

To implement an individualized, prescriptive program, give each student an initial assignment. Your prescription for Student A might read:

Student A will then know that he or she must meet with you for instruction before doing any work in skill 3.

Once the students have received their prescriptions, instruct them to select an assignment from *any* skill level below the one they have been assigned. Student A, for example, can select some practice work from any of the materials in the skill 1 box or the skill 2 box. This procedure will allow you to work with each skill group individually and give your students some review work to do while they are waiting for their groups to be called.

If you have any students who are assigned to work on skill 1, meet with their group first. They will need instruction before they are able to complete any of the assignments at the skill 1 level.

When you meet with each group, present a brief lesson on that skill and then allow the students to select materials from that skill level. The students will continue to work at that level until they have mastered the skill, at which time they will be assigned a new prescription.

As with any new program, having students practice the procedures is important. Take a few days to have small groups of students practice getting and replacing their prescriptions and locating and replacing materials in the correct order.

Management Materials

Because each student will be working according to a personal assignment, some form of communicating the assignment to the individual students is essential. Prescriptions can be written on blank pieces of paper:

Student A

Skill 3 Group

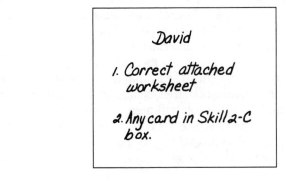

or on formal printed forms:

```
Rx for _____

to work on: _____

Do the following:


Date: _____ Completed: _____

Signed: _____
```

or on daily contracts (further described in Chapter 30):

```
                    Daily Contract

Date: _____

Student: _____

_____ Reading group

_____ Reading  workbook p. 40

_____ Spelling

_____ Handwriting  Unit 5

_____ Math  Skill 4-D

_____ Learning center

_____ Other:

      See me before you start on
      Math assignment.
```

Often, you will have a number of students working at the same level. Rather than writing individual prescriptions for a given subject area, you may list tasks on the board with the names of the students assigned to those tasks. Assemble the materials for a particular skill in a box and attach a list of students assigned to the materials.

In choosing a prescription method, consider the length of assignments, the availability of paper, the classroom organization, the management system you use, and how often you will need to change the students' prescriptions. Select a prescription format that is simple and manageable, one that won't bog down your instructional program.

If you choose to write the prescriptions out on individual papers, you can distribute them in one of the following ways:

1. Pass the prescription forms out to the students (or have a student pass the papers out) at the beginning of class.

2. Include the forms in the student's work file.

3. Place prescriptions in a mailbox or prescription holder. Mailboxes may be made of pint or half-pint milk cartons connected to one another, with the tops removed and the students' names written inside. To make a prescription holder, attach a library pocket for each student to a large piece of poster board and write each student's name on a pocket.

Finally, have each student prepare a file folder for storing unfinished assignments and materials. These files may be kept at the student's desk or at one or several storage locations, such as file boxes or drawers.

Instructional Materials

In addition to prescriptions and possibly prescription holders, you will also need instructional materials for students to work on independently. The materials you assemble can accommodate a variety of learning styles and preferences. For example, you can have the students practice addition facts by using worksheets, workbook pages, exercises in the adopted textbook, problems from other math books (including other adoptions, out-of-print textbooks, and books from other grade levels), flash cards, teacher-made task cards, activities in commercial kits, games, puzzles, manipulatives, or audiovisual materials.

The following guidelines will help you sort out and organize instructional materials to make them easily accessible to your students. The materials may be stored in a central location or in several locations. To avoid confusion, you may wish to keep materials for one subject, such as math, separate from materials in other subjects. If possible, keep similar materials together; for example, keep all books on the shelves, all worksheets in a file box or drawer, and all games in a cabinet.

In addition, try to keep all materials at the students' eye level or below, and avoid stacking objects one on top of another. Students should be able to obtain all materials easily.

Textbooks

Start with the adopted text. Assign the number one to this text. Even if each student has a copy, place an extra copy or two on the shelves (or wherever you store the books). Attach a piece of masking tape or an adhesive label to the spine and write the number one on each copy.

Assemble other books that have exercises in the skill areas you'll be covering. Even though the problems may be the same, students may find it interesting to work from a book used in another school, one that was used when you (or their parents) were in school, or especially one from a higher grade level. Number each book with a label on the spine. If you have more than one copy of the same book, assign the same number to each copy.

Workbooks

Most workbooks are used only once; these are called "consumable workbooks." For workbooks to be useful in a prescriptive program, each student should have one. You can also duplicate or laminate each page and file it as a worksheet, or have the students copy the work from the workbook on a separate piece of paper.

Even if students use their own copies of a consumable workbook, consider how you will collect their work. Since the back side of an assigned page may not have the same skill you want the student to work with for a particular prescription, you may want them to submit the entire workbook instead of tearing out the page.

If you use workbooks in the program, label each title with a number. If you have extra copies, put one or two in the storage area, with the label on or near the spine. Mark other workbooks from other adoptions or grade levels with different numbers; mark duplicate copies of the same workbook with the same numbers.

Dittos/Worksheets

Worksheets are another valuable instructional resource. When you find useful worksheets, assign each of them a number in sequence. The worksheets themselves need not be arranged in any particular order but each must be referenced with a number so that the students can find them. If possible, write the number on the original or master copy. Number a file folder for each worksheet you

plan to use. Arrange the files in order in a file box or drawer.

Make at least three copies of each worksheet. If you have a limited number of resources for a particular skill, or feel that a large number of students will be working with a particular worksheet, you may need more copies initially. Place the copies in the appropriate files—all copies in any given file should be the same. Staple one copy of each worksheet to the inside of its file folder. You may keep the originals in the file, or you may find it safer to keep them filed separately in the same numerical order.

If paper is in short supply, you may choose to mount one copy of each worksheet on a piece of construction paper. Number and, if possible, laminate each one. You may not find it necessary to file single, mounted worksheets in folders; they can be arranged in order in a box or in folders marked, for example, "1-9," "10-19," and so on. Students working with mounted worksheets will copy the work onto separate pieces of paper.

Counters, Manipulatives, and Games

Not all instructional materials will fit neatly on a shelf or in a file folder. When you use counters, manipulatives, and games, all of which usually include a number of loose pieces, you will need a storage system that will preserve the materials and allow the students to quickly find and easily return them.

Shoe boxes, coffee cans, sturdy gift boxes, and cookie tins with lids can be used to store such materials. Envelopes or self-sealing plastic bags may also work as containers, but they are not as durable and are usually more difficult to store. Assign each container a number. Write the number on adhesive labels or pieces of masking tape and stick them on the lid and sides of the containers.

Audio tapes, records, video cassettes, filmstrips, and other materials that are parts of your permanent classroom collection should be numbered if they will be assigned as a part of a prescriptive program. Also, number small items that may be easily lost, such as game pieces.

If your containers are not uniform in size and shape, you may wish to assign storage space to a group of them. For example, you can label one shelf or cabinet "Containers 1-9" and the next, "Containers 10-19."

Specific Skill Level Assignments

Grouping materials by skill may be difficult, if not impossible, because many of the materials will address a number of skills. To make the best use of a book that contains a number of exercises for a wide range of skills, go through the book page by page, determining which skills the exercises address. When you find a page or set of problems that corresponds to a particular skill, write the assignment, indicating the resource by number, the page, and if necessary, the specific items assigned. To keep practice activities separated by skill levels, you may wish to make a master list of assignments for each skill. For example:

```
        Possible Assignments: Skill #3–B

 1. Book 1, p.14, any 10 problems.

 2. Book 4, p.28, problems 3, 5–8, 10, 14–17.

 3. Cross number puzzle #3.

 4. Workbook 1, pages 4 and 5.

 5. Game #17.

 6. Game #24.

 7. Worksheet #56.

 8. Worksheet #103.

 9. Audiotape #4.

10. Any card from the skills kit—Orange level.

11. Book #11, p.89. Use counters in box #2.
```

Instead of using a master list, you may wish to write each assignment on a 4″ × 6″ index card. Using cards allows you to write assignments in greater detail. If you use task cards, you won't have to revise master lists every time you come across new materials or develop additional assignments. Students who do not complete assignments can keep the cards in their work folders and refer to them again during the next work period. Index cards also permit you to write out tasks on the card itself, eliminating the need for the student to get any additional materials.

Task cards should contain the following information:

1. The skill number.

2. The card number (the number of each assignment).

3. The resource needed, by number if applicable. (If all the work assigned appears directly on the card, there may be no need for any other materials). For example: Book 5, Worksheet 72, Box 11, and so on.

4. Page number, if applicable.

5. Problem numbers or choices, if applicable. For example: "First ten," "odd numbers only," "any ten," and so on.

6. Other necessary information. Examples: "You can use the counters in Box 4 to help." "You will need the tape recorder and headphones." "You may choose a partner for this activity." "Do this activity at the sink."

A few sample cards:

```
Skill 2-D                          Card #15

Copy the following sentences and add the
proper punctuation:

1. Sue said the cookies are in the jar

2. Stop thief he cried

3. Did you finish your homework asked
   Ms Deets

4. Well Daniel said we can still see a movie

          (continued on back)
```

```
Skill 72                            Card #3

You need Worksheet #6. Copy the problems
on a piece of paper and complete them.

          Watch out for zeros!

Make sure you put the worksheet back when
you're finished with it.
```

In preparing the assignment cards, write neatly and legibly. Colored markers, illustrations, or decorations (stamps or stickers, for example) can make the cards more attractive. Laminate all cards on both sides to increase their durability.

File the cards by skill in file boxes or pockets. You may want to use a separate container for each skill to reduce the possible jam that may occur if everyone needs a card from the same container.

Answer Keys

Not all prescribed tasks will produce a finished product. Watching a filmstrip or playing a game may provide excellent reinforcement and practice even though students may not have anything specific to hand in. When students do complete a product for which there are specific answers, an answer key can encourage self-checking, building independence and offering immediate reinforcement to the student.

Answer keys should be identified by the skill and assignment (or card) number and may be kept in order in a notebook or file box for students to look at when they need feedback or when they have finished an assignment. The possibility of cheating by simply copying the answers will soon become apparent to the students as a waste of time, unless doing so helps them achieve mastery. When the students arrange a conference with you to move on to the next skill level, they will be asked to demonstrate the skill. They won't be able to do this if they haven't achieved mastery. Once students recognize this, they tend to devote their time to learning the skill.

While the amount of work suggested here may sound overwhelming, consider the following points:

1. It is possible to start an individualized program with a minimum of materials. Even using exercises only from the adopted text or on the cards alone can get you going. This system has been designed for you to add to it as you find new materials.

2. Depending on the range of skills you've developed, you may even be able to use the program with students at different grade levels.

3. Once you have assembled the materials and created a number of assignments at each skill level, you are ready to individualize instruction in subsequent years as soon as you diagnose student needs.

Planning Sheet: Prescriptive Instruction

☐ Curriculum area selected: _____.

☐ Content sequence organized (Chapter 7).

☐ Diagnosis developed, assigned, and recorded (Chapters 11, 12).

☐ Initial placement for each student identified.

☐ Management materials constructed.

Describe prescription forms you plan to use: _____

_____

_____

_____

Distribution and storage methods:

    Description _____

_____

_____

    Materials needed _____

_____

_____

Student work files:

    Who will make them _____

_____

_____

    Where and how they will be stored _____

_____

_____

    Materials needed _____

_____

_____

_____

_____

_____

_____

_____

☐ Instructional materials assembled

BOOKS

Number assigned	Title	Quantity on hand	Where/how to acquire	Where/how to store

WORKBOOKS

Number assigned	Title	Quantity on hand	Where/how to acquire	Where/how to store

MANIPULATIVES AND GAMES

Number assigned	Title	Quantity on hand	Where/how to acquire	Where/how to store

WORKSHEETS/DITTOS/PUZZLES

Number assigned	Title	Quantity on hand	Where/how to acquire	Where/how to store

SPECIFIC SKILL LEVEL ASSIGNMENTS

☐ **ASSIGNMENT LIST**   ☐ **TASK CARDS**

Organization and storage of assignments: _____
_____
_____
_____

ANSWER KEYS

Organization and storage of answer keys: _____
_____
_____
_____

CHECKLIST FOR
DESIGNING ASSIGNMENTS

Slash (/) for assignments as they are completed.
X for assignments as answer keys are completed.

Skill Level/Skill Name	Assignments
_____	__1 __2 __3 __4 __5 __6 __7 __8 __9 __10 __11
_____	__1 __2 __3 __4 __5 __6 __7 __8 __9 __10 __11
_____	__1 __2 __3 __4 __5 __6 __7 __8 __9 __10 __11
_____	__1 __2 __3 __4 __5 __6 __7 __8 __9 __10 __11
_____	__1 __2 __3 __4 __5 __6 __7 __8 __9 __10 __11
_____	__1 __2 __3 __4 __5 __6 __7 __8 __9 __10 __11
_____	__1 __2 __3 __4 __5 __6 __7 __8 __9 __10 __11
_____	__1 __2 __3 __4 __5 __6 __7 __8 __9 __10 __11
_____	__1 __2 __3 __4 __5 __6 __7 __8 __9 __10 __11
_____	__1 __2 __3 __4 __5 __6 __7 __8 __9 __10 __11
_____	__1 __2 __3 __4 __5 __6 __7 __8 __9 __10 __11
_____	__1 __2 __3 __4 __5 __6 __7 __8 __9 __10 __11
_____	__1 __2 __3 __4 __5 __6 __7 __8 __9 __10 __11
_____	__1 __2 __3 __4 __5 __6 __7 __8 __9 __10 __11
_____	__1 __2 __3 __4 __5 __6 __7 __8 __9 __10 __11

Skill Level/Skill Name	Assignments
_____	__1 __2 __3 __4 __5 __6 __7 __8 __9 __10 __11
_____	__1 __2 __3 __4 __5 __6 __7 __8 __9 __10 __11
_____	__1 __2 __3 __4 __5 __6 __7 __8 __9 __10 __11
_____	__1 __2 __3 __4 __5 __6 __7 __8 __9 __10 __11
_____	__1 __2 __3 __4 __5 __6 __7 __8 __9 __10 __11
_____	__1 __2 __3 __4 __5 __6 __7 __8 __9 __10 __11
_____	__1 __2 __3 __4 __5 __6 __7 __8 __9 __10 __11
_____	__1 __2 __3 __4 __5 __6 __7 __8 __9 __10 __11
_____	__1 __2 __3 __4 __5 __6 __7 __8 __9 __10 __11
_____	__1 __2 __3 __4 __5 __6 __7 __8 __9 __10 __11
_____	__1 __2 __3 __4 __5 __6 __7 __8 __9 __10 __11
_____	__1 __2 __3 __4 __5 __6 __7 __8 __9 __10 __11
_____	__1 __2 __3 __4 __5 __6 __7 __8 __9 __10 __11
_____	__1 __2 __3 __4 __5 __6 __7 __8 __9 __10 __11
_____	__1 __2 __3 __4 __5 __6 __7 __8 __9 __10 __11
_____	__1 __2 __3 __4 __5 __6 __7 __8 __9 __10 __11
_____	__1 __2 __3 __4 __5 __6 __7 __8 __9 __10 __11
_____	__1 __2 __3 __4 __5 __6 __7 __8 __9 __10 __11
_____	__1 __2 __3 __4 __5 __6 __7 __8 __9 __10 __11
_____	__1 __2 __3 __4 __5 __6 __7 __8 __9 __10 __11
_____	__1 __2 __3 __4 __5 __6 __7 __8 __9 __10 __11
_____	__1 __2 __3 __4 __5 __6 __7 __8 __9 __10 __11
_____	__1 __2 __3 __4 __5 __6 __7 __8 __9 __10 __11
_____	__1 __2 __3 __4 __5 __6 __7 __8 __9 __10 __11
_____	__1 __2 __3 __4 __5 __6 __7 __8 __9 __10 __11
_____	__1 __2 __3 __4 __5 __6 __7 __8 __9 __10 __11
_____	__1 __2 __3 __4 __5 __6 __7 __8 __9 __10 __11
_____	__1 __2 __3 __4 __5 __6 __7 __8 __9 __10 __11
_____	__1 __2 __3 __4 __5 __6 __7 __8 __9 __10 __11
_____	__1 __2 __3 __4 __5 __6 __7 __8 __9 __10 __11
_____	__1 __2 __3 __4 __5 __6 __7 __8 __9 __10 __11
_____	__1 __2 __3 __4 __5 __6 __7 __8 __9 __10 __11

Chapter 27

. . . .

Skill Groups and Individual Conferences

NDIVIDUALIZED INSTRUCTION involves a number of teaching techniques. Once you have provided prescriptions for each student, matching the assignments to the learners' needs, you will have to provide instruction as students encounter new content.

Individual conferences, brief one-on-one student-teacher encounters, allow you to assess students' progress, provide feedback and reinforcement, and even present new material. When two or more students require instruction at the same skill level, skill grouping provides a means of working with only those students on that particular skill.

This chapter provides suggestions to help you conduct skill groups and individual conferences. The information will be especially useful if you have decided to incorporate prescriptive assignments into your instructional program.

Skill Groups

Chapter 24 introduced the idea of skill grouping as a small-group strategy in which group members are selected on the basis of common skill needs. Because they are so skill-specific, skill groups are subject to continuous change; when students acquire a skill, they move out of the skill group. Likewise, when other students are diagnosed as weak in a skill, they become a part of the group. Once all students have mastered the skill, the skill group ceases to exist and is replaced by groups formed to teach new and different skills.

A record-keeping system that indicates achievement for each student at specific skill levels can help you keep track of skill groups (see Chapter 10). For example, the visual clarity of the record-keeping system below makes it easy to identify which skill groups each student should be in. This chart represents the results of diagnostic

assessment. Mastery is marked with an *X* and partial mastery (remediation level) is marked with a *slash*, /. Boxes that are blank represent skills the student still needs instruction in.

Skill	1	2	3	4	5	6	7	8
Althea		X	X					
Bonnie		X	X	X	X	X		
Carlye			X					
Domita			X					
Eugene			X					
Franklin		X	X					

To select students for a skill group, simply scan down a column under a particular skill on the record sheet and identify any student who has not mastered the skill. In some instances you may want to include students who have just recently mastered that skill and who might benefit from the reinforcement.

When the skills listed are sequentially dependent (each skill builds on the previous skills), students are eligible for placement in a skill group only if they have mastered all previous skills. On occasion, a diagnostic test will indicate mastery of a complex skill when performance on preliminary skills is weak. In that instance, include the student in groups for instruction or review of the preliminary skills. If your contact with the student indicates that he or she does not understand the material, you may want to include the student in a skill group at that level, even though mastery appears to have been demonstrated according to the chart. If, on the other hand, the student seems to understand the concept, but did not perform well on the diagnostic instrument on the lower-level skills because of careless errors or misapplied processes, you may still want to include him or her in a skill group for review and assign practice work.

You have some flexibility in deciding whom to include in a group. Consider the types of errors made, the student's achievement on independent practice work, and observed performance. If you think the student will benefit from the instruction, include him or her in the group.

In the example chart, assume that the skills are sequentially dependent—in order to learn one skill, prior skills must be mastered. Note that all of the students have demonstrated at least some level of proficiency in skill 1 and that all but Domita and Eugene need no more instruction. Only the two students who have not mastered skill 1 need to participate in a lesson at that level. The instructional needs of the other four students would be best met in other skill groups. (Remember that occasional practice of all skills is recommended and can be assigned through prescriptions, as described in Chapter 26.)

Look down the column for skill 2. Note that the two students who need work at this level are the same who need work on skill 1. Since skill 2 is dependent upon achievement of skill 1, there will be no group called for this skill until either or both of the two students placed at skill 1 demonstrate mastery and can move on. Because students normally learn at different rates, it is possible that one of the students will master a skill before the other. In that case, you can move the student to skill 2 when he or she has mastered skill 1.

Since Bonnie, Carlye, and Franklin have mastered skill 3, they do not need to be called to the skill 3 group. Neither Althea, Domita, nor Eugene have mastered the skill, but Althea is the only one of the three who has mastered the previous skills. Hence, Althea is the only student from the record sheet above who would receive instruction at this level.

Suppose that it takes Althea several lessons and assignments to master skill 3, or that she has been absent and hasn't had a chance to make much progress. In the meantime, Domita has worked through the first two skill levels and is now ready for instruction on skill 3. Now when you call a group for skill 3, Domita and Althea will attend.

By now it may be clear that a skill 4 group would include Carlye and Franklin. Even though Carlye's performance on the diagnosis was stronger than Franklin's, it is appropriate to include both. You may find Carlye able to go back to her seat to practice after very little explanation, leaving you free to help Franklin a little longer. Bonnie would start out with instruction on skill 7, because she has mastered all of the prior skills in the list.

When you are working with students who have not fully mastered the material, then differences in entry level knowledge and understanding may require extending the instruction for some students in the forms of additional interaction, demonstrations, examples, observations, and/or practice. Likewise, variations in achievement levels within groups can be used as a basis for peer helping.

Guidelines for Conducting Skill Groups

When conducting skill groups, consider the following suggestions:

1. Teach skills in a sequence, if one exists. Teach and demonstrate only one new skill at a time.

2. Call to a group only those students who have a chance of succeeding at that particular skill. Make sure that the students in a skill group have a fairly solid understanding of any prerequisite skills. If you expose students to a skill that they are not intellectually ready for, they will probably fail to learn it.

3. Keep instructional meetings brief. You have many students to see and several groups to teach. Fortunately, the small size of most skill groups and the specificity of content allows for short, direct, intensive, and efficient teaching.

4. Introduce new material at the most concrete level possible. Gradually move toward more abstract representations of the content.

5. Introduce new material in the context of the skills already acquired by the student.

6. Practice new concepts with the students. Demonstrate procedures and clarify problems students may have by assigning independent practice tasks. Because skill groups rarely include large numbers of students, you also have the opportunity to observe performance and provide support and reinforcement on a personal and individual basis.

7. When instruction and interaction with students is over, have students return to their work areas to practice the skill they worked on in the group according to their prescriptions or an assignment given in the skill group meeting.

Conferences

In conducting an individualized, prescriptive program of instruction, you will sometimes need to work with individual students who appear to be between groups. Arranging a conference allows you to give extra help to students in need and provides an excellent opportunity to check a student's work and offer feedback. Students who are the only ones at a given skill level will need a conference before receiving instruction. Conferences are probably the best way to review and update prescriptions as well. Very often, they are a combination of teaching, checking, recording, *and* prescribing.

Have your record sheet handy during a conference to mark work accomplished and new skills mastered. You may want to design a conference form to keep track of the students' work, their performance, the instruction they received, and their progress. This form can be a personal and descriptive record of student progress. A sample conference form would be:

Date:	Student:		Skill #
What was done Prescription:	Student performance:		
Examples:	Instruction/remediation:		
Management and self-direction:	Student self-evaluation:	Teacher recommendations and new prescription:	

The conference form includes space for noting the date, name, and skill number. The box on the left, "What was done," provides space for you under "Prescription," to list the tasks (card or assignment numbers) the student chose (or was assigned) at that skill level. Under "Examples," write a sample problem or two. You can also use this space to have

the student work the sample problems, giving you the opportunity to observe the process he or she chooses.

Under "Student performance," write an evaluation of the student's performance—not a judgment, but a statement of achievement. You might comment on the aspects of the work that are giving the student problems or specific behaviors you observed. Describe what you have demonstrated or explained under the space marked, "Instruction/ remediation." Your comments might include specific steps emphasized, prior skills reviewed, or new skills introduced.

Space at the bottom of the form is available for you to note the student's management and self-direction. Comments in this box might describe the student's ability to take responsibility for working independently or requesting help as needed. "Student self-evaluation" refers to the student's perceptions of his or her progress and performance. This section might also include comments the student makes regarding his or her readiness to go on to the next skill.

The final box might contain a note such as "Recommend one more task at this level; then proceed to next skill," "Begin skill 17," or "Continue until next conference."

As you complete conference forms at each meeting, file them in the students' files.

Scheduling Conferences

Develop a management system that allows students to request conferences. Students will usually need a conference with you whenever they complete a prescription or individual work contract. A conference may be called when a student feels ready to move on to the next skill or when the student wants feedback on work before doing more practice in that skill.

Perhaps the simplest sign-up method is one that uses a chalkboard. Students sign up, one after another, as they need a conference. You then call the names one by one.

Make sure you also have a checklist for monitoring conferences. A student may get lost in the shuffle, especially if he or she has to compete with students who are more aggressive about signing up. To ensure that you are meeting with each student at least once a week, prepare a grid with students' names down the left-hand side and the dates of the first days of the weeks across the top. Whenever a student meets with you for a conference, you can give a star or sticker to that student to place on the grid.

A glance at the grid will tell you which students you haven't seen that week; you can then call those students for conferences. The grid can also help you monitor conference-happy students who may be spending more time in conferences (or signing up for conferences) than they spend working.

Conferences and skill groups are important steps in individualized, prescriptive instruction. Make time for both by devoting part of class time to skill-group instruction and the rest to holding conferences. Keep the conferences to three to five minutes each. Do not attempt to meet with each student or skill group every day. If your conference requests start piling up, see if you can't meet some of the conference goals—in particular, observation, feedback, and instruction—in a skill group.

Conducting the Conference

Before you call your first student for a conference, assemble:

The mastery record sheet.

A red and blue pen to mark the record sheet.

Some blank prescription forms.

Some blank conference forms.

The conference grid and stickers or markers, if necessary.

Conduct the conference sitting side by side with the student at a student-sized desk or table. Use the following procedure for conducting the conference:

1. Call the student to the conference.

2. Have the student bring his or her prescription and work to the conference.

3. Ask the student about the work done. Use general questions such as, "How did you like this activity card?" or "What did you work on?" Look over the student's work (which the student may have already checked), and check answers and processes. You do not need to check each problem; simply determine whether or not the student has mastered the skill.

4. Give the student a similar problem to answer or work through. Have the student solve the problem in front of you, explaining the process

as he or she goes along or as you ask questions about steps in the process.

5. Reinforce specific behaviors, focusing on what the student is doing right. Examples: "You set that problem up correctly." "You remembered your capital letters," "That is exactly how that problem is solved."

6. Offer instruction or further explanations to correct errors. Examples: "Let's go over where to put commas in a quotation." "Those zeros are tricky. This is what you need to do here."

7. Fill in the conference form. Discuss the student's progress and readiness to move on to the next skill. If the student is ready for the next skill, you can either assign practice work until the skill group is called, or introduce the new skill at the conference. Your decision will be determined by the need (or the student's desire) for practice, how soon you intend to call that skill group, how different or more difficult the next skill is, and the amount of time you have available (considering the number of students waiting to have a conference with you).

8. Record your recommendations and assign a new prescription. Determine the new assignment by the quality of the work done, the accuracy of the process demonstrated by the student, the number of tasks or the amount of work already done at that skill level, and the student's self evaluation. As a rule, if there was any need to clarify or reteach the skill, the same skill level should be reassigned. Reevaluate the student's progress at the next conference.

9. Mark the record sheet according to the guidelines in Chapter 10. Mark each assignment completed with a diagnonal red line. If the skill has been mastered, cross the diagonal to make an *X* with the red pen to indicate mastery.

10. File the conference form in the conference folder. Attach the completed prescription and the student's work (optional).

11. Mark, or have the student mark, the weekly conference grid.

12. Have the student erase or cross his or her name from the conference sign-up sheet and begin working independently on the new prescription.

Reflection and Evaluation: Skill Groups and Individual Conferences

Prepare the materials you need to conduct skill groups (mastery record sheet) and conferences (conference forms, checklist or grid, prescription forms). Implement the instructional procedures.

In what ways have your skill groups been successful? _____

What problems have you encountered? _____

_____

_____

_____

_____

_____

_____

What are you doing, or planning to do, to remedy those problems? _____

_____

_____

_____

_____

_____

_____

_____

_____

_____

Describe the conference procedure you are using: _____

_____

_____

_____

_____

_____

_____

_____

_____

_____

_____

What purpose(s) do your conferences serve? _____

_____

_____

_____

In what ways have your conferences been successful? _____

_____

_____

_____

_____

What problems have you encountered? _____

_____

_____

_____

_____

What are you doing (or planning to do) to remedy those problems? _____

_____

_____

_____

_____

In what ways are the processes of diagnosing, recording, prescribing, skill grouping, and conferring
working together?

_____

_____

_____

What changes do you anticipate in your management, materials, content, or records? _____

_____

_____

_____

How would you evaluate this program? Does it help you meet the needs of individual students? _____

_____

_____

_____

Chapter 28

Learning Centers

ARE YOU LOOKING for a way to organize your environment so there will be one or more places where students can work independently? Do you have materials you want to let students explore in their spare time? Do you have some exciting activities you want to use to supplement your regular routine? If so, you may want to set up learning centers.

A learning center is simply a place where students can perform some specific tasks. This place may be a corner arranged with pillows and carpets, a study carrel, an isolated desk or table top, a sink area, a group of desks pushed together, the space behind a bookshelf or couch, or even the inside of an old bathtub or huge box.

A classroom may contain one learning center, several learning centers, or nothing but learning centers. Centers are usually separated from the main part of the classroom or from one another by furniture, space, curtains, hangings, or shelves used as dividers.

Learning centers contain materials and instructions for tasks and usually have work space for one or more students. The center may be developed around one general content area (such as math, science, or art), a specific skill or skill area (such as addition, handwriting, or phonics), or even certain kinds of instructional material (such as newspapers, audiovisual materials, or commercial and teacher-made games or kits).

Learning centers allow for the maximum use of the environment and promote independent work skills and decision making. They can add variety, interest, and flexibility to any instructional setting or program.

Setting up Learning Centers

The organization and use of centers will vary from one classroom to another or even within one classroom, from one center to another. Several possible approaches to learning centers are presented below:

1. Vary the materials and tasks daily or weekly.

2. Vary the tasks daily or weekly, but use the same materials. Examples might include:
   ▸ using the newspapers: on Monday, find compound words; on Tuesday, find long *e* words; on Wednesday, write headlines out as complete sentences, and so on.
   ▸ using a button collection: on Monday, find ten buttons that are alike in some way; on Tuesday, tell how many buttons can fit flat inside each of these circles; on Wednesday, pick buttons to go with the clothes in this picture, and so on.

3. Using the same materials, allow students to select from a variety of possible activities. Keep the materials and activities at the center for an extended period of time. Examples might include:
   ▸ using the button collection, select two or more of the twenty-five task cards or questions.
   ▸ using handwriting practice cards, work on specific cards as needed or prescribed.

4. Provide a variety of materials, each with their own descriptions or directions. For example:
   ▸ choose one or more of these math games and manipulative materials.

5. To encourage student exploration, provide a variety of materials and references without specific directions.

Managing Learning Centers

There are many different approaches to managing the learning centers and working them into your daily or weekly routine. Some possibilities include the following:

1. Set up one center for the students to visit and explore as part of the daily requirements or weekly routines. Students can visit the center on an assigned rotation basis (for example, Group 1 on Mondays, or Group 3 from 9:30 to 9:50) or during independent work time. Let the students work at the center until they complete the task.

2. Put several or all of the daily independent work requirements in learning centers. Students can visit the centers on an assigned rotation basis. One center may be reserved for teacher-directed group instruction. Students can also visit the centers whenever they are not in a teacher-directed ability or skill group. They can select the centers that interest them.

3. Set up one center for students to visit *in addition to* their regular daily requirements or weekly routine. Consider the following types of centers:
   - *Inquiry or Open Enrichment Centers*—Students, guided by task cards or questions, explore the materials provided.
   - *Prescriptive Remediation Centers*—Only certain students are assigned to a center for remedial activities and skill practice based on a diagnosed or observed skill need.
   - *Prescriptive Enrichment Centers*—Only certain students are assigned to a center for enrichment activities based on some diagnosed or observed need.

4. Set up centers for contract activity selection (see Chapter 30).

5. Set up centers for integrated small-group activities (see Chapter 25).

Work Management Systems

The work in learning centers can be individualized to varying degrees, depending on the center's purpose, the students' needs, and the materials used. Some possible work management systems in which assignments may be individualized are described below:

1. Allow students to select activities by presenting materials with a number of possible tasks.

2. Allow students to select all the learning center activities they do.

3. Set out different work for different groups. Present a number of task cards or worksheets in different folders. Color code the cards or the folders to represent different quantities and/or levels of difficulty. Identify groups for that center by writing the names of the students on colored cards that correspond to the task cards or folders to which the students will be assigned.

4. Use the same color-coded materials described in number 3, but prescribe the work for individual students, using the colors of the tasks. For example:

   Jo—All Blue (*all work in blue folder or all blue task cards*)

   Bob—1 Red (*choice of one red task card or one worksheet from the red folder*)

   Celia—2 Yellow

   Martina—1 Blue, 2 Red

5. Provide a variety of materials and write prescriptions for specific tasks, cards, games, worksheets, and workbook pages.

Planning Sheet: Learning Centers

Duplicate this sheet for each center.

Theme: _____

_____

Purpose: _____

_____

_____

Location: _____

_____

Furniture needed: _____

_____

Maximum number of students: _____

_____

Students who will use the center: _____

_____

_____

Scheduling/availability: _____

_____

_____

Activities: _____

_____

_____

Objectives: _____

_____

_____

Materials: _____

_____

_____

Directions for students: _____

_____

_____

_____

Reflection and Evaluation: Learning Centers

Duplicate this sheet for each center.

How did the students respond to the center? _____

_____

_____

How did the students follow the guidelines for using and visiting the center? _____

_____

_____

In what area(s) do the students need practice while working at the center? _____

_____

_____

_____

In what ways did the center help with your instructional program? _____

_____

_____

In what ways did the center help the students develop independent learning skills? _____

_____

_____

In what ways did the center help you meet the needs of your students? _____

_____

_____

What are your plans for this learning center (maintenance, changes, continued use)? _____

_____

_____

_____

_____

_____

_____

_____

_____

_____

Chapter 29

Self-Selection Activities

WITH ALL YOU have to accomplish in a teaching day, why take the time necessary to let students select some of their own activities? The time you set aside for self-selection activities can be a valuable part of the day for several reasons. Through self-selection of activities, students can choose from a variety of materials that reinforce the skills they are learning in groups. By allowing students to choose their own activities, you can also learn about their preferences and priorities.

Selecting activities will help students develop responsible learning behaviors such as decision making, caring for materials, and on-task self-management. You can also motivate students to complete other tasks by offering them the opportunity to choose their own activities when they have completed an assigned activity. Finally, a self-selection program offers you a way to introduce new games and materials.

If you choose to include self-selection activities in your classroom, you will need to acquire appropriate materials and develop an effective management system. This chapter presents suggestions for both of these tasks.

Self-Selection Materials

To be most effective, the self-selection materials and activities you choose should be varied, stimulating, and in some way special for the students. Self-selection activities should provide opportunities to explore unusual topics. At the same time, the activities must be interesting and meaningful. Having personal conversations with students, administering interest inventories, and having a sharing time are some of the ways you can discover your students' personal preferences. Recognizing

that some of your students like motorcycles, horses, or crossword puzzles, for example, can help you choose materials that will interest them.

Self-selection time can be a time to introduce new materials or test activities you might want to use in an instructional setting. For instance, if you introduce a piece of audiovisual equipment or a game as a self-selection activity, by the time you want to use these items in independent, small-group activities, at least some of the students will be familiar with the materials.

You can also offer students opportunities to finish work or spend extra time with regular classroom activities if they choose. These options will be particularly attractive to students who want to catch up after an absence, make additional progress in a self-paced program, or avoid having to take work home.

Self-selection materials might include:

▶ teacher-made skill games.

▶ commercial games.

▶ electronic calculator or computer games.

▶ flash cards.

▶ card games.

▶ jacks, paddleball, or other eye/hand coordination games.

▶ paper-and-pencil puzzles (crosswords, dot-to-dot, or word searches).

▶ jigsaw puzzles.

▶ beads, manipulatives, or collections.

▶ art materials (cut-and-paste, clay).

▶ cassette tapes or records.

Self-selection activities might also include:

▶ watching filmstrips or videocassettes.

- ▶ sewing or crocheting activities.
- ▶ helping in another classroom.
- ▶ visiting and working in the library.
- ▶ using blocks, model cars, or toys.
- ▶ playing in a housekeeping or "store" center.
- ▶ playing with materials in a discovery or science center.
- ▶ letter writing to pen pals or writing in a journal.
- ▶ creative writing activities.
- ▶ free reading in the library.
- ▶ reading with or to a friend.
- ▶ completing assignments.
- ▶ creating a bulletin board.
- ▶ working on a newsletter.
- ▶ taking care of classroom plants or animals.
- ▶ cleaning out a locker, cubby, desk, or work space.
- ▶ creating a game, puzzle, or ditto for the rest of the class to use.

Unless you have inherited a well-stocked classroom or have had years to accumulate materials, start building up your supply of materials. Even after you have accumulated a good variety, you will want to look out for new materials and ideas to add to your supply.

Consider the following strategies and resources for acquiring materials:

1. Visit flea markets, garage or yard sales, discount or wholesale houses for puzzles, games, crafts, storage materials, and party favors.

2. Visit curriculum centers or learning materials resource centers to borrow games, materials, or ideas.

3. Browse through educational magazines and school supply stores for games and ideas.

4. Consider constructing and laminating at least one new game per week.

5. Bring in materials from your own home. (Here's an opportunity to encourage students' responsibility and respect for someone else's property.)

6. Invite the students to bring in their own materials to use for a few days.

Managing Self-Selection Activities

Limit the number of self-selection activities you offer at any one time. To let students know which materials and activities are available, construct a self-selection board, consisting of eight to twelve library pockets affixed to a 22″ × 28″ piece of posterboard. Do not write on the pockets. If possible, laminate the entire board and open the pockets with a razor blade or an X-ACTO knife.

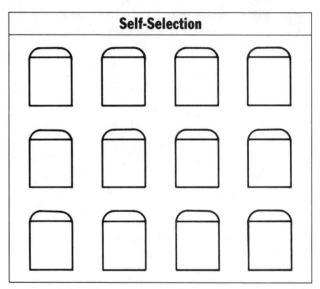

On the self-selection board, each pocket represents an available activity. Attach a card to each pocket with a paper clip. Each card should identify the activity and the number of students allowed to work on that activity at one time. If no number appears on the card, any number of students can select the activity.

Example:

In order to manage a self-selection process, the students will each need a marker to insert in the pocket of the activity they choose. Self-selection markers resemble bookmarks and are created by the student. Give each student a blank strip of paper, approximately 1½" × 6" and have the student write his or her name on it and decorate it with crayons. Laminate the strips to preserve them, and store them in a container near the self-selection board.

When a student is ready for self-selection, he or she simply takes the marker and puts it in the pocket for the activity of his or her choice. The student must check to see if the activity is restricted to a certain number of students; if it is, he or she must make sure that there are fewer markers in the pocket than the number of students allowed before adding another marker.

While this management system represents only one of several possible, it is described here because of its simplicity and flexibility. This system permits you to change the selection of activities very easily.

Implementing a Self-Selection Program

Some guidelines for conducting a self-selection program:

1. Have students practice marking choices, getting materials, returning materials, and returning markers. Do this several times.

2. Make participation in self-selection activities contingent upon certain criteria, such as completion of other classwork assignments, proper marking of activity choices, care and return of materials, and responsible behavior.

3. Allow students to begin selecting activities after they complete prerequisite work, even if only five minutes remain. Consider allowing open participation once a week with no prerequisite work completion requirements.

4. If certain students never seem to have time for self-selection activities because they find it difficult to complete their work on time, try to determine why this is happening. Is it because they are not motivated by the activities? Is the work too difficult? Do they simply have more to do than they can handle? If these students are not wasting time, consider reducing the work load, slowing the pace, or allowing them to complete work at home.

5. Be cautious to not overuse self-selection activities. If you find that a student has an hour and a half of free time each day, you may want to assign more work.

6. Change activities from time to time, but limit the number of new materials introduced at the same time.

7. Recycle activities by taking them out of circulation for a while and then returning them at a later date to maintain interest.

8. Include library time or free reading as an option.

9. If assignment completion is not explicitly required as a prerequisite to self-selection activities, include a "work completion" pocket for any students who have not finished their regular classwork or who wish to make additional progress.

10. Schedule self-selection activities at the end of the work period or at the end of the day.

11. Self-selection time can be scheduled formally (for example, daily from 3:00 to 3:20) or informally (as students complete their morning work). Self-selection time should probably not last more than thirty minutes, except for special occasions.

12. Be sensitive to students' responses to self-selection activities. Implement the period often enough to maintain interest and reinforce skills and desired behaviors. Take into consideration the level of student interest, participation, and cooperation when you make decisions about self-selection activity time.

13. Allow students to change activities by putting materials away correctly and then moving their markers.

Planning Sheet: Self-Selection Activities

☐ Make a self-selection board with interchangeable cards for labeling each pocket.

☐ Have students make markers. Laminate (or have students laminate) the markers.

☐ List the initial activities you plan to use and the materials you will need for each one.

_____

_____

_____

_____

_____

_____

_____

_____

_____

_____

_____

_____

_____

_____

☐ Self-selection schedule: _____

_____

_____

_____

☐ Criteria for participating in self-selection activities: _____

_____

_____

_____

_____

☐ Explain the self-selection process, management, criteria, and schedule to students.

☐ Have students practice marking activities, getting materials, and putting materials away.

Reflection and Evaluation: Self-Selection Activities

How long have you been using self-selection activities in your classroom? _____
_____

What changes have you made (or do you intend to make) in each of the following areas?

Types of activities and materials: _____
_____
_____

Number of available activities: _____
_____
_____

Frequency of rotation or change of activities: _____
_____
_____

Storage of materials: _____
_____
_____

Criteria for participation: _____
_____
_____

Scheduling: _____
_____
_____

Management: _____
_____
_____

Other: _____
_____
_____
_____
_____

How have self-selection activities helped with your instructional program? _____

_____

_____

_____

_____

_____

How have these activities helped your students build independent learning skills and self-management?

_____

_____

_____

_____

_____

How have the activities helped you meet the needs of your students? _____

_____

_____

_____

_____

_____

_____

_____

_____

_____

_____

_____

_____

_____

Chapter 30

. . . .

Work Contracts

WORK CONTRACTS are versatile tools for managing and individualizing instruction. They are useful at any grade level, for any subject, and for most tasks. One of the greatest strengths of work contracts is that they encourage the use and development of the students' decision-making and self-management capabilities.

How Contracts Work: Management Guidelines

A contract is an agreement. In classroom contracts, a student agrees to do a certain amount of work or type of task for a specific reward. This type of contract offers the student some choices. The student may be able to choose the order in which a set of activities is done, which activities to do, how many activities to do, or which topics to explore. Contracts may also allow students to propose projects and design activities of their own within a given set of guidelines. Examples:

▶ Jerry finishes his addition ditto and draws a "smiley face" in the box next to math on his contract checklist.

▶ Monique looks over the ten social studies tasks and circles four that she will agree to work on during the next week.

▶ After selecting "electromagnetism" as their topic, Janine and Robin design an experiment to demonstrate in class.

When you offer choices, make sure that they are all acceptable to you. Do not offer three topics with the hope or expectation that everyone will choose a particular one. Likewise, if you want each student to finish the reading workbook assignments first, set up the contracts to allow choices for activities *after* the workbook is complete.

The student's part of the agreement includes a commitment to a certain sequence or set of tasks. Completion of the sequence or tasks fulfills the contract. In most cases, both the agreement and reward are implicit and informal. The student need not make a formal commitment to a particular contract in all cases. Daily checklist contracts need only be marked as the work is completed. If a contract lists a certain amount of work to be completed by the end of a week, the student need not specify in advance the order in which the tasks will be done. As long as the work has been completed, the contract has been fulfilled.

Allow students to explore available choices and give them the freedom to change their minds if their initial choices don't work out for some reason. Unless you need to approve a self-designed activity or unless you need information for your planning, such as how long a student's presentation will be, you need not ask students beforehand what they will be selecting.

The reward a student receives for fulfilling a contract may simply be the satisfaction of having completed the task and colored or checked all of the spaces in a daily contract. More tangible rewards might include a star or sticker signifying completion of work; a certain grade that depends on the *amount* of work the student completes; progress to the next sequence or skill level; or a chance to participate in some enjoyable activity, such as working on a self-selection activity or visiting another classroom.

Contracts work best as aids for students' self-pacing, self-selection, and self-management. They are most successful when they offer rewards for completed tasks. Contracts should not include punishments for incomplete work. Not having access to the higher grade, to the next level, or to a desirable activity will be a strong enough negative consequence. If you have requested a commitment from students before they start working on a contract and you find that they have difficulty fulfilling their initial intentions, simply renegotiate the grade, reward, or deadline. It is often difficult for students to anticipate the difficulty of a contract assignment or determine how long it will take.

As with any other learning skill, start with simple forms that offer limited choices and gradually introduce more numerous and complex choices. Before you introduce the contracts, make sure your students have acquired any preliminary responsible learning behaviors necessary, and have practiced getting and replacing materials, making small choices, and working on their own. You may find it feasible, depending on your personal organization, management and goals, to have one group working on one type of contract while another group moves into a more complex or flexible format.

Contracts can help you manage the work in several subjects each morning or during an entire day. In some classrooms, contracts can last for a week or longer. You can also develop contracts for a specific subject area, allowing students to choose tasks for a class period, a week, or an entire marking period. This chapter presents sample contracts and some suggestions for accommodating individual needs and preferences.

Daily Fill-in Contracts

Fill-in contracts can be used on a daily basis. First explain the activities for the day. Ask each student to complete the tasks and color in the correct spaces.

This type of contract, because of its simplicity, is a good format to choose when you introduce contracts to your class. Select a design appropriate for your grade level and use the same form, at least for the first few weeks, before switching to another design. Once your students are comfortable with these contracts, the design can be changed to reflect a unit of topic you are covering in a particular subject, a topic of general interest, or upcoming seasons or holidays. Even young students can design contract forms with spaces for specified subject areas. The contracts can then be duplicated for the rest of the class to use.

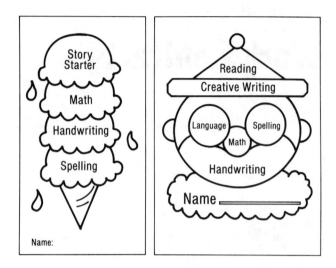

Opportunities for Individualization

These contracts can be individualized in several ways:

1. Students can decide which tasks to do first.

2. Work can be organized for skill groups. You can keep work at the spelling center or math tasks in color-coded folders or on color-coded task cards. Or, display the tasks in baskets, cans, shelves, pockets, or folders with students' names listed. Students can find their names and select the work in the appropriate container.

3. Work can be prescriptive at a particular center. You can assign each student the same tasks in spelling and language, but make math assignments on an individual basis.

Daily Checklist Contracts

Checklist contracts are similar to the contracts described above. Instead of coloring in spaces that represent assignments, however, the student simply checks a space next to each subject listed on the checklist as he or she completes the work in that subject. See *Daily Contract 1* (page 231).

Opportunities for Individualization

One advantage of a checklist contract is that specific assignments can be prescribed for individual students. In the *Daily Contract 2* example (page 231) the contract is used as daily prescription. The contract may also guide the student to a prescription kept elsewhere in the room.

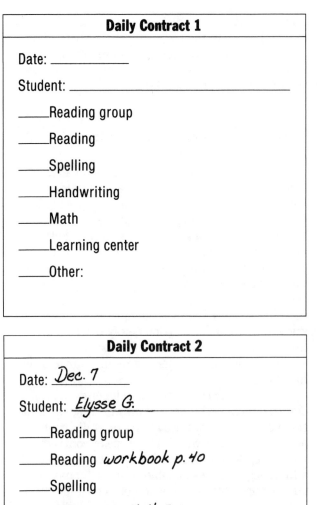

Daily Contract 1

Date: _____

Student: _____

_____Reading group

_____Reading

_____Spelling

_____Handwriting

_____Math

_____Learning center

_____Other:

Daily Contract 2

Date: *Dec. 7*

Student: *Elysse G.*

_____Reading group

_____Reading *workbook p. 40*

_____Spelling

_____Handwriting *Unit 5*

_____Math *Skill 4-D*

_____Learning center

_____Other: *See me before you start on Math assignment.*

Daily Group Contracts

Similar to a checklist, the group contract is designed as a grid. Down the left-hand side of the grid are the names of the students. Across the top are the assignment categories or subject areas. As students finish a task, they mark the grid, either by coloring in the appropriate square (perhaps with a special color for that subject area) or by marking the square with a sticker or with their initials. This strategy requires you to duplicate a grid daily.

The grid can also be made by using a large board or display with slots or pockets for each student under each subject or activity area. A student indicates the completion of an activity by inserting a card-marker (perhaps with a special color for that subject area) in the slot or pocket for that assignment. The cards are then removed at the end of the day and used again the next day.

Opportunities for Individualization

Daily group contracts may be used alone or in conjunction with individual checklists or fill-in contracts. They can accommodate individual needs in the same ways as individual contracts.

Weekly Contracts

Contracts can be constructed for use on a weekly basis and are most often set up as checklists. The only real difference between daily contracts and weekly contracts is the amount of paper. Instead of getting a fresh contract to check off each day, the students receive one checklist at the beginning of the week to use each day. Students should be comfortable and experienced with daily contracts before they begin using weekly contracts.

In general, weekly contracts are used when the same content areas are required each day. A simple list of subjects is shown in the example below; this is a good format to use when introducing weekly contracts to your class:

Name					
	Mon.	Tues.	Wed.	Thurs.	Fri.
Math					
Spelling					
Creative writing					
Language					
Reading					
Discovery center					

A more complex contract might contain a variety of assignments, some or all of which may be required each day. If an individual student is not required to do a math ditto on a particular day, the student can mark an X in that square for that day and do the other assignments on the contract. Likewise, if the art center is not set up or if no spelling tasks are being assigned to the class, each student can mark an X in those squares. The following example represents one possible format:

Student:	Week of:				
	Mon.	Tues.	Wed.	Thurs.	Fri.
MATH					
Ditto					
Learning center					
Prescription					
HANDWRITING					
SPELLING					
LANGUAGE					
Task card					
Learning center					
Creative writing					
ART					
READING					
Workbook					
Worksheet					
Game					
SELF-SELECTION					
OTHER					

Opportunities for Individualization

Weekly contracts leave little room for writing prescriptions or specific assignments on individual contracts. You will have to individualize assignments by writing separate prescriptions for individual students or by specifying assignments for groups and individuals at various work centers.

With these contracts, however, you can adjust the work load of individual students by adding or eliminating assignments on a daily or weekly basis. You might specify that one group do math prescrip-

tions on Monday, Wednesday, and Friday by marking an X in the boxes under Tuesday and Thursday. You may decide to eliminate language task cards for one group of students or add a book report requirement for another.

Weekly Composite Contracts

A weekly composite contract is an advanced form of the weekly contract. It also includes a week's worth of assignments, but allows students to decide when during the week they will do the various tasks. Unless the day is broken down into work periods during which students must complete one task and then move on to another, the students must also decide how much time to devote to each center of activity.

This type of contract demands that students know how to make decisions, stay on task, set limits, and pace themselves. Composite contracts for one subject area generally require far less self-management.

Composite contracts for self-contained classrooms list all independent morning work for the week, but do not list ability or skill group activities for that week. This type of contract is recommended for students who have demonstrated a high degree of responsibility and who have had success with other forms of work contracts. It is not appropriate for use in primary classrooms.

The first example of a composite contract on page 233 shows a list of all the activities the student must complete during the week. The numbers opposite each activity indicate how many assignments in that category should be completed. For example, this contract shows that the student will do one book report and five math task cards during the week. As the student completes each activity, he or she circles the appropriate number.

The second example of a composite contract on page 233 is used for only one subject area. It is effective in departmentalized settings or self-contained classrooms that have a specific time set aside for the particular subject area. As with any type of contract, this example requires that you plan a location for the storage and use of various materials, and that the students are able to find and use the required materials and audio-visual equipment; work independently (either alone or in a small group); make decisions; and perform the required tasks. Contracts such as this are ideal for

Student: _____ Week of: _____	
Activity	Number of Activities
Math task cards	
Math workbook pages	1 2 3 4 5
Math concept center	1 2 3 4 5 6 7
Spelling activities	1 2 3
Story starters	1 2 3
Discovery center	1 2
Listening center	1 2
Story card	1 2
Reading kit	1 2
Art center	1 2
Book report	1 2 3
Newspaper center	1
Language Arts task cards	1 2 3
Language puzzles	1 2 3 4 5
Handwriting prescription	1 2 3
Self-selection	1 2 3
Other:	

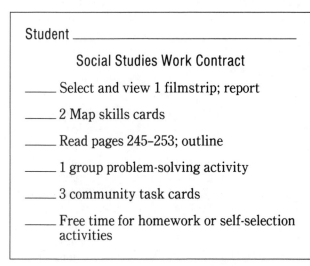

Student _____

Social Studies Work Contract

_____ Select and view 1 filmstrip; report

_____ 2 Map skills cards

_____ Read pages 245–253; outline

_____ 1 group problem-solving activity

_____ 3 community task cards

_____ Free time for homework or self-selection activities

secondary-level classes. The content and requirements can also be adapted for younger students who have the necessary self-management skills.

Opportunities for Individualization

In both examples, specific instructions for groups and individuals are not located on the contract form itself, but on prescription forms, on task cards, or in work center folders.

You can individualize the contracts by adjusting the amount of work required. Determine an acceptable work load for each student and cross out the rest, either by eliminating entire assignments (such as "Math dittos" or "2 Map skill cards"), or by reducing the amount of work required under an assignment heading (perhaps crossing out the last three numbers in the row after "Math workbook pages," or changing "2 Map skill cards" to "1 Map skill card").

To make the contracts more flexible, let students trade a card (do an extra language arts task card instead of a newspaper activity) or choose an activity after a certain number of assignments have been completed. You can also offer a choice of any four of the five activities listed on the contract. As always, introduce more complex formats only as students demonstrate competency on simpler formats.

Content Selection Contracts

In a content selection contract, the student is given choices of activities, materials, and/or topics. One of the simplest and most familiar form of a content selection contract is the book report assignment: students select the book or story they wish to report on and follow the format or guidelines you provide.

Another type of contract is based on a particular theme, such as electricity, weather, or maps. This contract offers a number of tasks through which the student can explore the topic. Out of a given number of tasks, the student must complete a certain number in order to fulfill the contract or receive a certain grade. Students can complete as many activities as they choose, depending upon the grade they are working for. As with any choices you set up in your classroom, make sure that all options available are equally acceptable to you.

You can also set up the tasks so that each one carries a specified number of points. The student must then select enough tasks to accrue the points necessary to fulfill the contract or receive a certain grade. In either case, set criteria for the completion of all tasks. Rather than grading each task, give full credit once the criteria are met, returning anything else with suggestions for completion.

A final type of content selection contract might simply offer the students a topic along with guidelines for researching the topic and designing a related project. This "free choice" option may also be included as an option in the theme contract described above.

Content selection contracts differ from the daily or weekly contracts previously described because they are not usually developed as the primary instructional management system. These contracts represent a specialized approach to a particular subject. They can be used for several days to supplement an instructional unit based on teacher-directed whole-group presentations. Content selection contracts are often assigned as homework, but they also function well as in-class assignments.

Opportunities for Individualization

Content selection contracts can be individualized to reflect students' preferences for certain topics, materials, processes, or types of problems. The choices you offer in structure or content are provided in the guidelines you set. For example:

"The book must be a biography."

"Problem #1 is required. You may choose three other problems from the list."

"Your final product must demonstrate a simple machine."

Group Content Selection Contracts

Tasks designed to be completed by small groups of students can be prepared in contract form as well. The process of completing the contract helps foster group decision-making skills and can be managed in several ways.

One method is to distribute the contracts to each student in the class and have the students look over the task choices. Identify a work area for each task and specify a maximum number of students for each group. Students then move, a few at a time, to the work area of their choice. Repeat this process over the next few days so students can participate in several different groups.

You can also divide the students into groups and allow each group to select an activity to do. The group can also decide which subsequent activities they will do. If they choose, the groups may all select the same activity on the same day. Unless materials required to complete the tasks are limited, this should not be a problem.

You can also divide the students into groups and have each group identify first and second choices. On the basis of the groups' choices, you can assign a different task to each group. A rotation format, such as the one used to manage integrated small-group activities (see Chapter 25), can also be used. Finally, you can have students self-select groups and activities with few restrictions.

Even more than individual content selection contracts, group contracts represent highly specialized methods of instruction that may enhance or supplement regular instruction.

Opportunities for Individualization

As with individual content selection contracts, group contracts can also accommodate student preferences. Because the activities involve the cooperation of several students, the choices may be more limited than in any other form of contract.

Planning Sheet: Work Contracts

Duplicate as needed.

Type of contract and format chosen: _____
_____
_____

Reason for selection: _____
_____
_____
_____

Purpose: _____
_____
_____
_____

What new or different learning skills and behaviors will this contract require of the students? _____
_____
_____
_____

What skills and behaviors have students demonstrated that indicate they will be able to handle the contract?
_____
_____
_____
_____

How do you expect the contract to benefit your management and instruction? _____
_____
_____
_____

How do you expect the contract to help you meet individual student needs? _____
_____
_____
_____

Attach a copy of the contract form for future reference.

Reflection and Evaluation: Work Contracts

Duplicate as needed.

Student response to and ability to use the contract: _____

_____

_____

_____

How has the contract been helpful in your management, planning, and instruction? _____

_____

_____

_____

_____

How has the contract helped you meet individual student needs? _____

_____

_____

_____

_____

What problems have you encountered? _____

_____

_____

_____

_____

What changes have you made (or do you intend to make) in using the contract? _____

_____

_____

_____

What are your plans for future use of contracts with your students (including other formats)? _____

_____

_____

_____

_____

UNIT VI

Instructional
Interaction

Chapter 31

. . . .

Questioning

TEACHERS ASK many questions to evaluate student knowledge and to stimulate
thinking. Questions for either purpose
may appear in the form of interrogative
sentences (actual questions) or requests. For example, you can determine whether or not a student can
spell "teacher" by presenting the task as a question
("How do you spell the word 'teacher'?"), or as a
request ("Write the word 'teacher' with the correct
spelling."). In this chapter, the word "question"
will refer to any communication requesting performance or information from students.

This chapter presents a variety of questioning
techniques designed to stimulate a wide range of
cognitive functioning. The underlying assumption
is that if students are presented with materials and
situations that challenge them to use complex thinking skills, they will better understand whatever
subject is being presented. The degree to which a
question stimulates thinking depends on the type of
question asked. Different types of questions require
different types or levels of thought processes.

Open and Closed Questions

"How much is five times three?"

"What is the date today?"

*"Who was the sixteenth president of the
United States?"*

"What ocean borders California to the west?"

All of the above are common classroom questions. All are alike in one way: each question has
only one correct answer. When you want specific
information, these kinds of questions, *closed
questions,* are appropriate. The problem with closed
questions is that they typically do not require
students to use high-level thinking skills. Most
people who tell you that five times three is fifteen do
so by means of simple recall. People who have been
multiplying five times three for years have incorporated this knowledge and would find it inconve-
nient to go through a complex thinking process each time
they confronted the problem—so recall has its

function. Much of the content you teach during the
year depends on the students' ability to build on
prior knowledge they access through recall. Closed
questions can also help you determine if the student
has the knowledge necessary to go on to more
complex levels of thinking.

However, recall answers will rarely tell you
more than whether or not the student can remember some piece of information. Closed questions
have only one right answer; the student who
answers is either right or wrong. Recall questions
are most valuable when they also require a student
to use skills other than memory to answer them.

For example, suppose that none of your students can name the sixteenth president because
none of them can *remember* the name of the sixteenth president—if they ever learned it in the first
place. Suppose you then tell them, "The sixteenth
president of the United States was Abraham Lincoln,"
and then repeat the question. Probably every
student who is paying even slight attention will be
able to recall the answer. Certainly some learning
has taken place, but the depth of the learning is
questionable.

Imagine that instead of telling the students
the answer, you turn a few of them loose in the
reference section of the library. By the time the
students have decided which reference to use,
what subject to look up, and what information is
relevant, they will have utilized several higher-level
thinking skills to come up with the correct answer.

Likewise, a student who determines the
answer to a multiplication problem by counting
with markers (or fingers) is using information, not
simply recalling information. This is also true of a
student who can name the Great Lakes after studying a map, or the student who can tell you the date
after consulting a calendar.

While closed questions only have one correct
answer, *open questions* may have an unlimited number of correct answers—or at least more than one:

"Give me an example of courage."

*"How did Dorothy know she wasn't in Kansas
anymore?"*

"What do we need to make tacos in class?"

These questions allow for a broad range of answers, any one of which might tell you whether or not the student understands the concept. For example, a student who tells you that his sister showed courage when she jumped in a cold river to save a cat has been able to apply the definition of the word "courage." Determining the answers to open questions requires that the students use the information in their memory, not just recall it.

When the majority of questions students face are one-answer, recall questions, students tend to try to look for the answer that will please the teacher rather than using analytical skills. Higher thinking processes are not only necessary for developing independent problem-solving skills, but they are essential to intellectual functioning as well as to concept and language development.

Many closed questions can be turned into open questions. Consider the difference between the types of thinking needed to answer the first question in each of the following sets and those needed to answer the questions or statements in italics:

How much is seven plus five?

Give me a math problem with the same answer as 7 + 5.

Use the markers to show me different ways to make 12.

What did the story say Cinderella wore?

What do you think Cinderella might have worn if the story had taken place during the Civil War?

Draw a "Before and After" picture of how you think Cinderella looked.

Which mountains run through Colorado?

Describe the geography of Colorado.

Compare the mountains in Colorado to the mountains in Pennsylvania.

Levels of Cognitive Functioning

M. J. McCue Aschner describes four types of thinking, or cognitive functioning, prompted by teachers' questions: *remembering, reasoning, creative thinking,* and *judgment*.[1] Although these

four types are not listed in a particular hierarchy, there is a correlation between Aschner's categories of cognitive functioning and the taxonomy of thinking skills presented by Benjamin Bloom.[2]

The most common type of thinking that occurs in a classroom is what Aschner calls *remembering*. Bloom calls this category *knowledge*, which includes the remembering "either by recognition or recall, of ideas, materials, or phenomena" (Bloom, p. 62). Knowledge ranks as the lowest level of intellectual skills in Bloom's taxonomy.

Aschner's second type of thinking, which he calls *reasoning*, corresponds to the categories Bloom calls *comprehension, application,* and *analysis*. Bloom believes that schools are more likely to emphasize functioning at the simplest level of the three, *comprehension*. Comprehension involves being able to "make some use of the materials and ideas" contained in a communication received (Bloom, p. 89).

Comprehension ranks as the second lowest level of intellectual skills in Bloom's taxonomy. The comprehension level differs from the knowledge level in that comprehension requires translation, interpretation, and/or extrapolation of information rather than simple recall.

Other questions that encourage reasoning include those from the *application* and *analysis* levels of Bloom's taxonomy. Application involves selecting an appropriate theory, method, principle, or idea, and applying it to solve a problem. Questions requiring application demand more complex reasoning skills than comprehension questions, because application requires the use of information in a different or new situation.

To analyze information, students must understand the content and form (organization and structure) of materials with constituent parts, and be able to describe the interrelation of those parts. Questions requiring analysis ask students to take apart a given communication and to examine the parts, their organization, and/or their relationship to one another. Tasks that require students to make comparisons, break down information, or search for sequences are examples of analysis tasks.

Aschner describes two other forms of questions—those that stimulate *creative thinking* and those that require *judgment*. These two

[1] M. J. M. Aschner, Asking Questions to Trigger Thinking, *NEA Journal* 50 (1961).

[2] B. S. Bloom, *Taxonomy of Educational Objectives: Handbook 1 Cognitive Domain,* 1956.

categories correspond to the two highest levels of Bloom's taxonomy: *synthesis* and *evaluation.*

Synthesis requires putting together elements and parts "to form a whole and combining them in such a way as to constitute a pattern or structure not clearly there before" (Bloom, p. 162). Evaluation involves using standards or criteria to make "judgments about the value, for some purpose, of ideas, works, solutions, methods, materials, etc." (p. 185). To some extent, evaluation requires all the other categories of behavior, but it may also be a "prelude to the acquisition of new knowledge, a new attempt at comprehension or application, or a new analysis and synthesis" (p. 185).

The chart below shows examples of Bloom's and Aschner's categories:

Aschner	Bloom	Examples
Remembering	Knowledge	Name the four food groups. What is the forty-ninth state? What is an adjective?
Reasoning	Comprehension	According to the graph, which month was the coldest? Translate the following paragraph into Spanish. Tell the story of *Cinderella* in your own words.
	Application	How many square yards of carpet do you need for a rectangular room 10′ × 17′? What will happen if you add red paint to blue paint? Find the following cities on the map.
	Analysis	How did the social code of the time restrict the behavior of the main characters? Rewrite the following sentences in a logical sequence. Given the following symptoms, determine which test procedures are necessary for diagnosis.
Creative thinking	Synthesis	Rewrite a fairy tale, placing its characters in the twenty-first century. Design a tent that could fit in your pants pocket. Compose a song to go with the story of *The Three Little Pigs.*
Judgment	Evaluation	Who do you think is best qualified to run for governor? Why? Decide which of these three houses is the best buy. Identify books that you feel contain evidence of sex-role stereotypes.

Learning Processes

Laura Atkinson suggests a set of categories of learning processes that teachers can develop through questions and comments or feedback.[1] These processes reflect many of the types of thinking described in the hierarchy above. As in the previous examples, the types of processes students use to learn about their world depend on the types of questions you ask. In the following chart, each of Atkinson's processes are described on the left. The right-hand column contains questions you might ask to stimulate that process if you and a group of your students were inspecting a button collection.

Sensory awareness: Learning through the senses.	How do these leather buttons feel? How do the plastic buttons sound different from the metal buttons when they touch the desk?
Labeling: Learning names for things and actions, how things are used and what they are for; learning words to describe.	What is the part underneath the button called? Which button works like a clasp?
Recalling: Remembering an experience with a particular object or activity; relating new items to familiar items; remembering sequence.	Where have you seen some of these buttons before? Which of these buttons look like other things? What do they remind you of?
Comparing: Identifying similarities and differences; comparing with the familiar; making analogies.	Find a button that is similar to the one on my dress. How are these two buttons different?
Projecting: Mentally placing an object or activity in another time, place, or situation.	Which buttons would be good on a heavy coat? Find a button a princess/army general/farmer might wear.
Classifying, categorizing: Seeing attributes and relationships; grouping objects.	Bobby has a pile of buttons. Find one that goes with his collection. Sort these buttons into different categories.
Predicting: Thinking about what may or will happen; developing an awareness of cause and effect.	Which of these buttons will last the longest? Do you think we will need buttons in 100 years? Why, or why not?

These processes also play an important role in concept development. Concept acquisition

[1] L. Atkinson, Developing the Intellectual Base, *Becoming A Teacher: A Book of Readings,* 1980.

depends on a child's experience and is aided by feedback from the teacher. Feedback in the form of questions and comments not only stimulates a child's thinking and learning processes, but also encourages language acquisition.

Questioning and Patience

Teachers in the habit of asking lower-level questions are probably also used to immediate, short responses. Often the silence after a question prompts the teacher to immediately rephrase or repeat the question. When your questions are thought-provoking, students may require more time to process the information and generate a thoughtful answer.

Teachers who are uncomfortable when their questions do not receive instantaneous responses may also unwittingly reinforce the students' belief in the need for short, correct answers. You may find that students need practice in using the silence after a question to think through a question. They may also need time to recognize that your questions do not have a single, correct response.

Be patient and encouraging. If you create a safe learning environment and give the students time to think, they will be much more likely to use the time to consider their own experience and exercise higher-level cognitive functioning.

Practice Sheet: Questioning

TASK 1

Each question listed below was written as a closed question designed to elicit a single correct answer. Rewrite the questions as open questions to make them more intellectually challenging. You may have to change the focus and objective of the questions to some degree. Write down several variations of each question.

What color is this apple? _____

_____

_____

_____

What is the dictionary's first definition for the word "proud"? _____

_____

_____

_____

What letter does the word "boat" start with? _____

_____

_____

_____

In what year did the Civil War begin? _____

_____

_____

_____

Who is the tallest student in the class? _____

_____

_____

_____

TASK 2

Look over the six tasks below. Number them in order of the degree to which you feel they stimulate thinking according to Bloom's taxonomy, beginning with the task that represents the *knowledge* category.

_____ Tell the story of "Nighthawk" in your own words.

_____ Here are twenty-five straws and some glue. Make the strongest structure you can with them.

_____ Explain how veins and arteries are different and how they are alike.

_____ Name the five senses.

_____ Multiply to determine how many cookies you need for everyone in the class to get three.

_____ Using Bloom's taxonomy, decide which of the following questions are most likely to promote higher-level cognitive functioning.

Explain your answers: _____

_____

_____

_____

_____

_____

_____

_____

_____

_____

_____

_____

_____

_____

_____

_____

_____

_____

_____

TASK 3

Using the definitions and examples for the following learning process categories, write a question or two about baking cookies. The purpose of your questions is to help the students with the following learning processes:

Learning through the senses: _____

_____

_____

_____

Labeling: _____

_____

_____

_____

Recalling: _____

_____

_____

_____

Comparing: _____

_____

_____

_____

Projecting: _____

_____

_____

_____

Classifying/categorizing: _____

_____

_____

_____

Predicting: _____

_____

_____

_____

_____

Reflection and Evaluation: Questioning

Duplicate as needed.

Prepare a lesson in which you expect to ask a number of questions. Think of a few questions you might ask, but also plan to allow the students' behavior, questions, and responses to influence your questions and comments. Tape record your lesson (and/or request to be observed) for a specified amount of time. Use the form below for your analysis:

Date: _____ Day: _____ Time: _____ ___ Observation ___ Tape

Subject/lesson: _____

_____

Objective: _____

_____

Describe the amount of talking done by you and the amount of talking done by the students: _____

_____

_____

Describe the amount of silence between your questions and the students' answers: _____

_____

_____

Describe the number of rephrased, restated, or repeated questions: _____

_____

_____

Describe the number of student responses to each question: _____

_____

_____

Describe the depth and length of student responses: _____

_____

_____

_____

_____

_____

_____

_____

List the questions you asked, word for word, during the course of the lesson. If you asked a great number of questions, select between ten and twenty. Copy them in the sequence in which they were presented, not at random. Identify closed (single answer, yes/no, recall) questions. Mark all questions to identify the thinking skills (Bloom/Aschner) and learning processes (Atkinson) that your questions were meant to stimulate.

_____

_____

_____

_____

_____

_____

_____

_____

_____

_____

_____

_____

_____

_____

_____

_____

_____

_____

_____

_____

_____

_____

_____

_____

_____

_____

_____

_____

_____

_____

Look at the activities you presented during any one day last week. Consider the objective(s) of several of the lessons, dittos, small-group activities, and so on. Identify the thinking skills and learning processes each was intended to stimulate. If one task had multiple objectives, write them out and identify the categories for each.

Task: _____

Objective: _____

Thinking skill: _____

Learning process: _____

_____

Task: _____

Objective: _____

Thinking skill: _____

Learning process: _____

_____

Task: _____

Objective: _____

Thinking skill: _____

Learning process: _____

_____

Task: _____

Objective: _____

Thinking skill: _____

Learning process: _____

_____

Task: _____

Objective: _____

Thinking skill: _____

Learning process: _____

_____

Task: _____

Objective: _____

Thinking skill: _____

Learning process: _____

Task: _____

Objective: _____

Thinking skill: _____

Learning process: _____

_____

Task: _____

Objective: _____

Thinking skill: _____

Learning process: _____

_____

In which categories were most of your questions? _____

_____

_____

_____

In which categories were most of your assignments and materials? _____

_____

_____

_____

What are your plans for maintaining or improving your questioning skills? _____

_____

_____

_____

_____

_____

_____

_____

_____

_____

_____

_____

Chapter 32

· ·

Values Activities

VALUES ARE CLASSIFIED in the affective domain, which also includes the development of principles, interests, and attitudes. In the classroom, values activities are particularly useful in programs developed to promote personal awareness and self-esteem. These activities can help students identify and express feelings and preferences, become aware of their own values, and develop their sensitivity to and acceptance of other people's values.

Values and Behavior

Just as your own values will affect your behavior as a teacher, so the values of your students will play a part in their behavior. Giving children the opportunity to discuss values, preferences, and feelings has additional benefits. Values activities:

▶ validate the unique character of each student.

▶ recognize each student as a "whole" being, as a thinking *and* feeling person.

▶ encourage self-expression.

▶ encourage vocabulary enrichment and language development.

▶ help students become aware of other people's feelings and values.

▶ help students become aware of their relationship to other people in society.

▶ help students develop responsible social and learning behaviors.

▶ help students develop and modify values in a social context.

In the book *Values and Teaching,* Louis Raths suggests that values and thinking are "inextricably linked: to encourage development in one area is to encourage growth in the other" (p. 200). If behavior is governed by an individual's values, then the potential impact of encouraging the development of values becomes clear. If you find a way to affirm students by helping them to explore, express, and exhibit their values in the "society" of your classroom, you will acknowledge the connection between values and behavior.

Values Activities in the Classroom

Traditionally, adults have influenced children's values by pointing to examples, using persuasion, limiting choices, enforcing rules, appealing to conscience, or using dogma to promote certain beliefs. While these methods may have controlled students' beliefs and behavior, they did not often encourage students to make thoughtful choices about their own values and beliefs.

Values activities in a classroom can range from having five-year-olds state their favorite colors to having a high school debate on politics. Values education takes place when management strategies are based on respect for the group. These strategies should offer choices and allow students to experience the positive and negative consequences of their own decisions.

Values awareness can come about as a result of cross-cultural experiences that include films, presentations, dances, art projects, holiday projects, or cooking activities. Likewise, activities involving students in your class with students of different ages provide excellent opportunities for affective and social development (see Chapters 34 and 35).

Discussions or writing activities can focus on "value-rich topics" such as friendship, family, money, love, rules, school, work, loyalty, honesty, cooperation, poverty, racism, sexism, stealing, jealousy, fear, envy or guilt (Raths, p.154).

Other values activities might include interest inventories, checklists, or questionnaires. Such surveys might propose open-ended questions such as those suggested below:

▶ Name your favorite food.

▶ If I don't have homework, I like to _____ after school.

▶ Name five things you would like to have with you if you were stranded on a desert island, assuming you had enough food, water, clothing, and shelter.

▶ I was so proud when I

_____ .

▶ My life hasn't been the same since

_____ .

Forced-choice questionnaires can also help students explore preferences by asking them to choose between two activities. Examples:

Play music or Listen to music

Watch a sports telecast or Watch the news

Make a picture with markers or Make a picture with paints

Go for a walk or Read a book

Asking students to rank items also helps them identify priorities and prejudices. Examples:

▶ Number the activities below from 1 to 10 in order of which you like best.

▶ Number this list of ten occupations from 1 to 10 in order of how important you think each one is.

▶ Name ten people in the world you admire most, and explain why. The people you choose may be from any period of history. Rank them from 1 to 10 in order of whom you most admire.

You can conduct a circle discussion of preferences or experiences by presenting a question, then moving around the circle for answers. Let the students offer brief responses or choose to pass. Full discussions, informally conducted, give students the chance to explore their values in greater depth.

Autobiographies, whether in the form of a composition, a "Me" book (pictures and statements depicting the student, house, family, pets, and so on) or a "Favorite Things" book (pictures and statements depicting such things as favorite foods, animals, toys, TV shows, or pastimes) allow students to focus on their values, preferences, personal experiences, and uniqueness. Diaries and journals are also excellent vehicles for personal expression.

Self-esteem activities may include any activity that helps reinforce a student's perception of his or her own capability. Making a special job or contingency available to each child at some time can help students experience responsibility and competence. A "Shining Star" bulletin board with pictures and statements showing students doing things they do well or that they are proud of, is also effective.

Another recognition activity involves having each student select a classmate at random. Ask the students to write three *positive* things about their selected classmates, perhaps including:

▶ what this person does well.

▶ what I admire about this person.

▶ adjectives describing this person.

Problems encountered in the classroom, particularly those involving personal interactions between students or between students and adults (parents or school staff) can be explored through large group discussions, but problem solving and role-playing in small groups may be even more effective. Discussions, whether in large or small groups, may include:

▶ identifying the problem and a realistic ultimate goal.

▶ brainstorming possible solutions.

▶ evaluating possible solutions in terms of probable outcomes.

▶ implementing selected solutions.

▶ evaluating outcomes.

Role-playing may also be used to explore the nature of a problem, different points of view, and possible solutions and outcomes.

The success of any of the activities described above will depend on a number of factors, including careful preparation (materials, organization), directions for students, and classroom management. Most important is the degree to which the activities and topics are matched to the needs and experiences of the students, the topic's relevance to their personal lives, and the developmental level of the students. Values activities that require the ability to understand another person's feelings may be especially difficult for younger children, but they are likely to promote growth and help students gain valuable social skills.

Planning Sheet: Values Activities

What behaviors or problems have your students exhibited that might be addressed by values activities?

_____

_____

_____

_____

_____

_____

_____

_____

_____

_____

_____

_____

What long-range goals do you have that may be achieved through some form of values activities?

_____

_____

_____

_____

_____

_____

_____

_____

_____

_____

_____

_____

_____

Planning Sheet: Values Activities

Duplicate for each values activity.

Identify possible values activities to use in your classroom. For each activity, write down the objective, the materials needed, the arrangement of the students (in a circle, in pairs, and so on), the way you will introduce the activity, the procedure for the activity, and any evaluation methods you plan to use.

Values activity: _____

_____

_____

_____

Objective: _____

_____

Materials needed: _____

_____

_____

_____

Arrangement of students: _____

_____

_____

Introduction: _____

_____

_____

Procedure: _____

_____

_____

_____

Evaluation: _____

_____

_____

_____

_____

_____

Reflection and Evaluation: Values Activities

Describe the students' responses to the values activities you implemented: _____
_____
_____
_____

In what areas were the students able to perform as desired? _____
_____
_____
_____

In what areas did the students experience difficulty? _____
_____
_____
_____

What did you do (or do you intend to do) to alleviate the difficulty? _____
_____
_____
_____

Describe the impact you believe the activities are having on your students':

    self-awareness _____
_____
_____
_____

    awareness of other people's feelings _____
_____
_____
_____

    behavior _____
_____
_____
_____
_____

In what ways are the activities helping you reach your goals? _____
_____
_____
_____
_____
_____
_____
_____
_____
_____
_____
_____

What other types of values activities do you plan to use and for what purpose(s)? _____
_____
_____
_____
_____
_____
_____
_____
_____
_____
_____
_____
_____

Chapter 33

Field Trips and Guest Speakers

CHILDREN DISCOVER their world through their community. You can expand your students' first-hand experiences by allowing them to encounter different dimensions of their surroundings, either by venturing outside the classroom or by bringing outside resources into your classroom. This chapter offers guidelines for planning and managing a field trip or a tour. Suggestions for including guest speakers in the classroom will be presented as well.

Field Trips and Tours

Field trips and tours enable teachers to provide experiences that would be impossible to offer in a classroom. A field trip differs from a tour in that students are prepared for field trips to a greater degree. A tour may simply be a visit, but on a field trip, students should have a sense of purpose and be prepared to find answers to questions raised in the classroom.

The first step in planning a field trip or a tour is to identify possible resources—the sites to be visited by your students. Each site you consider should be evaluated in terms of the following questions:

1. What is the purpose or objective of your visit? How does the visit tie in with your current curriculum goals?

2. How would you describe the resource? What does it have to offer your students or your curricular program?

3. What are the days, dates, and times that the resource is open or available?

4. Are there special events that occur at that site? When?

5. Where is the resource located? What is the distance to and from the school?

6. How would you reach the site? Consider bus routes from your school, names and phone numbers of bus lines for rental, or walking or driving directions.

7. How much time will you need for the trip (including travel)?

8. What supplies are needed? Consider things the students might need to bring to be more comfortable (hiking shoes, a bag lunch) and things they might need to complete or participate in activities on site (a notebook, an empty can, some string, extra money to buy drinks or souvenirs).

9. Are there any special considerations, such as the number of adults required, minimum age of students, or accommodations for the handicapped?

10. Do you have a telephone number and contact person for the resource?

11. What is the cost per student and per adult?

12. What are your plans to introduce the resource and prepare the students for what they will encounter on the trip?

13. What specific questions or information can the students look for on the trip?

A "Community Resource Reference Form" has been provided in the planning section at the end of this chapter (pages 259–260). By duplicating the form and completing it for each resource you consider, you can begin to build a resource file for future planning and reference.

Planning and Managing Field Trips

Successfully carrying out a field trip involves a number of planning and management considerations. Most experienced teachers have many horror stories about problems that developed during field trips. Yet many of the logistical and discipline-related problems that may occur on a field trip can be avoided by careful advance planning. Consider the following guidelines:

▶ Obtain administrative approval *before* announcing the trip to students.

▶ In picking a date, avoid Mondays. Over the weekend, kids often forget to bring their lunches, spending money, and so on.

▶ Recruit, screen, and *instruct* parent chaperones so that they will be able to contribute significantly to the trip. Don't wait until just before leaving to tell parents what you expect of them. Send a note home beforehand that outlines: (1) what you expect parents to do, (2) rules you have discussed with students, and (3) any other pertinent information.

▶ Divide students into task groups well before the trip is to take place. Each task group should have a specific responsibility; for example, records (keep records or journals), supplies (obtain necessary items for or from the trip), photography, public relations (write thank-you notes), and maintenance (cleanup).

▶ If taking a tour, select an impressive place. If you were bored on your last trip to the sewage treatment plant, for example, your students will probably be bored, too.

▶ Take everyone, including your trouble-makers. Leaving someone behind for disciplinary reasons could lead to deep-seated resentment that you may never overcome.

▶ Send parental permission slips home unless the school uses a blanket permission form covering all field trips for the year.

▶ Even with signed permission slips, you may be legally liable if you agree to supervise students in too large an area. Trying to supervise students in two large halls of a museum could make you liable if something happened to someone. Err on the safe side and take one adult for each group of five children.

▶ Use name tags (including the school name). This is often essential for young students. It also enables chaperones to call students by name.

▶ Avoid going in private cars whenever possible; the legal hazards (insurance coverage, and so on) are considerable.[1]

Guest Speakers in the Classroom

People can also be important community resources.

Dozens of people in your community, including the parents of your students, may have specialized interests or knowledge that can be valuable to your students. The first step in utilizing community resource people to enrich your students' learning is to identify the people and the special interests or talents they have to contribute.

Consider the following questions when you identify someone as a potential guest speaker:

▶ What is the person's name, address, and telephone number?

▶ How was the person identified as a resource?

▶ What is his or her area of specialization? What does the person have to offer to your students?

▶ Are there special presentations, materials, media, activities that the person can make, or make available?

▶ What is the topic's grade level appeal?

▶ When is the person available? Will there be a fee for the presentation?

[1] Guidelines from Welton and Mallan, *Children and Their World: Strategies for Teaching Social Studies,* Second Edition, Copyright © 1981, Houghton Mifflin Company, used by permission.

- What time and materials are needed for the presentation or demonstration?

- Are there any special needs or considerations?

A "Resource Person Reference Form" has been provided on page 261. This form can be duplicated and added to the binder or folder you prepared for the community resource reference forms.

Working with Guest Speakers in the Classroom

As with planning for a field trip, identifying a guest speaker for your classroom is relatively easy, but several problems may arise. The resource person may have difficulty selecting relevant materials for the presentation, or speaking in a way that is understandable and of interest to the students, pacing material for the students, or being prepared to talk without the benefit of audiovisual aids.

Before inviting someone from outside the classroom to speak to your students, consider the following guidelines:

1. Meet with the resource person, particularly one who insists on talking to your class. Make sure the person is not simply looking for an opportunity to use the school as a platform for a special cause.

2. Before issuing an invitation, be certain to check school policies and inform the principal of your intentions.

3. Work with your class to establish a need or desire for whatever information the resource person can provide.

4. Provide the resource person with a list of questions or topics your class has developed before the presentation.

5. Prepare name tags for the students, so the speaker can call each person by name.

6. Lay the ground rules for behavior as you would for an off-campus trip. Remind the students that they are hosts and that the speaker is a guest.

Planning Sheet: Field Trips and Tours

Identify possible options for class field trips. Name five or more places for each category below.

School community resources within walking distance: _____

_____

_____

_____

_____

_____

_____

_____

Community resources within twenty-five miles that require transportation: _____

_____

_____

_____

_____

_____

_____

_____

_____

Resources beyond twenty-five miles: _____

_____

_____

_____

_____

_____

_____

Duplicate the form on the following page for each resource you plan to investigate. Complete each form and put all the information sheets into a special binder or folder for future reference.

Community Resource Reference Form

Place: _____

___ Walking distance   ___ Up to twenty-five miles   ___ More than twenty-five miles

Description: _____

_____

_____

Availability: _____

_____

_____

Special events and dates: _____

_____

_____

Address/location: _____

_____

_____

Distance from school each way: _____

_____

_____

How reached: _____

_____

_____

Time needed (including travel): _____

_____

_____

Contact person: _____ Phone: _____

Address (if different): _____

_____

_____

Cost per student: _____ Cost per adult: _____

Special considerations: _____

_____

_____

Supplies needed: _____

_____

_____

_____

_____

Purpose/objectives: _____

_____

_____

_____

_____

Introduction/presentation: _____

_____

_____

_____

_____

Questions/what to look for on trip: _____

_____

_____

_____

_____

_____

_____

_____

Follow-up comments: _____

_____

_____

_____

_____

_____

_____

_____

_____

Resource Person Reference Form

Name: _____ Phone: _____

How identified as a resource: _____
_____

Address: _____
_____

Area of specialization: _____
_____

Special presentations, materials, media, activities available: _____
_____
_____
_____
_____
_____

Grade level appeal: _____

Availability: _____ Cost: _____
_____

Materials required: _____
_____

Preparation required: _____
_____

Special needs or considerations: _____
_____

Questions for speaker: _____
_____
_____

Follow-up comments: _____
_____
_____
_____

Reflection and Evaluation: Field Trip

Duplicate as needed.

Where did you go? _____

_____

_____

What was your reason for selecting this place? _____

_____

_____

In what ways did this trip tie in with your curriculum? _____

_____

_____

Describe your planning (without students): _____

_____

_____

Describe your preparation *with* the students: _____

_____

_____

_____

If you invited parents along, what did you do to prepare them to be helpful? _____

_____

_____

_____

Describe the field trip itself: _____

_____

_____

_____

_____

_____

_____

_____

Describe your follow-up questions and activities: _____

_____

_____

_____

_____

_____

How was the walk (or ride) to the site a learning experience—what was noted, discussed, or pointed out along the way?

_____

_____

_____

_____

Why would you or would you not return to this place? _____

_____

_____

In what ways was this trip a success? _____

_____

_____

_____

What problems arose? _____

_____

_____

_____

How would you plan or manage a similar trip differently? _____

_____

_____

_____

_____

What have you learned that will help you plan or manage future field trips? _____

_____

_____

_____

_____

_____

Reflection and Evaluation: Guest Speaker

Duplicate as needed.

Whom did you select to visit your class? _____

_____

What was your guest invited to share with your class? _____

_____

How was your guest's presentation to be tied in with your curriculum? _____

_____

_____

Describe the planning you did (without students): _____

_____

_____

_____

Describe your preparation *with* the students: _____

_____

_____

_____

What did you do to prepare or help the guest? _____

_____

_____

Describe the presentation and the student's response: _____

_____

_____

_____

_____

_____

_____

_____

_____

_____

Why would you or would you not invite this person to speak with another class, or to speak to your class again?

_____

_____

_____

In what ways was the speaker's presentation a success? _____

_____

_____

_____

What problems arose? _____

_____

_____

_____

Would you plan, prepare, or manage anything differently for future speakers? _____

_____

_____

_____

What have you learned that will help you plan or manage future guest visits and presentations? _____

_____

_____

_____

_____

_____

_____

_____

_____

_____

_____

_____

_____

Chapter 34

. . . .

Combined-Class Activities

AS THE FOLLOWING examples illustrate, peer interaction can involve two or more students working together on a joint project or helping each other in a same-age or cross-age situation:

▶ Peggy, Joe, and Mark build a city out of building blocks.

▶ Joan, Debbie, Bill, and Leo assemble a diorama for the science fair.

▶ Ellie quizzes Dominique on her spelling words.

▶ Ignacio reads a story to a group of children in kindergarten.

▶ Pat helps Rochelle and Jackie learn their colors.

▶ Donna helps a group of first graders put on their coats and hats to go home.

Effective peer interaction benefits both students and teachers.

This chapter and the one that follows focus on helpful peer interaction in a cross-age situation. Although peer interaction programs can be highly successful in a self-contained classroom, having students visit another classroom offers additional benefits. Elements of the combined-class model presented in this chapter may also be adapted for two classes of the same age, or for a single self-contained classroom.

Benefits of Peer Interaction

Peer interaction can enrich the learning environment and help you with classroom management. Through peer interaction, students often develop responsible learning behaviors. Other benefits include:

▶ improvement of the student helper's attitudes toward school and learning.

▶ increased motivation.

▶ improved attendance.

▶ increased attention span.

▶ increased participation.

▶ increased time-on-task.

▶ increased self-control.

▶ increased self-esteem.

▶ more effective social interaction.

▶ increased altruistic behavior.

▶ better understanding of personal feelings, needs, and capabilities.

▶ cognitive growth such as acquisition of new skills and a greater understanding of concepts.

While peer interaction assists the students being helped, the greatest benefit is to the students in the helping roles.

Peer interaction programs not only benefit the students, but also help teachers by:

▶ providing opportunities to develop flexibility and adaptability.

▶ providing opportunities to meet the individual needs of students.

▶ enhancing curriculum through varied enrichment and reinforcement activities.

▶ enhancing instructional and management techniques.

- providing processes to stimulate positive social, emotional, and academic student behavior.

- providing high-interest, high-motivation activities to reinforce positive student behavior.

Overview of the Combined-Class Model

The model presented in these two chapters was designed for cross-age implementation involving students in a class at one grade level working with students in a class at a different grade level. The model includes two overlapping phases with a gradual transition from one to the other. This chapter presents Phase I of the program, which involves the simultaneous participation of the two classes in one or more combined-class experiences. This phase generally begins with a few orientation, or getting-acquainted activities, and moves into a more formal activity period during which the students work together in cross-age small groups. Phase I serves as the training phase that enables helpers to participate effectively in the second phase of the peer interaction program.

Phase II, discussed in Chapter 35, involves individual student helpers who assist the teacher and students in the lower-grade classroom in a variety of classroom activities, some of which involve peer tutoring.

The Purpose of Combined-Class Activities

A successful peer interaction program requires competence in social interaction. Social skills can be presented, practiced, and achieved during Phase I. While peer interaction programs traditionally focus on peer tutoring, this model provides a developmental approach to a variety of student interactions, of which peer tutoring is only one.

The first phase, the combined-class activity phase, emphasizes goal-setting and developing interactive behaviors. The purpose of this phase is to familiarize the older students with the new environment, the receiving teacher (the teacher receiving the older helpers), and the younger students. The combined-class activity provides opportunities for students to practice skills that will be useful in later interactions, particularly those involving helping and tutoring.

Identifying Your Needs and Resources

Before exploring the various attributes of the model, consider the following questions to help define your own focus and resources:

1. Do you feel that your students need to improve the quality of their learning behaviors?

2. Would you like your students to improve the quality of their social interaction skills?

3. Do you believe that students can develop responsible learning behaviors through interacting with other students?

4. Is there a class of younger students in your building? (If your students are the youngest in the school, consider the benefits of having older children coming in to your class to help.)

5. Would you be willing to work with the teacher of that class, if he or she is interested, on planning and developing an activity (or set of activities) that would involve the participation of both classes?

If you have access to a class of younger students with a teacher willing to participate, before the two of you begin discussing details such as scheduling and management, be sure to discuss the following considerations with the receiving teacher. Is that person willing and able to:

- participate and plan with you?

- support your goals?

- accommodate students from the two classes for combined-class activities?

- set criteria for helper behavior in the receiving classroom?

- enforce rules positively and consistently?

- reinforce positive helping behavior?

- work toward a program requiring individual helpers (Phase II)?

Finally, consider the degree to which the program will fit within school guidelines and long-range curricular goals. Discuss the program with the principal to generate suggestions and support.

Introducing the Program

Once you have decided on a context for conducting a peer interaction program, you need to orient and train your students to work with other children. This process can be simple and informal and will be best achieved by actually having the students work together. Nonetheless, planning *with* your students, before attempting a combined-class activity, will increase the likelihood that the combined-class activity—and subsequent activities—will be successful.

Some possibilities for introductory activities:

1. Talk to your students about working with students in another class. Generate some discussion about the students' feelings, questions, and ideas. The receiving teacher can do the same.

2. Have the students in each classroom exchange visits and observe each other in their own classrooms. Have the students in each classroom introduce and share something about themselves.

3. When students will be traveling to another classroom, discuss good traveling behavior and practice making a nondisruptive entrance into the receiving classroom.

4. In separate groups, or with the two classes combined, have students work together to list the characteristics of a good helper.

5. Discuss and/or role-play relevant topics and situations, such as:

    ▶ expectations.
    ▶ accepted behavior in response to rules.
    ▶ the privilege of being a helper.
    ▶ courtesy and politeness.
    ▶ listening and respecting feelings.
    ▶ procedures and safety.
    ▶ getting help and solving problems independently.
    ▶ encouraging independence in other students.
    ▶ reinforcing and acknowledging cooperation and performance.
    ▶ handling noncooperative participants by allowing them to withdraw or change activities.
    ▶ setting a good example.
    ▶ guiding other students by asking and responding to questions.
    ▶ giving good directions and being patient.

    ▶ allowing for the special needs of younger students.
    ▶ sharing interests and bringing skills to the new classroom.

6. Offer some suggestions for successful helping, such as:

    ▶ call the younger children by their names.
    ▶ say "please" and "thank you."
    ▶ set a good example.
    ▶ take care of materials.
    ▶ smile and be friendly.

Informing Parents

Because the peer interaction program involves one or more special activities requiring the students to be out of the regular classroom at times, prior contact with parents is recommended. Initial contacts can be made through telephone conferences, individual personal contact, or a group orientation program. Teacher- or student-written newsletters may also be used for initial contacts and for keeping parents informed of ongoing activities. You may also want to send teacher- or student-written invitations to parents to request their attendance for observation or participation in a particular activity.

Depending on your school policy and the needs and expectations of the community in which you teach, you may need to use permission slips for some activities. Permission slips are especially recommended for activities involving cooking, videotaping, recording, travel, or some holiday celebrations.

Parent orientation contacts might include the following information:

▶ An explanation of the purpose and goals of the intended program.

▶ Information about scheduling, program duration, and anticipated costs.

▶ A description of the types of interactions and activities planned, particularly in terms of long-term curricular goals.

▶ An announcement that the student has been selected as a helper for working in another classroom.

▶ A description of the role the student will play as a helper in the other class, the specific activities or types of activities assigned, and expected benefits to that helper.

▶ Assurances, in context, that peer interaction is a valuable form of learning.

Planning the Combined-Class Activity

By now your students should be quite familiar with the students in the other class. The orientation activities, in which students from both classes participated, provide a natural transition to the more formal combined-class activities.

The combined-class activities usually take place in the receiving classroom, usually the homeroom of the younger students. The activities are intended to promote communication and interactive competence and to help students become familiar with the environment that they will be working in during Phase II of the program.

For this program, the two classes, combined, are divided into six cross-age groups of approximately equal size. Small-group arrangements tend to require more interaction, sharing, and cooperation. In this model, four of the groups work on activities in learning centers (or different, designated spaces in the environment), while two groups work on a special, teacher-directed activity at another location in the room. By rotating through the centers in two rotations, each group will get to work at two centers *and* at the special activity center.

The following checklist describes the steps for planning a combined-class experience:

Step 1: Plan Groups

Divide the combined group into six cross-age, heterogeneous groups of six to nine students in each. Each group should contain approximately the same number of older students and the same number of younger students. Attempt to distribute the students according to their leadership capabilities; their abilities to listen, follow directions, and get along with others; and their degree of independence and self-control. Since helping and cooperation within each group are primary goals, selecting leaders within each group is not recommended.

Plan your groups with the receiving teacher. Color code your groups and make color-coded name tags for each student.

Step 2: Determine Location

Determine the location for the combined-class experience. While the receiving classroom is recommended, as it will be the location for future Phase II activities, some combined-class activities may take place elsewhere. The location should be able to accommodate both classes in small, separate work areas or centers, allowing for a high degree of interaction in the groups. The location should also provide a space for the "special activity" as well as spaces for the other groups to work on alternative activities.

Step 3: Choose Activities

Select a special, teacher-directed activity that can accommodate two groups at one time. Cooking or art activities work especially well. The special activity may allow the students to complete the same task (for example, each group makes caramel apples or different kinds of cookies), but consists of three separate activities, each completed during a different rotation. For example, each group might complete a step in making applesause (wash and cut apples, core apples and measure other ingredients, cook and serve applesauce), or complete a different part of a meal instead (prepare salad and drinks, make the main course, make desserts).

Plan alternative activities for students to work on when they are not working on the special activity. Gear all activities to the ability level of the *younger* students, but require participation by all group members. The best activities are those that require or allow the students to work together. Alternative activities should not require teacher assistance. Some possible alternatives include:

▶ playing in the blocks center.

▶ listening to a record or tape in the listening center.

▶ making a group collage.

▶ playing with puzzles and manipulatives.

▶ playing with games from the receiving classroom.

▶ coloring.

▶ cut-and-paste activities.

▶ playing "store."

You will need four alternative activities.

Step 4: Plan Rotation Schedule

Set up a rotation schedule such as the following:

Group	Starting Center	First Rotation	Second Rotation
Red	Special activity	Alternative #3	Alternative #1
Orange	Special activity	Alternative #4	Alternative #2
Yellow	Alternative #1	Special activity	Alternative #3
Green	Alternative #2	Special activity	Alternative #4
Blue	Alternative #3	Alternative #1	Special activity
Purple	Alternative #4	Alternative #2	Special activity

This schedule has two rotations, two groups of students working on the special activity with one or both teachers, and four alternative activities conducted in separate work spaces in the room. Each group participates in three activities: the special activity and two assigned alternatives.

Step 5: Prepare Materials

Prepare or gather materials for the activities in the combined-class experience. Determine how you will share the cost and responsibility with the receiving teacher and whether you will ask students to bring in any money.

Step 6: Introduction

Plan a brief introduction to the students in which you and the receiving teacher will address the two groups simultaneously. To begin the combined-class experience, you will need to do the following:

▶ Explain the process of rotation to the students.

▶ Explain the activities they will be doing in the centers (special activity and alternative activities).

▶ Remind the students of the need for group cooperation, sharing, and independent problem solving.

▶ State the criteria for student behavior, reviewing expectations in a positive light and avoiding threats and negative examples.

Step 7: Plan Follow-up

Plan a follow-up session to occur after the rotations. In the follow-up, have both classes participate in recalling and describing the previous activities. If possible, record students' comments on poster-sized paper and have the students illustrate their remarks.

Step 8: Plan Timing

Determine how much time you will need to conduct a brief introduction, the rotations, and a follow-up. Attempt to schedule enough time for all the rotations to occur in one session.

Step 9: Arrange Environment

Determine the best arrangement for the environment. If the environment will need to be specially arranged for the combined-class experience, decide when this will occur. Discuss the responsibilities of each teacher and determine the need for student or adult helpers to set up the environment.

Step 10: Determine Teachers' Roles

Plan for both teachers to be present during the combined-class experience. Determine the teachers' roles in the room. Depending on the degree of cooperation among the groups, the difficulty of the special activity, and the availability of parent volunteers or aides, one teacher may elect to work with the special activity group while the other monitors the students working on alternative activities. Teachers may switch roles from one rotation to another. When the students are working well on their own, both teachers may be able to work with the special activity.

Implementing the Combined-Class Experience

The following guidelines are offered to help you manage the activities according to your plans:

1. Before getting the two groups of students together, make sure each student is wearing a color-coded name tag.

2. Take the students to the location for the combined-class experience. Have the work centers and areas set up before your students arrive.

3. Address the total group (both classes) in your introduction.

4. Direct the groups to the activities assigned for the first location. Dismiss groups one by one to the alternative activities first, according to the color of their name tags. The teacher conducting the special activity can escort the remaining two groups to the special activity area.

5. Guide and direct the various activities as needed.

6. Conduct the rotation as scheduled. Before allowing students to move from one activity to the next, make sure each group is cleaned up, ready to move, and knows exactly where to go.

7. Upon completion of the special activity, gather the total group together and conduct the follow-up exercises as planned. Encourage sharing and discussion to develop content vocabulary, recall, sequencing, and other communication skills.

If a student misbehaves during the activity, you may wish to remove the student from the situation to a "quiet space" until he or she is ready to participate in the group again according to the criteria set in the introduction. By doing this, you are placing the responsibility for the student's behavior where it belongs—on the student. The privilege of working with the group remains contingent upon the student's cooperative behavior within the group.

To be most effective in preparing students to become peer helpers and tutors, arrange several combined-class experiences. Not all need be conducted in small-group rotations. Opportunities for joint-class participation in school activities may occur over a period of several months, even once the individual helper phase has begun. Keep in touch with the receiving teacher so you will be aware of possibilities for working together. If one class has completed work on a play or puppet show, the other class can be invited to watch the performance. Models, murals, guest speakers, or special student presentations can also be shared. Both classes can get together for holiday activities, singing or music activities, or just to watch a film. A combined-group walking tour or field trip also presents opportunities for interaction and growth. You may wish to videotape or photograph students at work (obtain permission when necessary). Share the photos and videotape with the students, staff, and parents.

Planning Sheet: Combined-Class Experience

What purpose(s) would you like a combined-class experience to serve? _____
_____
_____
_____
_____
_____
_____
_____

In what way(s) is the receiving teacher committed to your goals and willing to work with you? _____
_____
_____
_____
_____
_____

In what way(s) does the administration support your goals? _____
_____
_____
_____

In what way(s) is the receiving classroom environment able to accommodate your space needs? _____
_____
_____
_____
_____
_____
_____
_____

Describe your plans for presenting the program to parents: _____
_____
_____
_____
_____
_____
_____
_____

Describe the activities you plan to use to introduce your students to the idea of working with children in another classroom:
_____
_____
_____
_____
_____
_____
_____
_____

Describe the orientation (joint-class, getting-acquainted) activities you have planned:

Activity _____
_____

Materials needed _____
_____

Location _____
_____

Responsibilities (yours and receiving teacher's) _____
_____
_____
_____

Activity _____
_____

Materials needed _____
_____

Location _____

_____

Responsibilities _____

_____

_____

Activity _____

_____

Materials needed _____

_____

Location _____

_____

Responsibilities _____

_____

_____

Activity _____

_____

Materials needed _____

_____

Location _____

_____

Responsibilities _____

_____

_____

Activity _____

_____

Materials needed _____

_____

Location _____

_____

Responsibilities _____

_____

_____

PLANNING THE COMBINED-CLASS EXPERIENCE

Step 1. Describe your grouping arrangement: _____

_____

_____

_____

_____

_____

_____

_____

_____

_____

_____

_____

_____

_____

_____

_____

_____

Step 2. Where will the combined-class experience take place? _____

_____

Why was this location selected? _____

_____

_____

Step 3: Describe the activities you intend to use.

Special activity: Location/center:

Starting place _____   _____

First rotation _____   _____

Second rotation _____   _____

Alternative #1 _____   _____

Alternative #2 _____   _____

Alternative #3 _____   _____

Alternative #4 _____   _____

Describe the rotation schedule you plan to use: _____

_____

_____

_____

_____

_____

_____

_____

_____

Step 4. What materials will you need for:

the introduction? _____

_____

the special activity? _____

_____

alternative #1? _____

_____

alternative #2? _____

_____

alternative #3? _____

_____

alternative #4? _____

_____

the follow-up activity? _____

_____

Will you be asking your students to bring in any money, and if so, how (vebal request, note to parents)?

_____

_____

_____

_____

_____

What materials will you supply? _____

_____

_____

_____

What materials will the receiving teacher supply? _____

_____

_____

_____

What materials, if any, will the students supply? _____

_____

_____

_____

Step 5. Describe the introduction you have planned: _____

_____

_____

_____

_____

_____

_____

_____

_____

Step 6. Describe the follow-up session you have planned: _____

_____

_____

_____

_____

_____

_____

_____

_____

_____

_____

_____

_____

Step 7. When will the combined-class activities take place (date)? _____

At what time will they begin? _____

How much time are you allowing for:

   your introduction? _____

   each rotation? _____

   your follow-up? _____

What schedule adjustments, if any, do you need to make that might affect the schedules of other teachers, the cafeteria, or the school?

_____

_____

_____

_____

Step 8. What changes or preparation of the environment will need to be made to accommodate the whole-group introduction and the follow-up, small groups, and rotation?

_____

_____

_____

_____

_____

When will these preparations be made? (Make sure that the environment will be ready when the students arrive.)

_____

_____

_____

_____

Who is responsible for these preparations? _____

_____

_____

_____

_____

_____

_____

_____

Step 9. How many adults will be working in the room during the combined-class experience? _____
_____

Describe the responsibilities and duties of the adults, specifying where they will be stationed and what they will be doing:

_____
_____
_____
_____
_____
_____
_____
_____
_____
_____
_____
_____
_____
_____
_____
_____
_____
_____
_____
_____
_____
_____
_____
_____
_____
_____
_____

Reflection and Evaluation: Combined-Class Experience

In what ways were your introductory activities successful? _____

_____

_____

_____

In what ways were your orientation (getting-acquainted) activities successful? _____

_____

_____

_____

During the combined-class experience, how were the following evident?

Positive social interactions _____

_____

_____

Sharing and cooperation _____

_____

_____

Ability to work on tasks independently _____

_____

_____

Ability to handle and clean up materials _____

_____

Ability to move from one work area to the next and get to work _____

_____

_____

Participation in the follow-up by students in both classes _____

_____

_____

Appropriateness of special activity _____

_____

_____

Appropriateness of alternative tasks _____

_____

In what ways did the implementation reflect your planning? _____

_____

_____

_____

In what ways was your grouping strategy successful? _____

_____

_____

_____

In what ways was the environment well arranged and accommodating? _____

_____

_____

_____

How well did you and the receiving teacher stick to your time schedule? _____

_____

_____

_____

To what degree were you and the receiving teacher consistent in your management of student behavior?

_____

_____

_____

_____

_____

_____

What modifications might be made for future activities of this nature with regard to:

    planning? _____

_____

_____

_____

    introduction activities? _____

_____

_____

_____

orientation (getting-acquainted) activities? _____

_____

selection of the special activity? _____

_____

selection of alternative tasks? _____

_____

arrangement of the environment? _____

_____

movement of students from one area to another? _____

_____

grouping? _____

_____

time management and scheduling? _____

_____

behavior management? _____

_____

_____

_____

What are your plans for future combined-class experiences with these groups?

_____

_____

_____

_____

_____

_____

_____

_____

_____

_____

_____

_____

_____

_____

Chapter 35

Peer Helping and Tutoring

THIS CHAPTER will help you extend the combined-class experience into the second phase, using students as peer helpers and tutors to work with the teacher and the younger students in the receiving classroom. Phase I activities were intended to build the communication and interaction skills necessary for this phase. By now, your students should be very familiar with the environment of the receiving classroom, the teaching style and expectations of the receiving teacher, and the special needs of the younger children. Your students have met and worked—in small groups—with many of the children they will now be helping on a more personal basis. Because of this preparation, individual helpers need only adapt to new materials and the management of this phase of the program.

Types of Helping Interactions

In Phase II, students may assist the teacher and the younger students in a wide variety of classroom activities. While your students may work with the younger children right from the start, student helpers can also help the teacher in the receiving classroom without actually working with the other students. Noninteractive projects which might include preparation of materials (mixing paints, cutting paper, sorting), care and assembly of equipment (playground, blocks, kitchen, audiovisual), or simple cleanup (putting materials away, sweeping, washing paint brushes) are especially valuable for students who may need additional orientation to the receiving classroom. These tasks reinforce the student's self-concept as a helper and build confidence as he or she further adjusts to the environment.

When the student is comfortable, nonacademic interactive tasks will allow him or her to work with an individual or small group of younger students. Valuable experience can be acquired by helping students to wash their hands before lunch, put on outdoor clothing, line up to go home, or open milk cartons and utensil packets during lunch. Nonacademic tasks reinforce the helper's sense of capability and responsibility while building the interactive skills necessary for academic interactions.

Between the combined-class activities and nonacademic helping, the transition to academic tasks should be smooth and simple. Again, the helper works with a small group of students or on a one-to-one basis. At this point, this model seems like a peer-tutoring program. The word "tutoring," however, suggests teaching, and while many helpers will naturally assume a teaching role, the emphasis of the interaction is on *helping* and *modeling*, primarily for the purpose of reinforcement. Teaching in the sense of instructing or presenting new concepts is *not* advised; instead, students should share and reinforce familiar information.

Most of the academic tasks involve activities, materials, and procedures already used in the receiving classroom. A helper might take part in listening to a story, playing in the blocks center, playing store, or playing an instructional game with one or more younger students. Completing an art activity, watching a filmstrip, or playing with puppets are other tasks helpers and "helpees" can do together.

Helpers can read or tell a story to a younger student or group of students. Even helpers who have not experienced much success in reading in their regular classroom can often perform well—and build a great deal of confidence—in this area in the receiving classroom. Helping a younger child understand and complete a particular task or assignment will also help reinforce the older student's understanding of the skills involved.

Helpers may initiate activities or suggest other ways they would like to help, particularly as they begin to perceive themselves as responsible helpers.

In Phase II, most of the activity occurs in the receiving classroom. As the "sending" teacher, your primary responsibilities will be scheduling students' visits, introducing the phase to your students, and helping the receiving teacher set up the management system. Once the program gets underway, the receiving teacher should provide opportunities for your students to help. The helping activities can be assigned informally, if desired, and with a minimum of preparation. You can provide support by setting and reinforcing participation criteria and helping the receiving teacher build the skills needed. Management guidelines for scheduling, assigning tasks, monitoring procedures, and implementing the program are provided below.

Scheduling the Program

Consider the following suggestions for selecting students and setting up a schedule for helper visits:

1. Try to give each student a chance to be a helper. Give preference to students not often chosen for special privileges and/or to those who would benefit most, particularly slow learners or students with behavior problems.

2. Make sure the schedule is convenient for you and the receiving teacher. Try to set up a fixed schedule, assigning students to specific days and times. For example, one helper might know that for the next grading period, he will be expected in the receiving classroom on Thursdays from 1:30 to 2:00.

3. Assign one to three helpers for each time slot, depending on the needs of the receiving classroom. If you send more than one, try to balance the personalities and abilities in each group of helpers you send.

4. Plan for helping periods of twenty to forty-five minutes each.

5. If possible, assign "floaters" to cover special needs that pop up from time to time or to replace absent helpers. Create opportunities for floaters to help. Assure the floaters a regular position on the next schedule rotation.

6. Change the fixed schedule every four to six weeks to allow all students to participate in the regular schedule at varying days and times.

7. Try not to release helpers to the receiving class when they will be likely to miss instruction in their own classroom. Independent work periods, self-selection, or recess are probably the safest times, providing the students stay caught up on their work or don't mind missing the other activities.

Assigning Tasks to Helpers

In most instances, the receiving teacher will be responsible for planning the tasks the helpers will be involved in. You may wish to recommend particular students for specific tasks, or ask if there are any tasks available to strengthen particular skills. Try not to overburden the receiving teacher, however.

The receiving teacher, with your help, will determine how tasks will be assigned to the helpers. Three strategies are suggested below:

1. The receiving teacher briefly explains the tasks to student helpers as they enter the receiving classroom. This method is most valuable for general tasks such as "read to the five students in the language center," "sweep the play area," or "find a student for the listening activities."

2. Create an assignment board with several pockets that offers tasks to helpers. Each helper will get to choose a pocket.

   ▶ The receiving teacher makes a number of activity cards that simply state or illustrate directions such as "read a story," "listen to the record," "blocks," "store," "cut paper," "help with shapes puzzle," "any game," or "any center." These cards are placed in the pockets.

   ▶ If a specific location is preferred, a location card (perhaps a different color than the activity cards) may also be put in the pocket to tell the students where they should work.

   ▶ Student cards, each labeled with the name of a student in the receiving classroom, are put in the pockets to tell the helper who to help. Student cards should be a different color than the activity and location cards. Student cards can also include a photo of the student along with the name. Additional cards marked "any student," "any two students," or "any three students," for example, should be handy for times when the helper can choose among available students.

▶ The receiving teacher can prepare as many pockets as anticipated helpers, perhaps with one or two extra to allow for a choice or an alternative if the first activity selected is completed early.

▶ The flexibility of this method allows the receiving teacher to request noninteractive tasks (no student cards in the pocket) or let helpers assigned to specific students select the tasks (no activity card) or location (no location card).

3. Establish a "helper center" containing tasks and materials a helper and a helpee (designated or self-selected) may select together.

Monitoring the System

You will need to develop sign-in and monitoring materials to keep track of helper visits and elicit feedback from helpers. Start by preparing a weekly sign-in sheet for helpers to sign upon entering the receiving classroom. Include the date and time of arrival. Next, prepare a "helper slip" or evaluation checklist for the helper to complete. A sample helper slip follows.

Helper _____

Date _____ Time[1] _____

☐ Partner(s)[2] _____

_____

☐ Group   ☐ No partner

Task _____

_____

    ☐ The task was completed.

    ☐ We worked well today.

    ☐ My partner could do the task.

    ☐ My partner needs more work with this task.

    ☐ I would like a conference with the teacher.

Comments:

[1]or class period.

[2]Up to two partners may be named; for three or more, check "group" and name the students on the back of the card.

Designate a place for students to deposit completed helper slips so that the receiving teacher can see how things went that day. Then, prepare a file box for storing them. After looking over the day's helper slips, file (or have a student file) them under the name of the partner or under the headings of "two partners," or "group," or "no partner."

To ensure that each of the younger students receives help, use a checklist. When student helpers select partners during free-choice activities, the checklist will show which students have been helped that week. Students can only select a partner from those whose names have not been checked or initialed.

Implementing the Program

Follow these suggestions for introducing and managing the peer-helping program:

1. As with Phase I, this program must be "sold" to the students. Even before the program begins, convince students that participation in the program is a special privilege contingent on performance and behavior. At the same time, the challenge must appear accessible and rewarding.

2. To introduce this phase of the program:
   ▶ specify rules and guidelines clearly.
   ▶ explain the schedule.
   ▶ describe the sign-in procedures, including those for task and student selection, as well as the use of the checklist.
   ▶ describe the procedures for completing and filing the helper slips. Remind students of their responsibility to leave time to complete the forms and provide feedback to the receiving teacher on the outcomes of their interactions with the younger students.

3. Once the program begins, be sure to supervise, observe, and interact with student helpers as needed.

4. The receiving teacher should also check with each helper at some point during their visit to make sure everything is going well and to demonstrate interest and concern.

5. Sincere and consistent reinforcement should be available from both you and the receiving teacher. Greeting the students and saying "thank you" provides a positive model for

student helpers. Ideally, reinforcement should come from every level of faculty and staff. A supportive school environment seems to provide the most effective atmosphere for reinforcing the program's goals.

6. Discipline should be consistently maintained in a positive manner. Avoid warnings and "second chances"; infractions should be met with a calm, polite, and immediate request for the helper to return to his or her own classroom until next time. If discipline continues to be a problem, short-term suspension from the program is recommended.

7. The receiving teacher should monitor and discuss the helpers' choices. From time to time, on a regular basis, the receiving teacher can recognize the older students' contributions by conferring with individual helpers. These brief interactions also allow for discussion of the helpers' experiences and input. Because participation is a privilege, using tokens, points, or other tangible rewards for participation is *not* recommended.

Evaluating with the Receiving Teacher

You and the receiving teacher will both find it helpful to meet regularly to exchange information. In addition to discussing schedules, materials, activities, and other needs, you can let the receiving teacher know of behaviors, patterns, or changes in the performance of any student in the helping program, particularly if the changes are positive and probably the result of the interactions in the program. The receiving teacher can also provide information about the performance of student helpers by regularly observing and evaluating their performance.

Develop a "helper observation form" with the following comments for the receiving teacher to check off as noted:

▶ Helper made a nondisruptive entrance into the room.

▶ Helper went immediately to the helper center (or to get partner or materials).

▶ Helper signed in correctly.

▶ Helper followed correct procedure for getting task.

▶ Helper selected partner and got right to work.

▶ Helper gave clear directions to partner.

▶ Helper and partner stayed on task.

▶ Helper followed correct sequence for completing the task.

▶ Helper set a good example.

▶ Helper interacted positively with partner.

▶ Helper thanked and reinforced partner.

▶ Helper checked with teacher about problems.

▶ Helper and partner put materials away.

▶ Helper filled out evaluation checklist.

▶ Helper is welcome back in this classroom.

▶ Other observations and comments.

Be sure to go over this form with the helper involved. The most valuable aspect of providing this type of feedback is that the observation form clearly spells out the qualities of a good helper. The positive evaluation statement on the form provides excellent reinforcement for the helpers on their actual performance. These observation forms also provide important information about student growth and performance for you and for the counselor, principal, and parents.

Planning Sheet: Peer Helping and Tutoring

What purpose(s) would you like this phase of the peer interaction program to serve? _____

_____

_____

_____

_____

In what way(s) is the receiving teacher committed to your goals and willing to work in accord with the suggested guidelines?

_____

_____

_____

_____

_____

Describe your plans for scheduling. Identify the days and times you have set aside during which student helpers will be available. How long will the helpers stay in the receiving classroom?

_____

_____

_____

_____

Which students will visit at the same time, and when will their visits be scheduled? _____

_____

_____

_____

_____

_____

_____

_____

_____

_____

_____

_____

Identify "floaters" to help out if regularly assigned helpers are absent or if the receiving teacher needs special assistance:

_____

_____

_____

Assuming this schedule works well, how long before you plan to change it? _____

_____

What changes (for example, additional visits, different times, longer times) do you anticipate making?

_____

_____

_____

_____

_____

Describe the receiving teacher's plans for:

noninteractive tasks? _____

_____

_____

_____

nonacademic (interactive) tasks? _____

_____

_____

_____

academic tasks? _____

_____

_____

_____

_____

_____

_____

_____

_____

_____

Describe the sign-in procedures and materials you plan to use: _____

_____

_____

_____

How will the students know:

what they should be doing in the receiving classroom? _____

_____

_____

who they should be helping? _____

_____

_____

where they should be working? _____

_____

_____

Have you constructed:

the necessary sign-in materials? _____

_____

a checklist for the students in the receiving classroom? _____

_____

helper slips? _____

_____

helper observation forms? _____

_____

_____

In what ways do you plan to support and maintain Phase II helper participation with continued or on-going Phase I combined-class activities?

_____

_____

_____

_____

_____

_____

Reflection and Evaluation: Peer Helping and Tutoring

Evaluate the implementation of the program in the following areas:

Scheduling _____

_____

Selection of helpers _____

_____

Activities _____

_____

Signing in _____

_____

Task or partner selection _____

_____

Helper slip completion _____

_____

Behavior management _____

_____

Helper observations by the receiving teacher _____

_____

Students' responses (helpers) _____

_____

Students' responses (younger students) _____

_____

Parents' responses, if any _____

_____

Administration's responses, if any _____

_____

_____

_____

_____

_____

_____

What changes have you made in the schedule, procedure, or activities? _____

_____

_____

In what ways has the program affected your students' attitudes, behaviors, or skills (cognitive and interactive)?

_____

_____

_____

_____

What changes do you anticipate making in this program? _____

_____

_____

_____

What would you do differently if you set up the program (Phases I and II) to implement next year?

_____

_____

_____

_____

_____

_____

_____

_____

_____

_____

_____

_____

_____

_____

UNIT VII

Instructional Environment and Materials

Chapter 36
....

Classroom Environment

IS YOUR CLASSROOM environment rich and dynamic? Does it contribute to the instruction you provide or simply warehouse the students and materials? Is it teacher-oriented or student-oriented? Does it demand interaction and literacy from your students? Does it encourage responsibility and decision making? Does it stimulate thinking?

A classroom environment consists of both architectural elements (basic structure) and arranged elements (materials added to the basic structure). As a teacher, your control over the architectural environment may be limited, yet some teachers have modified architectural elements by building lofts, permanent storage units, platforms, or ramps. You can sometimes alter the structure by changing the room's colors, knocking out walls, or adding windows, permanent dividers, and doors.

For the most part, however, you will be working with the arranged elements of the environment. These elements are modified in response to the changing needs of students. The arranged environment will need to be dynamic, continually changing to accommodate the changing needs of your students.

As you consider the impact of the environment on your instruction and the behavior of the students in your class, remember that the environment appears different to a child than it does to an adult. The adult's perception of the classroom is more encompassing than that of the child's and includes stored materials that cannot be seen by the child. Although the adult's environment exists, essentially, from the knees up, the child's environment may not include some of the space above his or her head.

The Student-Centered Environment

A relationship exists between the classroom environment and students' behavior. Changes in the environment are likely to produce changes in students' behavior. Similarly, problems in students'

behavior may sometimes be attributed to problems in the environment. A poorly arranged environment can lead to confusion, overcrowding, and lost or damaged materials. Other problems may develop because the environment lacks the necessary materials or stimuli, or because materials and stimuli are inadequate or inaccessible to students.

A student-centered classroom environment will help students develop responsible learning behaviors. To create this kind of environment, consider the following suggestions:

1. Arrange materials and supplies for student access. If supplies are visible and accessible, the students can take and use what they need without your assistance.
   - Keep supplies at the students' eye level or below.
   - Store materials in clear containers, particularly if the student cannot see into the top of the container.
   - Label opaque containers with pictures or samples of contents glued on the outside.
   - Provide access to the materials that students can use independently, including books, games, printing sets, typewriters, computers, and audiovisual supplies.
   - Identify specific spaces for materials (with labels, pictures, or outlines of materials on storage surfaces).
   - Require that the students take responsibility for caring for and returning materials.

2. Provide opportunities for students to perceive and respond to written words used in schedules, labels, student writing, sign-up sheets, instructions, and activity cards.

3. Make books available for free reading, for enrichment activities, or for reference.

4. Provide for self-management of daily administrative routines, such as attendance, lunch count, or borrowing the hall pass.

5. Make available a variety of learning opportunities and materials. Examples:
   ▸ Work centers at which students can work on prepared tasks and activities.
   ▸ Assignments that students can complete using their own texts and materials and/or those in the room.
   ▸ Inquiry or discovery spaces where students can explore and investigate materials.
   ▸ Self-selection areas where students can choose their own materials and activities.
   ▸ Provisions for different learning settings, including space and opportunities for working independently near other students, for interacting and completing tasks with other students, and for working or reading alone in a quiet or private space (such as a study carrel, overstuffed chair, corner with pillows, corner desk or small table).
   ▸ Provisions and environmental arrangements that help students move freely, make decisions, get supplies, and select tasks easily.

Decisions you make about the learning environment should be based not only on what you plan to teach, but also on the student behavior you wish to elicit. The arrangements of furnishings and learning materials you provide will influence the processes your students use in learning. Different arrangements will require the students to use different learning behaviors.

Small Changes

A dynamic environment constantly changes in response to the students' growth and changing needs. Most of the changes you make in your classroom will be small ones. Even the introduction of new charts, posters, student work, displays, active bulletin boards, games, books, kits, paints, or pillows constitutes a small change in the learning environment. Small changes might also include new door signs, schedules, or board messages that are changed daily; or slight modifications in management that involve new materials or traffic patterns.

You may need to draw the attention of the students to new materials, particularly when students are not used to looking for changes, or when new materials require some explanation. You may also have to point out materials that are not immediately visible, such as new books in the library or new games in the self-selection area.

Once the students become aware that the signs on the door are new each morning, for example, they will begin to anticipate fresh messages greeting them when they arrive each morning. Use a door sign or board message that a majority of the students will see in order to draw attention to the new rabbit cage, cloud chart, or easel. Messages such as "What's new in the room?" "Look in the science center for a surprise!" and "What's in the bag?" will stimulate curiosity. Don't forget to leave paper or space on the sign, in the center, or on the board so that students can respond.

Students tend to ignore materials left hanging or displayed in the room for more than a few days. Even those bulletin boards you labored over for days will be overlooked in a very short period of time unless the students are interacting with the display or have a reason to notice them every day. You can maintain the students' interest in the materials by drawing their attention to them, making small changes every few days, or assigning tasks that require the students to use or look at the materials.

Make small changes in the environment to visually introduce new materials, maintain efficiency or improve classroom management, encourage student involvement in the environment, and stimulate the students' thinking.

Large Changes

Large changes will have more impact on your students' behavior than the smaller modifications and additions mentioned above. Large changes might include a complete reorganization of furnishings or a major modification that would require new materials, new furnishings, or new traffic patterns in the classroom. Adding a new learning center, creating work spaces, or implementing a new program will most likely be large changes.

Major changes in the environment and routine will probably demand major changes in the students' behavior. Unless the changes are very clearly explained and students practice the new routines, major changes can cause major problems. Frequent large changes can cause insecurity, disorientation, and disruption. While both small and large changes can enrich the classroom and stimulate students' growth, major changes should be undertaken primarily to accommodate instructional and behavioral goals that require them.

Worksheet: Classroom Environment

Draw your classroom's floor plan in the space below. Identify:

- ■ traffic patterns (red lines).

- ■ areas not used by students (shaded).

- ■ areas where students usually work to complete tasks (mark with *X*).

- ■ areas where students spend self-selection activity time (label).

- ■ areas where small group instruction takes place (circle).

Describe your room in terms of the following elements of a student-centered classroom:

Student access to materials and supplies _____

_____

_____

_____

_____

Variety of learning materials for students to use independently as part of classroom instruction and/or for self-selection

_____

_____

_____

_____

_____

Identification of specific spaces for specific materials _____

_____

_____

_____

_____

Frequently changed displays of student work _____

_____

_____

_____

_____

Opportunities to respond to written words in the room (message boards, and so on) _____

_____

_____

_____

_____

Self-management of daily administrative routines _____

_____

_____

_____

_____

Variety of work areas and strategies for learning (for example, learning centers, self-selection activity areas, independent reading areas)

_____

_____

_____

_____

_____

Maximization of efficient movement and self-management _____

_____

_____

_____

_____

What is the impact of your environment on:

the development of students' self-management and responsible learning behaviors? _____

_____

_____

_____

_____

the students' interaction with one another and their development of interactive competence? ____

_____

_____

_____

_____

the students' learning, stimulation, and motivation? _____

_____

_____

_____

_____

_____

_____

Planning Sheet: Classroom Environment

What small changes or additions have you made in your classroom recently? _____

_____

_____

_____

_____

_____

_____

_____

_____

_____

_____

_____

What small changes do you anticipate making within the next few weeks? _____

_____

_____

_____

_____

_____

_____

_____

_____

_____

_____

_____

_____

Identify some major changes you have made in your classroom recently and describe the goals you hoped to achieve in doing so:

_____

_____

_____

_____

_____

_____

_____

_____

_____

_____

_____

_____

_____

What major changes, if any, do you anticipate making within the next few weeks? _____

_____

_____

_____

_____

_____

Why do you feel these changes are needed? _____

_____

_____

_____

_____

_____

_____

_____

_____

Reflection and Evaluation: Classroom Environment

In the spaces below, identify the changes or additions you make to your learning environment day by day for the next four weeks.

WEEK 1

Monday

Tuesday

Wednesday

Thursday

Friday

WEEK 2

Monday

Tuesday

Wednesday

Thursday

Friday

WEEK 3

Monday

_____

Tuesday

_____

Wednesday

_____

Thursday

_____

Friday

_____

WEEK 4

Monday

_____

Tuesday

_____

Wednesday

_____

Thursday

_____

Friday

_____

Did you find that keeping a record of changes in your environment was useful? Why or why not?

_____

_____

_____

_____

Were there more or fewer changes in the last month than in the past? _____

_____

Were the changes generally small or large or both? _____

_____

What effect did the changes you made on the physical environment have on the following:

Your awareness of individual learning styles _____

_____

_____

Number of language and information sources _____

_____

_____

Improved teacher-student interaction _____

_____

_____

Improved student-student interaction _____

_____

_____

Better care of supplies and materials _____

_____

_____

Increase in self-motivated learning _____

_____

_____

Increased integration of subject areas within the curriculum _____

_____

_____

Accomplishment of other curricular and instructional goals _____

_____

_____

_____

_____

Now, draw your classroom's new floor plan in the space below. Identify:

- ■ traffic patterns (red lines).

- ■ areas not used by students (shaded).

- ■ areas where students usually work to complete tasks (mark with *X*).

- ■ areas where students spend self-selection time (label).

- ■ areas where small group instruction takes place (circle).

How is this floor plan different from the previous one you drew? What new evidence do you have to indicate that your environment is student-oriented?

Student access to materials and supplies _____

_____

_____

_____

Variety of learning materials _____

_____

_____

_____

Identification of specific spaces for specific materials _____

_____

_____

_____

Recent and frequently changing displays of student work _____

_____

_____

_____

Opportunities to respond to written words _____

_____

_____

_____

Self-management of daily administrative routines _____

_____

_____

_____

Variety of management strategies for learning _____

_____

_____

_____

Maximization of efficient movement and self-management _____

_____

_____

If you were to fill out a similar report next month, how would you expect it to be different from the one above?

_____

_____

_____

_____

_____

_____

How would you expect it to be similar? _____

_____

_____

_____

_____

What generalizations can you make from your observations about the relationships between the environment, learning, and student behavior?

_____

_____

_____

_____

_____

What instructional goals do you have that will require further changes in the environment? _____

_____

_____

_____

_____

_____

_____

_____

_____

Chapter 37

. . . .

Interactive Displays

USING WALLS and bulletin boards as display space for room decorations can make your classroom attractive, but you may be wasting a valuable instructional resource. While decorations brighten up an environment, they are likely to be ignored after a few days. Even displays of students' work should be changed and rotated frequently to avoid this problem.

As discussed in Chapter 36, it is important to maintain an active, dynamic environment that will be more than simply a backdrop for your instruction. This chapter offers guidelines for using displays as instructional resources in the classroom. These displays require interaction from the students and become a part of the learning materials they use.

This chapter presents strategies for developing instructional resources such as door signs, pocket activities, activity boards, and active bulletin boards.

Door Signs

An important goal in developing your classroom environment is to provide materials that stimulate interest and require students to read. Signs in and around the room that address students, ask them questions, or state directions give students a reason to read.

Door signs that are changed daily can be an effective way to encourage reading. Mounted at student eye level on the door to your classroom, these signs greet the students each new day. Door signs can say almost anything. Some types and examples are suggested below:

▶ Greetings:
Good morning, class. Welcome back from spring break.

▶ Notices or announcements:
Happy birthday, Mary.
Early dismissal today!
Joshua's mother had a baby! Is there a baby at your house?

▶ Reminders:
Remember that your library books are due tomorrow.
Don't forget to go straight to the gym after recess.
Tomorrow is St. Patrick's Day. Wear something green.

▶ Requests that demand some immediate behavioral response:
Get a book from the library shelf before you sit down.
Look in the hamster cage to see a surprise.

Door signs can also pose questions that can be answered in the blank space on the sign itself or on a separate piece of paper. These types of signs might include:

▶ Closed preference questions:
Who do you think will win the Pittsburgh-Cleveland game tonight?
Which flavor of ice cream do you like best: chocolate, vanilla, or strawberry?

▶ Open preference questions:
Where would you go if you could travel anywhere in the world?
Draw your favorite shape below.

▶ Survey questions:
How many sisters do you have?
Do you have a dog?
Have you ever been to Mexico?
What do you know about sheep?

▶ Skill-related questions:
What in the room is round?
Name a liquid.
What words can you make from the letters in BIRTHDAY?
Name several things that are red.

▶ Feeling questions:
Report cards will be handed out tommorow. How do you feel about that?
How do you feel when you watch the snow fall?

Using Door Signs Effectively

The following suggestions may help you use door signs successfully in your classroom:

1. Use signs regularly. The signs should be up for the students to see as they enter the room in the morning. If you have more than one door, make different signs for each. You may also use similar signs in other locations around the room.

2. Make signs large enough to include room for student responses. Signs may be made from $12'' \times 18''$ construction paper in different colors. The signs are simple to make, but they should be attractive, appealing, and visually clear.

3. If signs are all the same size and shape, you can assemble them in a book and place it in the class library. If the signs are about the same size, but cut in different shapes, they can be mounted and then made into a book. This book can be used as a reference in the future.

4. Vary the content and type of signs from day to day. Involve individual students on special occasions, such as on birthdays, when someone's dog has puppies, or when a child is due back after a long illness.

5. Use door signs to introduce concepts or ideas you will be working on later in the day, or to reinforce concepts you have been working on.

6. Try to construct messages on the door sign that require some form of interaction on the part of the students. Signs that offer students a place to respond in writing or those that request some immediate action are preferable to simple greetings or reminders which require no response.

7. Allow some time for students to respond. This time may be when they enter the room, when they take a break from independent seat work, when they are on their way to and from the room with the pass, and/or during self-selection time.

8. Draw some attention to the door sign at the beginning of each day. Read the message or have a student read it to the class. In many instances, this will allow nonreaders to participate and encourage them to want to become readers.

9. Draw some attention to the sign at the end of the day. Acknowledge and briefly discuss the students' responses to motivate them to continue responding.

10. Encourage, but do not require each student to respond. Do not tell students that responding is *not* required; simply reinforce those who do.

11. Rather than having students write out their responses, set up a door sign now and then that requires students to graph their responses. Examples:

Do you have a pet?

Yes □□□□□□□□□□□□□□□□□□ □□□□□

No □□□□□□□□□□□□□□□□□□ □□□□□

or

What type(s) of pet(s) do you have?

Dog □□□□□□□□□□□□□□

Cat □□□□□□□□□□□□□

Bird □□□□□□□□□□□□□

Fish □□□□□□□□□□□□□□

Horse □□□□□□□□□□□□□□

Hamster □□□□□□□□□□□□□

Other □□□□□□□□□□□□□

None □□□□□□□□□□□□□

Students respond by coloring in the squares that apply.

Pocket Activities

Pockets or hanging containers can turn display space into a storage or distribution center. You can use one pocket in one part of the room, several in different small places around the room, or perhaps an entire set of pockets in a larger space.

Pockets may be made of laminated paper, cardboard, fabric, or hanging plastic files. They may contain supplemental materials to be done in spare time, puzzles for self-selection, or related activities for selection in a learning center. In the following example, a pocket activity is displayed between the door and the chalkboard.

The example below shows a more elaborate use of pockets:

By grouping a number of pockets together, you can present a set of work contract materials, learning-center activities, supplementary-unit tasks, or self-selection puzzles. A similar display can be constructed without the balloons.

Activity Boards

Activity boards are mini-bulletin boards with assignments on them. These boards provide colorful and attractive presentations of a variety of tasks. Once prepared and laminated, they can be used again and again. You can hang them on bulletin boards, wall space, or on the back of a book-shelf. When you no longer need to use a particular activity board, you simply take down the complete display and store it as is. It will be ready for display again the next time you need it.

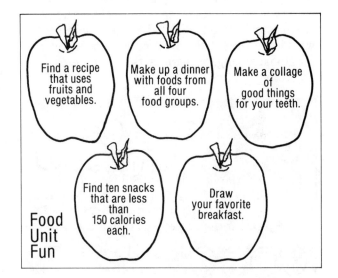

Activity boards can be used as a creative writing center or as one of several integrated small group activities. Use them in conjunction with pocket activities to provide the necessary information for completing other activities.

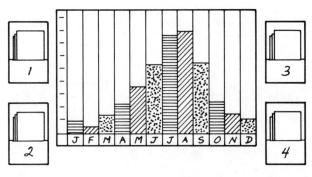

Active Bulletin Boards

Active bulletin boards differ from activity boards because they require more than reading and choosing. While pockets simply store materials, active bulletin boards require movement or manipulation of the materials that make up the bulletin board display.

Below is an example of a very simple bulletin board containing a random arrangement of numbered dots which the students move around and arrange so that the numbers are hung on the board in sequence. Instead of dots, you can construct this active bulletin board using animal or seasonal shapes, such as ducks, bears, umbrellas, pumpkins, or Christmas trees. The shapes can also be marked with letters of the alphabet for sequencing, words for alphabetizing, or math facts to be ordered according to sums.

A sentence train, such as the one below, is more sophisticated. A boxcar at the end of the train holds cards that contain sentence fragments. By sticking the cards in the appropriate cars, students can construct different sentences.

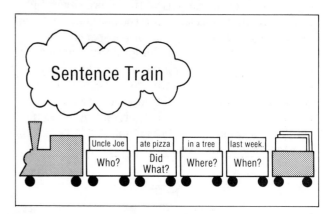

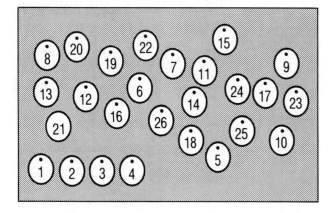

Planning Sheet: Door Signs

Plan a number of door signs you would like to use during the next two weeks. Keep in mind that you may wish to add signs about events or changes that occur in your classroom during this time, or to introduce or practice concepts you will be teaching. Design each sign to elicit responses from students.

1. _____
2. _____
3. _____
4. _____
5. _____
6. _____
7. _____
8. _____
9. _____
10. _____

For two weeks, use and change the door signs daily according to the guidelines presented in this chapter.

Ideas for other door signs: _____

_____

_____

_____

_____

_____

_____

_____

_____

_____

_____

_____

_____

_____

_____

_____

Planning Sheet: Pocket Activity

Duplicate as needed.

Number of pockets: _____

Location(s): _____

_____

_____

_____

Contents: _____

_____

_____

_____

_____

_____

Purpose: _____

_____

_____

_____

_____

_____

Use: _____

_____

_____

_____

_____

_____

_____

_____

_____

_____

Planning Sheet: Activity Board

Duplicate as needed.

Concept: _____

_____

_____

_____

Purpose: _____

_____

_____

_____

Location: _____

_____

_____

_____

Contents and appearance (draw proposed design below):

Use: _____

_____

_____

_____

Planning Sheet: Active Bulletin Board

Duplicate as needed.

Concept: _____

_____

_____

_____

Purpose: _____

_____

_____

_____

Location: _____

_____

_____

_____

Contents and appearance (draw proposed design below):

Use: _____

_____

_____

_____

Chapter 38

Homework

ASSIGNING HOMEWORK—school-related tasks completed out of school—is a well-established educational tradition. Most teachers assign some homework as early as kindergarten and first grade. Teachers of older students, particularly those in departmentalized programs who only work with each group for forty to fifty minutes, generally prefer using the limited class time for actual instruction. The homework they assign is intended to give the students practice in what they have been taught that day or to let them prepare for a lecture, demonstration, or discussion to come.

In elementary schools, students often have opportunities to read and practice new skills in the classroom. Since more time is devoted to in-class work in the lower grades, homework is sometimes assigned less frequently or only for special purposes.

Why Assign Homework?

In some schools, administrative policy or pressure from parents may influence a teacher's attitudes and decisions regarding homework assignments, but teachers usually assign homework to reinforce concepts introduced in class and to allow students additional practice of skills.

Homework extends learning beyond the classroom. Having students work on problems and processes used in school also enables parents to keep in touch with what their children are being taught. In addition, assigning homework builds responsibility and independent learning skills. For younger students, getting used to doing homework is excellent preparation for the type of learning they can expect in the higher grades. For all students, homework communicates the idea that learning is a process that goes beyond the classroom.

Assigning Homework

Consider the following guidelines for assigning homework:

1. Give homework assignments consistently; for example, make a spelling assignment every Monday and Thursday, or every Wednesday. If you are consistent about making assignments, the students are more likely to return them.

2. Give specific directions for homework assignments. Make sure the assignment sheet you send home is clear and legible. Remember that you will not be there to answer questions.

3. Go over assignments in class and do examples. If possible, observe and instruct as needed. If the students cannot do the work in your classroom, without instruction, it is unlikely that they will be able to do the work at home.

4. Avoid assignments that require parents to teach or explain. Depending on the community in which you teach and the content of the assignments you send home, your students' parents may or may not be able or available to help. If possible, students should do the work independently, with parental support and supervision.

5. Match the length, frequency, and difficulty of assignments given as homework to the age and abilities of your students. Keep assignments very short and success-oriented, especially at first. With the exception of big projects, be careful not to extend the school day by several hours.

6. Require that homework be turned in at a certain time. Follow-up may include checking to see if the work was done, going over the work or portions of the work in class, checking to see if the students used or brought in home resources, or discussing the students' reactions to the assignment and the processes they used.

7. Don't give homework as punishment.

Homework Calendars

One method of assigning homework that meets all the objectives described above is a homework, or home-job, calendar. Homework calendars are constructed as any monthly calendar, and each day is marked with one task for students to do at home.

Homework calendars are easy to plan, prepare, distribute, and follow up on. They are extremely flexible in the types of tasks they require and they adapt to any grade level or content area.

Homework calendars offer opportunities to apply skills and knowledge gained in school in a different context and setting. They connect learning to the students' life outside school and often involve parents in the students' learning.

Because homework calendar assignments tend to be informal and personally meaningful, students will probably complete them. Calendars require the students to do something every day, offering them the opportunity to exercise responsible learning behaviors daily.

The types of tasks available on a homework calendar can vary considerably. Items sampled from over a dozen typical homework calendars for primary students included the following tasks.[1]

Helping tasks:

Turn off a light someone forgot about.
Clean your room.
Help make dinner.

[1] Items provided by intern teachers enrolled in the 1981–1982 Albuquerque Public Schools/University of New Mexico Graduate Intern Program.

Make your bed and someone else's.
Help set the table.
Take out the garbage.

Interactive tasks:

Give someone in your house a hug.
Smile at someone you like.
Say something nice to someone you don't often talk to.
Call a friend on the phone.
Go for a walk with a friend.
Say something nice to someone in your family.

Sharing tasks:

Play a game with a friend.
Read your favorite story to someone else.
Tell someone a riddle.
Cut an apple in half and share it with someone.
Sing a song to someone.

Holiday- or calendar-related tasks:

Write the numbers of the days on this calendar.
Tell someone how many days there are in February.
Find out something about George Washington.
Tell three people the name of the month.
Make a shamrock for someone.
Make a heart mobile.
Make a special valentine.

Skill-related tasks:

How many △ shapes can you find in your house?
Measure your bed.
Add up the numbers in your phone number.
Count the number of doorknobs in your house.
Find the area of your living room.
Write the numbers from one to ten backwards.
Count to 100 by threes before you fall asleep tonight.
Find five wooden objects in your house.
Make a blue collage using pictures from an old magazine.
Select something green to wear tomorrow.

Make a list of red things in your house.

Weigh yourself.

Touch your toes ten times.

Find out how long it takes to boil one cup of water at low heat.

List seven things that require electricity.

Draw a map from your house to the school.

Write your name and address.

Write a springtime haiku poem.

Look at the moon and draw its shape.

Say the days of the week in Spanish.

Count from one to ten in French.

Write a letter to someone.

List ten words that rhyme with "hug."

Draw a comic strip.

Constructing a Homework Calendar

Design the calendar according to the age or grade level and needs of your students. Follow this procedure to develop your own homework calendar:

1. Use the calendar grid on page 321 for your homework calendar master. Note that the calendar also includes weekends.

2. Fill in the name of the month. You or the students may write in the days of the week (in English or some other language).

3. Identify a space for writing the dates by placing a slash or an empty shape (related to a holiday of that month, for example) in the corner of each box. You or your students may fill in some or all of the dates. Examples:

4. Select a variety of tasks. Some tasks should relate to concepts and skills you are teaching in your room that month.

5. Design several tasks that require students to complete a project that can be brought to school and shared with the class. Mark these tasks with a star.

6. Write the tasks in simple words in the appropriate calendar boxes. Print neatly. Illustrate the tasks if possible. Examples:

7. Duplicate the calendar (one for each student).

Using Homework Calendars

The teachers who prepared the calendars from which the previous examples were taken introduced homework calendars to the students and their parents through an in-class presentation and a newsletter sent home. The newsletter explained the goals of the homework calendars and requested the parents' support and involvement.

Be sure to set aside time each day to let students share how they carried out their tasks on the previous day. Even when a task does not require students to bring a completed project from home, students benefit from explaining how they completed their tasks.

Reflection and Evaluation: Homework

What do you feel is the purpose of assigning homework? _____

_____

_____

Do you ever assign homework? _____

If no, why not? _____

_____

If yes, complete the chart below:

Subject area	Type of work assigned*	Purpose of assignment	Frequency	Can the work be done in school?	Do you grade the work?

*For example: dittos, workbook pages, problems in the text or from the board, readings, research, other.

If you expect parents to help:

how? _____

_____

_____

to what extent? _____

_____

_____

how will you let them know? _____

_____

_____

At what age or grade level do you think homework should first be assigned? _____

_____

_____

What types of assignments? _____

_____

_____

For what purpose? _____

_____

_____

In what ways are your homework assignments consistent with the suggestions in this chapter? _____

_____

_____

_____

_____

_____

_____

_____

_____

_____

_____

Planning Sheet: Homework Calendars

Duplicate as needed:

Month: _____

Special calendar design features: _____

_____

_____

Concepts to be developed: Homework activities to be assigned:

_____   _____

_____   _____

_____   _____

_____   _____

_____   _____

_____   _____

_____   _____

_____   _____

_____   _____

_____   _____

_____   _____

_____   _____

_____   _____

_____   _____

_____   _____

_____   _____

Duplicate, enlarge if desired, and fill in the chart on the following page to create your calendar.

Reflection and Evaluation: Homework Calendars

How did you introduce the homework calendars:

to your students? _____

_____

to their parents? _____

_____

How did the students respond to the calendar and activities? _____

_____

_____

_____

_____

How did you manage the follow-up? _____

_____

_____

_____

_____

How would you assess the students' interest, involvement, and the frequency of task completion?

_____

_____

_____

_____

What response, if any, did you receive from the parents? _____

_____

_____

_____

_____

What did you find especially positive about this project? _____

_____

_____

_____

_____

_____

What problems arose? _____

_____

_____

What can you do to alleviate those problems? _____

_____

_____

In what ways do you intend to continue using homework calendars as a part of your instruction?

_____

_____

_____

How do you anticipate that future calendars will be different:

in design? _____

_____

_____

_____

_____

_____

in tasks? _____

_____

_____

_____

_____

_____

in management? _____

_____

_____

_____

_____

_____

Chapter 39

Developing Instructional Materials

INSTRUCTIONAL MATERIALS include any objects or materials a student uses to gain or apply knowledge, including textbooks, felt boards, math counters, games, or computers. You probably use a variety of materials to stimulate learning or to appeal to a variety of learning mode preferences. Materials may be selected to provide students firsthand experience with concrete objects, or to offer them a variety of approaches to content that they will encounter repeatedly.

It is reasonable to expect that a student will become bored doing the same math problems over and over again, even when such practice is warranted. Assigning the student a puzzle or game that provides practice in essentially the same math problems may not only maintain interest, but also stimulate or reinforce learning in a new way.

Educational Games

The greatest strength of educational games is their power to motivate. When students learn while they are playing a game, they *enjoy* learning. Moreover, because educational games tend to motivate, stimulate interest, and give pleasure, students are likely to spend more time learning a particular concept or skill.

Games can also:

▶ help students understand the purpose of rules.

▶ clarify difficult concepts and processes.

▶ promote social interaction.

▶ integrate students of diverse ability levels.

▶ teach several skills and meet multiple educational objectives at the same time.

▶ fulfill the students' need for active participation.

▶ simulate the real world.

▶ provide students the opportunity to act and experience the consequences of their actions.

▶ focus attention.

▶ reduce the teacher's role as the sole source of instruction.

▶ provide opportunities for students to learn by doing.

▶ be useful at the simplest or the most complex stages of learning.

▶ be helpful for students of all ages.

▶ apply to all areas of the curriculum.

If you are planning to buy or invent a game, there are a number of points to consider. Depending on your objectives, even the simplest game can provide an opportunity for learning. Yet a game that offers the players many options for decisions, matches the content and the format, and requires skill instead of chance, may elicit more sophisticated forms of learning and involvement.

Game Formats and Adaptations

Many popular and familiar game formats are adaptable for use as classroom skill reinforcers. Several of these games are described here.

Bingo

Each student will need a game board constructed as a 5- × 5-square grid. Each square in the grid is marked with a different reading vocabulary word, color, Dolch word, science vocabulary word, second language vocabulary word, numeral, or answer to a math problem. No two game boards are exactly alike. Some answers will appear only on one board, and the same answers will appear in different locations on different game boards.

One person, usually the teacher, slowly calls out a variety of words, numbers, or colors. The students look for these items on their boards. The first student to mark a certain designated formation of squares on his or her game board, usually any horizontal, vertical, or diagonal row (four corners may also be marked) calls out, "Bingo!" and wins the game.

Tic-tac-toe

This game is played by two students. Each of the two players will need a different colored set of cards marked with math problems. The game board is constructed as a 3- × 3-square grid. Each square in the grid is marked with an answer to one of the math problems.

To play, the two students take turns drawing a card from their individual sets and placing the card on the square with the appropriate answer. If an answer is already covered, the student can place his or her card over the card on the correct answer (this requires the student to compare math problems that have the same sum). The first player to get three cards of one color in a row, wins the game.

Other content possibilities include picture words and beginning sounds, numerals and objects, long- and short-vowel symbols and long- and short-vowel words, or states' names and their geographical features.

Concentration

This game of memory requires a set of cards that are identical (or blank) on the back sides. The front sides of the cards are marked so that they may be paired, either as identical matches or as matches of different but related things.

Pairs or small groups of students may play the game. To play, students mix up the cards and then arrange them face down in rows on a desk or other flat surface. The students take turns trying to make a match by turning up two cards. If the cards match, the student gets to keep the pair and take another turn. If the cards don't match, the student turns the two cards face down again. When all the cards have been paired, the student who has the most cards wins the game.

The game can require students to match colors and color words, pictures and initial consonants (or final consonants, blends, vowels), words and definitions, words and second-language counterparts, scientists and inventions, states and capitals, adult and baby animals' names, or any concepts that can be paired.

Guessing games

Guessing games challenge students to respond to questions such as, "How many beans are in the jar?" and "I'm thinking of something in the room that is four inches long. What is it?" In addition to developing learning processes such as observing, estimating, or predicting, guessing games may be used as skill or concept builders: "I see something that begins with a *B*," "I'm thinking of a number between 57 and 81," or "I'm thinking of a city in the southwest."

Guessing games may require simple answers, or may allow students to ask questions (observe, measure) to narrow the range of answers before guessing.

Board games

Board games offer another format with many possibilities. Movement around a trail of squares or steps on the board may depend on directions on a card, a throw of a die or number cube, a spin on a spinner, or the student's ability to say a word on a card or answer a question. To increase the interest and complexity of the game, you can add options (forks in the trail or choices in directions marked in a square or on a card), shortcuts (bridges or secret passages allowing for movement between spaces on the trail), and pitfalls (specially marked cards or spaces on the trail that require giving up a turn or token).

The purpose of the game depends on the design of the board. The object may be to get from one end of the trail to another, or to start at one end and travel around the board until a certain number of tokens are collected or tasks completed. In addition to the board, the game materials also include a different place marker for each student and any materials (cards, spinners, dice) needed for the students to move around the board.

Board games can be developed for students of any age or grade level and with almost any content.

Making Your Own Games

Hundreds of puzzles, games, and simulations are commercially available. Calculators and computers may offer an array of games for skill practice and programmed learning. Yet there may be times, due to financial constraints or students' specific needs, when you will want to make your own games. Fortunately, material supply stores, teacher centers, and teacher supply catalogs carry items such as blank playing cards, posterboard, markers, and laminating film so that teacher-made materials can be durable and attractive.

If you choose to make your own games, consider the following guidelines:

- ▶ Construct games to serve some objective or meet a particular need.

- ▶ Make game materials, concepts, and directions consistent with and approriate for the ability levels of students in the class.

- ▶ Include with any game a list of materials that always belong with that game.

- ▶ If possible, label each piece of a game or puzzle.

- ▶ Keep all pieces of a game or puzzle together in one container (covered box, sealing plastic bag, or can with lid).

- ▶ Make the materials as attractive and professional-looking as possible. Use markers or paints to add color. Avoid bleeding when using felt-tipped markers by outlining in permanent black markers and filling in with water-soluble colored markers.

- ▶ Laminate all game materials.

- ▶ Assign a specific location for storing games and insist that the games be put away correctly each time they are used.

- ▶ Keep rules to a minimum.

- ▶ Don't make the students rely on a set of written rules. To introduce a new game, play it with a small group of students. Unless the game is particularly complex, allow them to teach the game to the rest of the students in the class. Include rules for reference and for your own needs.

- ▶ Don't make the students depend on you for solutions or correct answers. Whenever possible, provide answer keys or self-correcting materials with the game.

Puzzles

Puzzles may appear in a variety of formats. Many puzzles are completed by individual students as paper-and-pencil activities. Several types of puzzles are presented below.

Crossword puzzles

These puzzles require students to fill in horizontal and vertical series of boxes with the letters of words in response to clues (definitions, synonyms, translations). The puzzles allow students to practice spelling and word comprehension skills. The number of letters in the answer and, once some words are filled in, certain letters of those words, help students figure out the answers. Clues may be antonyms, homonyms, capitals or geographical features, battles or events, characters from a story identified by quotes or descriptions, and so on.

Cross number puzzles

Set up in the same format as crossword puzzles, these puzzles can be used to practice any math operations with whole numbers or decimals. The number of digits and place values are possible clues.

Word (or number) search

A word or number search requires students to find a sequence of letters or numbers on a page full of letters or numbers. The numbers or letters are arranged horizontally, vertically, or diagonally (forwards or backwards). This type of puzzle also develops perceptual skills. The word search is usually accompanied by a list of words to look for. It may include a secret word, defined instead of listed, or directions to find a missing word by eliminating other words. The number search is accompanied by a list of numbers to find.

Dot-to-dot puzzles

These puzzles allow students to create a picture by connecting dots numbered or lettered in sequence. They can be used to practice a numerical sequence (including counting by ones, twos, fives, or tens), a sequence of sums, a sequence of historical events by date or description, a sequence of story events, or a sequence of letters or words.

Coloring puzzles

Coloring puzzles require students to create a picture by coloring or shading only those spaces containing a designated item, concept, or quality (vowels, long vowels, odd numbers, multiples of three, names of states or capitals, correctly spelled words, words that rhyme, and so on).

Coded puzzles

To complete these puzzles, students decode a given message by matching or determining the meaning or equivalent of each symbol in the coded message. The coded message may be written with letters, numbers, symbols, or even math problems. For example, each math problem sum could correspond to a different letter, which, when written in sequence, would spell out a message.

Graphing puzzles

Used to strengthen graphing skills, these puzzles ask students to construct a dot-to-dot drawing on a grid from given coordinates.

Matching Puzzle Pieces

This format offers students several puzzle pieces to match. The game might require that students find two pieces with exactly the same content (to refine visual discrimination) or find two pieces that are different but related. Any content that can be paired can be used, including capital and lowercase letters, Roman and Arabic numerals, digital and analog clock faces, numerals and their names spelled out, numerals and corresponding dots or figures, dates and events, math facts and answers, inventors and inventions, states and capitals, or words in English and their foreign language equivalents. This type of puzzle may appear in several formats.

Domino format

All pieces are the same shape and size, as in dominoes or playing cards. One side of each piece is marked with something that matches another piece. If the backs of the pieces are blank or otherwise identical, these materials can be used in a concentration game.

Jigsaw format

The matching pieces physically fit together to complete a shape or form. You can make the puzzles by starting with a set of whole cardboard or wooden pieces, all the same shape and color, and then cutting them into two pieces with different squiggly or jagged cuts. One half of the puzzle is marked on each corresponding piece. When two matching pieces are put together, they complete the shape to form, for example, a rectangle, a heart, a circle, an Easter egg or Christmas tree, or an animal shape. Jigsaw format puzzles have the advantage of being immediately self-correcting and reinforcing.

Completion format

The pieces go together conceptually to complete a picture or an object. The puzzle may be completed, for example, by putting the scoop of ice cream on the correctly marked cone, or matching a sock and a shoe.

Word Tricks

These are short, simple puzzles that require working with letters and words to find solutions. Several different formats are suggested below.

Rebus

Students are asked to add or subtract words or letters according to drawn clues and plus and minus symbols to find the answer.

Scrambled letters

Students are given a word or a sequence of letters to rearrange to make a word. For example, given AOTC, the students might find COAT or TACO. Or, by rearranging the letters in the word SMILE, students might create LIMES, SLIME, or MILES.

Transformations

Students are given a beginning word and an ending word, for example BOY and MAN. Starting with BOY and changing one letter each time, the students will find the words in the transformation sequence (BOY-BAY-MAY-MAN).

Reversals

Students are given a definition for a word and a second definition for the same word spelled backwards. For example, reverse "cooking container" (PAN) to get "a brief sleep" (NAP).

Beheading

Students are given a definition for a word and a second definition for the same word without the first letter. For example, behead "not quick" (SLOW) to get "not high" (LOW).

Add-a-letter

Students add a specified letter to a given word and rearrange the letters to make a new word. For example, add a "Z" to ONE, FORE, and RIPE to get ZONE, FROZE, and PRIZE.

Add-a-vowel

Students add a specified vowel in the correct places to make a sentence out of a meaningless series of letters. For example, add an "E" to PTSSATR to get PETE SEES A TREE.

Acrostics

Students use the letters of a word spelled vertically to spell out horizontal words. Definitions are given for each horizontal word, and the number of letters in each word may be indicated by a dash for each letter.

Collections

Other concrete materials can be extremely useful in your classroom. Sand tables, water tables, even a washtub filled with rice and various sized containers can offer young students opportunities to understand new concepts and integrate learning skills through hands-on experiences with concrete objects. Collections of objects from the students' own environment can help you achieve similar goals.

You may want to illustrate a concept such as shape, color, or texture by collecting items that express that particular concept. For example, one collection might be made up of round items, another of soft items, another of red items, and another of plastic items. Collections might also contain a variety of similar items: a collection of buttons, a collection of postcards, or a collection of keys, for example.

A collection should contain as many different items as you can find that fit in the group. For example, a button collection might contain large buttons, small buttons, buttons with shanks, buttons with two holes or four, buttons of all different colors, metal buttons, wooden or bone buttons, antique buttons, buttons in the shape of animals or hearts, smooth and textured buttons, and so on. A button collection might also contain a few items which are not specifically defined as buttons, but which serve the same purpose, such as buckles, or other fasteners.

The object of the button collection is not to teach about buttons, but to use the concrete attributes of the buttons to develop concepts such as shape, color, texture, or size, along with related vocabulary, and to stimulate mental processes such as sorting and classifying, labeling, imagining, recalling, or comparing. Collections, which can be left out for students to explore or used in a teacher-directed small group experience, help develop language skills, cognitive skills, and social skills.

The familiarity of the objects in the collection allows you to start with the students' own experiences and then ask questions that encourage them to think. For example, probably all children are familiar with some form of button, although their experiences will differ. Students in very warm climates might not recognize a large heavy button used on a coat; students with parents in the military might be more familiar than other students with the metallic buttons used on uniforms. Beginning with what students already know, you can structure questions and tasks to help students learn. Questions such as, "How is this button different from the ones on your shirt?" or "Where do you think this button came from?" require students to move beyond their immediate environment and experience. Holding up a large, square, plastic, shiny, red button with two holes and asking students to "find a button like this one" might draw a variety of responses; one student may find an exact match while another selects a small, round, wooden button that is similar because it has two holes. Each student will see the objects in his or her own way. Structuring questions with no right or wrong answers provides students with a low-risk environment in which they can develop cognitive skills.

Assembling and Using Collection Kits

To assemble kits, you will need to develop a sharp eye for objects to collect. Enlist the aid of friends, students, and other faculty members by informing them of your needs. A letter to parents and a notice in the teachers' lounge announcing that you are collecting buttons this month and would appreciate contributions can help you build a number of collection kits to use in your classroom. (You may generate even more enthusiasm from the faculty if you also announce that you will be happy to share the collections with them.)

You will need to set aside a bit of storage space. A box in the office or faculty lounge and perhaps one in your classroom can serve as a place for contributors to leave materials, but once the collection kit is assembled, store the materials in a separate container. Continue to build your collections as you find new materials.

Collect many items covering as wide a range as possible. Sometimes borrowed objects or special items such as fragile, antique, or personally significant objects may make their way into your collection. Even then, keep the special materials separate from the rest, and identify them as special for the students. You might want to make the students aware of the sources or contributors of the special items. Remind them to handle these items with care.

Although you can use the materials without much background information, a little research will help you present the materials in greater depth. For example, even the dictionary definition of the collection's concept—in this case, buttons—can help you develop the concept. Including a definition will remind you of the many meanings of the concept as you develop the collection and present it to the students. Given the definition of the concept, you can ask if zippers or Velcro are buttons, how they are alike and different, or what fasteners other than buttons can serve the same purpose. Likewise, learning about the history of buttons, or how they are made, sold, or packaged, can help you expand the students' experiences and answer questions that might arise.

To help with your planning, prepare a file card for each collection, noting the name of the collection, the dictionary definition, a list of possible materials to include, and a list of instructional possibilities. You may want to include activities using the objects, or write questions that encourage language development, concept and skill development, thinking, predicting, or creativity. Preparing the cards when you develop the collections will help ensure that the collections fill a clearly defined purpose.

Before introducing the collections, set criteria regarding their use and about the handling of materials. If the collection contains many small objects, you may wish to include a towel to protect the objects and to define the space for using the materials. Introduce the collections in small, teacher-directed groups before leaving them for the students to work with independently.

Community Resources

Even if you've been teaching for years or were fortunate enough to start out in a well-stocked classroom, at times you will want materials such as films and art supplies for a short time only. In some cases, you may want to obtain items that your school does not provide, such as carpet remnants or math counters, or discover inexpensive resources for basic items such as pencils, erasers, or paper.

Always be on the lookout for resources to use for materials, collections, and activities. Many businesses offer leftover or demonstration materials to teachers, sometimes for the cost of taking them away. You may be able to find some useful items: a broken clock or telephone for your students to dismantle, old locks and clasps for motor skills development, maps or charts for unit lessons, keychains or tokens for rewards, and plastic chips or corks for math counters. Businesses can sometimes provide scrap paper, display materials, and storage containers. If you call in advance, a local ice-cream store may even be willing to wash out cardboard containers for you.

If you are lucky enough to have one in your area, a teaching materials resource center will be rich in resources for making and laminating your own materials. Visit a children's bookstore or a professional library regularly for inspiration and ideas. Begin to keep track of the resources in and around your community. Who has a label-making machine? Is there a bookstore in town that sells or exchanges used books? What are the television stations willing to provide? Remember to write a note to yourself about any resources you discover. Don't overlook such places as the education office of a public utility, a wallpaper store, or the city dump. Resources you find now may come in handy later.

Planning Sheet: Developing Instructional Materials

Duplicate as needed.

Name of game or puzzle: _____

Concept/skill: _____

_____

Grade level(s): _____

Objectives: _____

_____

_____

Description of game:

    Materials include _____

_____

_____

    Number of players _____

_____

    How is it played? _____

_____

_____

_____

_____

_____

Description of puzzle:

    What is given (clues, word lists, numbers)? _____

_____

_____

_____

_____

    How is the puzzle completed? _____

_____

_____

_____

_____

Reflection and Evaluation: Instructional Materials

How have the students responded to the materials?

Games _____

_____

_____

_____

_____

_____

Puzzles _____

_____

_____

_____

_____

What changes have you made in the content, design, or use of the materials?

Games _____

_____

_____

_____

_____

_____

Puzzles _____

_____

_____

_____

_____

How have the materials contributed to your instruction and your ability to meet individual needs and preferences?

_____

_____

_____

Bibliography

Abercrombie, N.; Hill, S.; and Turner, B. *The Penguin Dictionary of Sociology*. London: Allen Lane Publishers, 1984.

Aschner, M. J. M. Asking Questions to Trigger Thinking. *NEA Journal* 50 (1961).

Atkinson, L. Developing the Intellectual Base. *Becoming a Teacher: A Book of Readings*. Ed. Odell, et al. Lexington, MA: Ginn Custom Publishing, 1980.

Avedon, E. M., and Sutton-Smith, B. Eds. *The Study of Games*. New York: John Wiley & Sons, 1971.

Bloom, B. S. *Taxonomy of Educational Objectives: Book I Cognitive Domain*. New York: Longman, 1956.

Bluestein, J. E. Developing Responsible Learning Behaviors through Peer Interaction. Ph.D. diss., University of Pittsburgh, 1980.

_____. Rx: A Prescriptive Approach to Math Instruction. Albuquerque, 1981.

Bluestein, J. E., and O'Brien, P. Handbook for Developing Student Volunteer Programs and Joint Class Activities. Pittsburgh, 1979.

Champagne, D. W., and Goldman, R. M. *Teaching Parents Teaching*. New York: Appleton-Century-Crofts, 1972.

Curwin, R. L., and Fuhrmann, B. S. *Discovering Your Teaching Self: Humanistic Approaches to Effective Teaching*. Englewood Cliffs, NJ: Prentice-Hall, 1975.

Dreikurs, R., and Grey, L. *Logical Consequences: A New Approach to Discipline*. New York: E. P. Dutton, 1968.

Dunn, R., and Dunn, K. *Educator's Self-Teaching Guide to Individualizing Instructional Programs*. New York: Parker Publishing Co., 1975.

Gerrard, T. *Com-Packs: Kids' Committees for Integrated Learning*. Albuquerque, NM: I.S.S. Publications, 1987.

Gibson, J. T. *Educational Psychology*. 2d ed. New York: Appleton-Century-Crofts, 1972.

Gordon, A. K. *Games for Growth: Educational Games in the Classroom*. Chicago: Science Research Associates, 1972.

Gordon, T. *T.E.T. Teacher Effectiveness Training*. New York: David McKay Co., 1974.

Grey, L. *Discipline Without Fear*. New York: Hawthorn Books, 1974.

Homme, L. *How to Use Contingency Contracting in the Classroom*. Champaign, IL: Research Press Co., 1973.

Krathwohl, D. R.; Bloom, B. S.; and Masia, B. B. *Taxonomy of Educational Objectives: Book II Affective Domain*. New York: David McKay Co., 1974.

Lee, D. M., and Rubin, J. B. *Children and Language: Reading and Writing, Talking and Listening*. Belmont, CA: Wadsworth Publishing Co., 1979.

Loughlin, C. E., and Suina, J. H. *The Learning Environment: An Instructional Strategy*. New York: Teachers College Press, 1982.

Mager, R. F. *Preparing Instructional Objectives*. 2d ed., rev. Belmont, CA: David S. Lake Publishers, 1984.

Morlan, J., and Espinosa, L. *Preparation of Inexpensive Teaching Materials*. Belmont, CA: David S. Lake Publishers, 1988.

Osborn, D. K., and Osborn, J. D. *Discipline and Classroom Management*. Athens, GA: Education Association, Early Childhood Education Learning Center, 1977.

Paul, A. S.; Smith, A. V.; and Henderson, R. W. *Intellectual Kits: Tools for Instruction in the Tucson Early Education Model*. Tucson: Research and Development Center, University of Arizona, 1974.

Pearson, C., and Marfuggi, J. *Creating and Using Learning Games*. Belmont, CA: David S. Lake Publishers, 1975.

Peter, L. J. *Individual Instruction: Prescriptive Teaching System*. New York: McGraw-Hill, 1972.

Presbie, R. J., and Brown, P. L. *What Research Says to the Teacher: Behavior Modification*. Washington, D.C.: National Education Association, 1976.

Raths, L. E.; Harmin, M.; and Simon, S. B. *Values and Teaching*. 2d ed. Westerville, OH: Charles E. Merrill Publishing Co., 1978.

Welton, D. A., and Mallan, J. T. *Children and Their World: Strategies for Teaching Social Studies*. Boston: Houghton Mifflin, 1981.